CW00545222

The Lotus Elite

Patrick Stephens Limited, part of Thorsons, a division of the Collins Publishing Group, has published authoritative, quality books for enthusiasts for more than twenty years. During that time the company has established a reputation as one of the world's leading publishers of books on aviation, maritime, military, model-making, motor cycling, motoring, motor racing, railway and railway modelling subjects. Readers or authors with suggestions for books they would like to see published are invited to write to: The Editorial Director, Patrick Stephens Limited, Thorsons Publishing Group, Wellingborough, Northants, NN8 2RQ.

The Lotus Elite

Dennis E. Ortenburger

Foreword by John Wagstaff

Patrick Stephens Limited

First published in 1990

British Library Cataloguing in Publication Data
Ortenburger, Dennis E.
The Lotus Elite.
1. Sports cars, history
I. Title
629.2222

ISBN 1-85260-100-0

Patrick Stephens Limited is part of the Thorsons Publishing Group, Wellingborough, Northamptonshire NN8 2RQ, England.

Typeset by Burns & Smith Ltd, Derby

Printed by The Bath Press, Bath, Avon

10 9 8 7 6 5 4 3 2 1

Contents

Foreword

by John Wagstaff

When Dennis Ortenburger asked me to write the Foreword to this book I was both honoured and flattered. Honoured because his first book, *The Original Lotus Elite*, was a sell-out and recognized as something of a landmark in single marque books because of the extent of Dennis's research.

The author has recorded in this completely new book a wealth of newly uncovered history, both of the car and its creators. It is full of new technical details, previously unpublished photographs and anecdotes—it is the definitive work on the Lotus Elite. All the more amazing as Dennis, who works as a Local Government Officer, lives half a world away in Southern California with his wife Marlene and their two sons, Kipp and Renn.

Despite being an unashamed Anglophile, Dennis has only visited England twice and it was during his first visit that I met him when he was researching the original book. He impressed me at the time with his dedication and personal integrity and, of course, his amazing knowledge of the subject. His subsequent books on the Lotus 7, Lotus 11 and Frank Costin—the aerodynamicist—stand as a monument to his ability as a researcher.

Dennis has always been a dedicated admirer of the late Colin Chapman, almost to the point of reverence. He was, I know, tremendously saddened by his sudden death and particularly by the hints of subsequent scandal that threatened to shadow his memory. Dennis saw him as an automotive genius whose contributions surpassed those of the legendary Ettore Bugatti and Enzo Ferrari.

I met Colin Chapman only two or three times, although I did know his father, Stan Kennedy-Chapman, quite well. He acted as Team Manager for Team Elite at Le Mans in 1960 and was extremely kind to me; in fact, we corresponded for some time afterwards.

My interest in fast cars really began during the time I was in the Royal Air Force when the only way of getting home from a windswept coastal command station in North-east Lincolnshire was by public transport, most of the time spent in freezing railway waiting rooms and bus shelters. What I needed was some machinery to tame the twisting lanes of the Lincolnshire wolds followed by the straight Roman roads from Lincoln to my home in the Midlands. A combination, I was to discover later, not dissimilar to the Nürburgring and Le Mans, but all on the same journey.

Unfortunately, I was only 18 at the time and desperately short of funds. The nearest I came to having a car was the occasional use of a fellow airman's 900cc side valve Ford Popular with a three-speed gearbox and a maximum speed of about 70 mph. However, it had suspension modifications which enabled it to corner incredibly quickly and a journey which by train or bus took half a day was now little over one hour. This, I suppose, was my first realization that high average speeds are not always achieved by lots of power—something which every Lotus Elite driver will appreciate.

After leaving the Air Force I bought a TR2 with money loaned to me from my mother and my first race was at an opening meeting at Mallory Park in 1956. This was followed by a Lotus 11 and then, in 1959, my first Lotus Elite. I was invited by David Buxton to form a team of Elites to contest some national and international races. There followed five marvellous years of competing with the car.

A few years ago I was fascinated to learn that during one rainy afternoon someone from Club Elite in America had fed into a computer all the published European race results, and arrived at the conclusion that between 1959 and 1965 I had probably raced more miles in a Lotus Elite than any other driver. This included many club and most, if not all, of the British and European National and International long-distance sports car races, of which seven or eight were of 1,000 kilometres or more. I was also lucky enough to accomplish three placings at Le Mans.

The original Lotus Elite has always been a very important part of my life and to be so closely involved in its racing history is something of which I am very proud. I occasionally walk down to the garage, sit in my old Team Elite car and take a trip backwards in time to reflect on those wonderful days in the early 1960s. Finally, to be invited to write the Foreword to this superb book closes a chapter in my life full of rich and rewarding memories of occasions and friends, both past and present.

John Wagstaff
Langley Priory

Acknowledgements

The research for this book wasn't done in the normal way, which is to gather information and photographs within time limits set by production and publication schedules. Rather, it was the result of over two decades of enjoying my Elite while participating in discussions, collecting photographs and picking up other information as part of a continuing hobby. This also included acting as my own mechanic, fibreglass technician and paint and body specialist. Admittedly, the last year, or two, prior to publication got a little hectic as the last bits and pieces of certain stories were tracked down, but these were also very important because they filled in the blanks of what otherwise would have been simply a scrap-book collection of snapshots and disjointed memories.

The number of individuals on whom I've relied to provide this information is, as you can see, quite large. Despite my persistent requests for ever more information, their enthusiasm remained both spontaneous and genuine, and my sincere appreciation is extended to all.

First on my list is my wife Marlene who culled nearly every word of this manuscript from a patchwork collection of tapes, handwritten notes and hastily typed pages. Her patience and skill is second only to the editors of Patrick Stephens Limited who coaxed the finished draft into a readable story. Three Elite experts including Peter Kirwan-Taylor, Anthony Bates and Mike Ostrov critiqued the first draft and checked it for errors. Kirwan-Taylor also supplied personal records, Bates secured interviews and conducted original research in England, and Ostrov compiled the extraordinary Elite registry which is combined with the chassis list in Appendix II.

David Morgan, the Secretary of the Historic Lotus Register, also did research in England. Several personalities who were with Lotus in the early days, including Tony Caldersmith, Len Street, Mike and Frank Costin and Jay Chamberlain, contributed heretofore unknown insights into the design, early production and marketing of the car. Ian Walker, Roger Nathan and John Wagstaff described their experiences with racing Elites and John told the story of Team Elite and, of course, wrote the Foreword for this book.

Alvin Cohen related his observations of the Elite as a crew member of Roger Nathan's racing team and his study of early Elite colour schemes. Koichi Sugita explained the effect the Elite had on the Japanese enthusiast and that country's car designers. Barry Swackhamer told of his Elite restoration and Richard Spelberg Jr, Steve Earle and Charlie English allowed my use of their extensive literature collections. Bill Hutton and Miles Wilkins detailed the Elite clubs on both sides of the Atlantic and they explained how they got into businesses that catered for Elite owners. Felix Brunelle analysed the early paint and finish problems and Phil Cannon told of his adventures in a modsport Elite.

Gary David, Barry Swackhamer and Rich McCormack revealed the delights of the Elite miniatures and Derek Bentley detailed the Rochdale, the world's second GRP monocoque. A group of Elite historic racers took time to tell of their exploits and these included Bob Green, Judy and Mike Freeman, Robin Longdon, Brian Caldersmith and Frank Starkey, who also provided his double-dimpled Elite for study.

Numerous photographers contributed their work and they included my son, Kipp, Michael Brown, Harold Barker, Nigel Brown, Larry Fisher, Adrien Schagen, the late Henri Beroul and LAT Photographic. John Chatwin and Nick Raven, respectively the Chairman and Secretary of Club Elite, assisted in the registry and provided material from the Club's newsletters. Joe Dykzeul made prints for much of the original graphics, and Avnon FilmLab printed all of the author's photography. And finally, there were the magazines which permitted reprints of articles, covers and data panels. They were *Road & Track*, *Car and Driver*, *Autosport*, *Autocar*, *The Motor* and *Motor Sport*.

There were others who contributed smaller, but no less important, pieces of information and they are named in the text. Without the help of all, this book couldn't have been written.

Introduction

Most automobile enthusiasts have a favourite car or two, and can usually point to the time and place they made first acquaintance. I'm no different, of course, and can remember at the age of 18 seeing an automobile so full of wonder that it stopped my conversation in mid-sentence.

It was 1961 and I was in a car jammed full of teenage athletes on our way to a high school track meet. Someone shouted, 'Hey, look at that!', and we skidded to a stop and piled out in front of a tiny automobile showroom. There it was, painted an unbelievable shade of lavender blue and parked on a raised concrete pad, and for the first few minutes no one uttered a word. Eyes darted everywhere for a clue as to what it was. Somehow it didn't even look like a car, at least not like anything we were used to seeing.

Ah, but it was beautiful and as aerodynamic as a bullet. And yet, at the same time it was almost delicate, someone said 'like a glider', although it looked solid enough. 'Look here, the body is continuous, it's smooth underneath.' And so the conversation went, with all of us agreeing in the end that the car looked like it was doing a hundred just standing still.

Finally someone caught sight of the nose badge—Lotus—and saw a sign in the showroom that read 'Jay Chamberlain—authorized distributor for the Lotus Elite'. We eventually pulled ourselves away and made it to the meet before the first race, but the memory lingered for a long time. I even made the promise every young enthusiast makes at least at one time or another, that one day I'd own one myself.

In 1966 I purchased chassis number 1461. The excitement, incidentally, never went away, but neither did the apparent mystery about the car which led me to begin a casual investigation, at least at first. I enjoyed the car from the beginning but wondered at remarks like, 'Well yes, you own a Lotus Elite', as if to say there was something odd about the car, or me for owning it. I was puzzled why my mechanic refused to touch it and why everyone had the inside story on differentials falling out and dealers who disappeared in the dead of night.

In 1976, a friend of mine by the name of Rich McCormack saw my collection of Elite lore and hardware which, by then, filled half-a-dozen three-ring binders, a steamer trunk and two walls in my garage, and persuaded me to write a book about the car. As it happened, Rich owned a publishing company called Newport Press and the following year *The Original Lotus Elite, Racing Car for the Road* hit the car book stores.

The problem was that as I met more of the people associated with the Elite in the early days and delved deeper into my own car (largely as a result of a decade of historic racing), there seemed to be much more to the story than appeared in my first attempt at book writing. This was confirmed by comments from the experts like, 'Your book is fine as far as it goes, but how about explaining the double-dimpled Elites, or telling us about the tragic race at Sebring and why the car came in so many wild colours?' Being the compulsive type, I renewed my research and began collecting information again. I also bought an early Maximar Series I and took it apart (and put it back together again) to see for myself how different a car it was from the Bristol body/chassis.

In 1988, Patrick Stephens, who knew the Elite very well from his vantage point of Advertising Manager for *Sports Car and Lotus Owner* magazine back in the 'fifties, asked if I was ready to write the rest of the Elite story. So here is what I've come up with to further explain Colin Chapman's magnificent fibreglass monocoque GT. A car that, despite being almost too advanced to be successfully constructed (in 1957), set standards and trends in aerodynamics, styling, performance, handling and racing which to this day have never been equalled, let alone surpassed.

Dennis Ortenburger
Woodland Hills, California

The author gathering Elite information at Laguna Seca in 1988. (Kipp Ortenburger)

Chapter 1

An Elite style

Described by some experts as 'the Golden Age of Sports Cars', the decade ending in 1965 (not surprisingly, this is also the cut-off date for several historic racing organizations) marked the end of an extraordinary period of automotive history. The time was filled with the proliferation and the development of an amazing variety of high-performance two-seaters from an equally plentiful number of manufacturers.

The decade was great fun for motoring enthusiasts because so much was happening in so many corners of the world and there were dozens of periodicals to tell them about it. Admittedly, it was also pretty innocent, with no concern over impact standards or air pollution or energy conservation, but to countless enthusiasts these years provided them with affordable and spirited transportation. By definition, sports cars were as suited to commuting as they were to milder forms of competition which included rallies, road racing, hill climbs and sprints, although a fast run from Paris to Monaco while in sporting mood probably met the requirements as well.

The Golden Age was ushered in by the demands of a motoring public weary of both the terrible cost of and the long recovery from a World War. A new generation of enthusiasts hungered for fast, good-handling cars and automobile manufacturers were anxious to provide them.

The early 1950s witnessed an extraordinary upsurge in motorsport, and in England dozens of the old circuits came alive to the sight and sounds of racing cars. At about the same time, the American Air Force was indirectly subsidizing sports car racing in the US by allowing the SCCA to use several of its airfields as courses. In both countries throngs of spectators hungry for the aroma of Castrol 'R' and the sight of wheel-to-wheel competition lined up to purchase tickets.

Most sports car manufacturers, whether brand new or long established, supported competition, either by direct involvement or by assistance to privateers. Names like Abarth, MG, Triumph, Elva, Austin Healey, Siata, Berkeley, Sunbeam, Fairthorpe, OSCA and a host of others became relatively common, not only in the pages of *Autosport* and *Road & Track* but also in urban streets and country lanes

There is little doubt that if you were old enough to drive in 1955 you experienced, in some measure, what the car magazines in those days called 'The Sports Car Movement'.

Lotus Engineering Co Ltd

The excitement of an enthusiastic public and a revived car industry encouraged a large number of newcomers to try their hand at building high-performance road cars. One of these was Lotus Engineering Company Limited which was located on the north edge of London, at No 7 Tottenham Lane, Hornsey.

In 1957 Lotus was a successful racing car builder. The company had been founded by Colin Chapman only five years earlier but it had already scored a class victory at the 24 Hours of Le Mans and was acknowledged to be the leader in racing car aerodynamics, not to mention chassis and suspension design.

From the very beginning, Chapman's designs were a complete break with convention. His ideas were fresh, solidly engineered solutions to the engineer's dilemma: strength versus weight. Of course, he also had a particular gift of visualizing how suspension geometry worked, and the application of his insight resulted in cars that cornered like few others. Despite the youth of his company and its chairman (Chapman was 29 in 1957), Lotus was on the cutting edge of racing car technology and the public not only knew it, but also eagerly anticipated the launch of every new model. Chapman didn't keep them waiting long because from 1953 he gave the racers a completely new car every year.

As we learned in Gerard Crombac's monumental book on Colin Chapman (*Colin Chapman, The Man And His Cars*, Patrick Stephens 1986), Chapman's first love was racing, but in order to support this passion he needed to build road cars as well. He had already experienced the potential for this kind of market with his Lotus Mark 6 which was first introduced in 1952. The Six was a stark little square rigger which raced mainly in the 1172cc class (powered by the Ford 10, four-cylinder side valve engine). Chapman eventually built about 100 of these cars and was astounded at the number of customers who asked for a canvas hood and frame to drive the things on the road!

Lilliputian facilities

To the enthusiasts who knew the layout of the Lotus works it was amazing that the company could build one car at a time, let alone produce them in series. Colin Chapman's 'factory' consisted of a couple of small buildings and an office that faced the minor road called Tottenham Lane. The property, incidentally, was adjacent to the Railway Hotel, and both were owned by Chapman's father, Stanley.

Despite his cramped quarters, Chapman was anxious to begin work on his first purpose-built road car. In 1956 he introduced the Eleven, which went on to become the most successful small-capacity sports racer of all time. He then turned his attention to a new kind of sports car which had been introduced a few years earlier but was developing into a highly regarded type of automobile. It was called the GT or Grand Touring car.

A modern photo showing No 7 Tottenham Lane occupied by C.S. Bacon & Son, Incineration Engineers. Railway Hotel on the left. (George Rance)

The Grand Touring car

As described in my previous Lotus book for PSL, *The Lotus Eleven* (1988), in the 'fifties the GT or Grand Touring designation came to be used to describe certain enthusiasts' cars. These were two-seater coupés which were designed for high-speed travel in complete comfort. The word 'comfort' was defined a little differently in those days, however, and had no relation to modern usage which usually refers to megawatt stereo systems, climate controls, power steering, electric windows, digital instruments and the like.

Then, it meant instead an ergonomically designed interior that enabled a driver to conduct the car's business of high-speed travel efficiently. This included seats with good lateral support, a steering wheel with a good 'feel' (usually wood) and set at the proper height, angle and reach for 'arms over' manoeuvres, a brake and throttle pedal arrangement that permitted 'heel to toe' techniques, a gear lever that fell closely to hand and an interior that was made comfortable by full carpeting, good ventilation and unobstructed visibility out of the front and sides of the car, the road ahead being more important than who was coming up behind.

The GT designation also required a willing engine, a suspension and chassis that yielded predictable handling and excellent cornering power, good brakes and enough luggage space to accommodate a weekend's journey for two. A Grand Touring car was meant for those who delighted in driving as much as in arriving, and it was not uncommon, for example, to hear of drivers of these cars taking the long way round to their destination just for the fun of it. Coincidental with the development of the 'Gran Turismo' concept was the announcement of an international racing category for GT cars divided into several displacement classes. Chapman had already made up his mind to challenge one of them with a car he and his wife Hazel had already named.

What's in a name?

Colin Chapman's penchant for car names beginning with the letter 'E' began with the Eleven, although in that instance it was done to avoid any confusion over the appearance of the number in print (would '11' be seen as the Arabic number eleven or the Roman numeral two?).

All successive race cars, incidentally, were identified by type number, whereas the road cars were given names and numbers. As it happened, Colin and Hazel had great fun coming up with the name 'Elite', which was finally chosen because of its definition, 'the choicest part', its 'Park Avenue' appeal and its alliteration which they felt would become a Lotus tradition. Peter Kirwan-Taylor recalled that the name was often mispronounced 'Elight'.

Initial specifications

A common practice of Colin Chapman was to develop a set of criteria for a car before any design lines were put on paper. These general specifications often included competition goals, notes on construction, critical dimensions and the like. Chapman and his confidant, Peter Kirwan-Taylor (of whom we will learn more later) recorded five of them for the Elite.

The first was that the car would be completely suitable for road use and rallies (such as the Monte Carlo), but also that it would be capable of a class win in Le Mans. If these sound mutually exclusive, remember the definition of a sports car and the fact that Chapman never did anything only mildly competitive—he went after the biggest prize of all, Le Mans. The importance of this 24-hour race will be examined in detail in Chapter 8, but for now suffice to say that the French classic was the most important race in Europe and the prestige of simply competing was enormous.

The next specification was that the Elite would be a glass-reinforced plastic (fibreglass) monocoque (ignore for the moment that this type of construction had never been attempted before), with certain aerodynamic refinements such as a ducted radiator and a fully enclosed undertray.

The car would have the same suspension system as Chapman's first open-wheeled car, the Lotus 12 Formula 2 car, that is wishbone independent front suspension and Chapman struts at the rear. The 12 would also contribute its wheelbase and track together with its bump and rebound.

Scuttle height would be determined by the profile of the new Coventry Climax single overhead cam engine.

And lastly, the cabin dimensions and the overall height of the car would be determined by a 4½-inch ground clearance and the height of an average-sized driver and passenger (of course, Chapman used his own 5 ft 7 in frame as the model) on a seat the distance of which from the floor pan was 1½ inches. Oddly enough, this last specification proved to be the only one Chapman failed to accomplish to the letter. No matter, his immediate problem was what his revolutionary automobile was going to look like.

The stylist, Peter Kirwan-Taylor

The Lotus Elite was acknowledged by expert and casual observer alike to be one of the best-looking automobiles ever built. To some eyes it

The Elite looked good even when viewed from a low angle, as this American press picture shows. (Western Distributors)

In 1989 Peter Kirwan-Taylor (far left) was still active in the financial world and was a director of five companies. (Photographer unknown)

was the prettiest car in all of automotive history. What made it so was a graceful, fluid shape that had a certain delicacy accentuated by 15-inch diameter single-laced wire wheels (ie having 48 spokes as opposed to the 60 of a double-laced wheel). Remarkably, the Elite had no bad angles whether viewed from above or below, straight on or in profile. What is also surprising is that this masterpiece was not the culmination of the life's work of a trained automotive designer, but rather a development of schoolboy sketches done by a 27-year-old chartered accountant by the name of Peter Kirwan-Taylor.

Of course, Peter Kirwan-Taylor was no ordinary accountant. In fact, when he entered university he could as easily have pursued engineering as economics. His stepfather, who had an engineering degree from Cambridge, held, among other lofty positions, the first chair on the Executive Board of Lagonda Motors. Kirwan-Taylor was thus exposed to automobiles and automobile engineering before he was in his teens. As it happened, the Chairman of Lagonda had also been director of both Folland and Westland Aircraft, so Kirwan-Taylor's stepfather conducted business with the aircraft industry as well.

During frequent business trips to Folland and Lagonda with his stepfather, Kirwan-Taylor came to know Folland's new Chief Designer, Teddy Petter. Petter's knowledge of aerodynamics and his enthusiasm for the subject was so infectious that he persuaded his young pupil to study the subject. One of the texts he read was published in 1951 and was titled *Aerodynamic Drag*, and Chapter 9 covered the air drag of four-wheeled vehicles. Interestingly, Kirwan-Taylor still has this book in his library.

By the time Kirwan-Taylor entered Cambridge University (where he managed to squeeze in a class on mechanical drawing) he not only had a knowledge of automobile design but also understood aerodynamics, which, as we will see later in this chapter, contributed significantly to the Elite's stunning good looks. One of his pastimes between classes was to fill up sketch books with drawings of futuristic-looking automobiles.

Kirwan-Taylor ultimately chose to major in economics, much to the relief of his father who was a financier and London merchant banker.

Kirwan-Taylor, in his special-bodied Mark 6, leads another Mark 6 through a corner. His ideas on radiator ducting were still being developed as evidenced by the bonnet blowing open at the back edge. (Photographer unknown)

Accounting seemed a more stable way of making a living, and proved to be the right choice—in 1989 Kirwan-Taylor was a director of no fewer than five companies and Chairman of the Board of yet another.

All of which seems a long way from Colin Chapman and Lotus, but in 1953 Kirwan-Taylor decided he wanted to go motor racing and bought a Lotus Mark 6 kit. It was during frequent trips to Tottenham Lane to sort out assembly that he met Chapman. From the start, Kirwan-Taylor didn't care for the bodywork on the Six so he decided to design his own. The result was a very tidy roadster (done in light alloy by Williams and Pritchard) that introduced him to the problems of ergonomics, scuttle versus engine height, wing clearance for suspension travel and the like. Even more significant, however, was that Chapman liked both the design and Kirwan-Taylor and the two became lifelong friends. Peter's racing career, incidentally, consisted of a couple of outings in the Six which he described as being 'satisfying and very nearly spectacular'.

How the shape evolved

In 1955 Kirwan-Taylor learned that two of his friends, Peter Lumsden and Paul Fletcher, wanted to enter a Lotus Eleven at Le Mans. He suggested a closed body shape for maximum aerodynamic advantage and went to see Chapman with his ideas. It was then that Chapman took him aside and let him in on his proposal for a fibreglass monocoque coupé. He also explained that a closed body on the Eleven's spaceframe chassis presented several problems he did not want to take the time to solve like weight distributions and how to manage entry over high chassis sides and with what kind of doors. Chapman wanted to start with a clean sheet of paper and he invited Kirwan-Taylor to help.

Peter's job was to come up with a body shape and from Chapman's general specifications he saw few limitations. The engine was extremely compact which allowed a low scuttle height. The chassis, at least for the moment, presented no constraints to suspension movement or passenger accommodation and, best of all, a monocoque construction, with its interior panels and bulkheads, lent itself to an enclosed undertray and efficient radiator ducting.

For a time Kirwan-Taylor subscribed to nearly every motor magazine published in English and attended every motor show at home and on the Continent in order to bring himself up to date on the work of current stylists. Chapman wanted elegance for his GT but nothing so trendy or outrageous that the design might become prematurely dated or, worse, not sell.

There were several cars that intrigued Kirwan-Taylor and their influences can be seen in the Elite. They were the Alfa Romeo Superflow, particularly the front end without the headlight covers, and the Alfa 3½ litre by Boano, which featured partially covered wheel arches and a high waistline.

Interestingly, Kirwan-Taylor's initial sketches (no airbrush artistry here, Peter always worked with graph paper!) showed the Elite with vestigial fins. These devices were a popular styling device of the day, but they could also be quite functional in the stabilization of a car's centre of pressure if their size and placement were just right; remember that the current Lotus sports racer, the Eleven, used fins for this purpose. Kirwan-Taylor finally erased them after a discussion with Lotus's resident aerodynamicist, Frank Costin, but more on his contribution to the Elite a little later in this chapter.

Kirwan-Taylor was influenced by the Ferrari Superfast; notice the rear portion of the side window and the back bumper. (Photographer unknown)

The front of the Elite also owes much to the front of the Alfa Romeo 3 litre. (Photographer unknown)

Some aerodynamic factors

By the time the Elite was designed, Colin Chapman had already achieved considerable recognition for successfully venturing into the void of automobile aerodynamics. There was a tremendous body of knowledge available for aircraft, of course, but the automobile lagged far behind. This was because the car presented several problems, all related to keeping it on the ground (as opposed to aircraft which are all about lift) and maintaining stability on its intended course, despite the effects of cross-winds, cornering (when a car turns it generates its own cross-wind) and heavy braking.

The techniques for simple streamlining or drag reduction had been known for years, as had the significance of drag coefficients. The perfect shape in an airstream, for example, is the elongated tear-drop which has a Cd (coefficient of drag) of 0.04, whereas the proverbial brick yields a Cd of 1.17. The problem was that when a car got down to the really low numbers, stability suffered dramatically and it wanted to spin in a corner or even on a straight if there was a wind blowing. Car builders quickly discovered that there were many factors at work in successfully piercing the air, and only one was reducing drag. Some of the Elite's later contemporaries, incidentally, had very good Cds; the Porsche 911 was 0.34, the Citroen DS19 0.31 and the early Jaguar E Type coupé was 0.44. That of the Lotus, however, was a remarkable 0.29.

Of the many aerodynamic factors at work in a low-drag automobile, and perhaps the most important, is the car's centre of pressure. Simply stated, this is the point on a car body where the force of a cross-wind is the greatest. As long as this point stays near the car's centre of gravity there is no problem, but if it moves forward directional stability is reduced. And, sure enough, as drag gets lower, the centre of pressure moves forward!

There were two solutions to positively locate the centre of pressure at or near the centre of gravity. One was the use of fins which, in cross-winds, behaved like sails. The other solution was to shape the car as an aerodynamic entity with the positioning of its masses calculated to positively locate the centre of pressure. Frank Costin used both of these solutions on his early aerodynamic Lotus sports racers. As we will see, for the Elite he only needed one.

Another styling feature common in the mid-'fifties was the reverse-angled 'A' pillar which supposedly achieved improved visibility through the windscreen. Kirwan-Taylor remarked, 'We flirted with it and thank goodness dropped it'.

The Elite's bumpers received a good deal of attention and Kirwan-Taylor decided that they should be fashioned after current European trends on GT cars which meant they would be small and light in weight. Several Grand Touring cars had bumpers made of aluminium, but this material was deemed too soft for the Elite; chrome-plated steel was too heavy and out of place, so the decision was made to use stainless steel.

While the Elite's bumpers were never designed to ward off collisions or create parking spaces, they were otherwise quite functional. The car had front and rear body seams, incurred in the moulding process, which were thus neatly hidden by the stainless steel pieces. The front oval incorporated ducting which facilitated air flow to the radiator and the side pieces functioned as splash shields that kept deep water from being thrown up on to the windscreen. The rear bumper worked similarly in keeping road debris and spray off the number plate and rear lights. Best of all, of course, was the fact the bumpers were handsome and entirely in keeping with the elegance and grace of the Elite's body shape.

The Elite was fitted with twin exhausts at the rear because Chapman liked the look and believed the visual effect suggested power. This was despite the fact that the exhaust manifold, whether high performance four-branch or standard cast iron, terminated in a single pipe which ran in a recess the length of the underbody from the engine bay to the rear wheel wells. This pipe had to be split with 'Y'-section tubing to achieve the desired appearance.

The aerodynamicist, Frank Costin

Frank Costin was a Chief Aerodynamicist for the de Havilland Aircraft Company Limited who enjoyed a light diversion by designing

The Elite's front bumpers neatly cover a seam on the body/ chassis. (George Rance)

The rear bumper also covers a manufacturing seam and protects the registration number from road debris. (George Rance)

97E

34C

Left *Aerodynamic evolution: the Lotus Nine.* (Author)

Middle left *Aerodynamic perfection: the Lotus Eleven.* (Author)

Bottom left *Frank Costin altered the body shape to incorporate the reverse camber line.* (Author)

streamlined body shapes for Colin Chapman's sports racing cars. He was responsible for the Lotus Mark 8, 9 and Eleven, and by 1957 was recognized as the leader in the application of aerodynamic principles to racing cars. His designs for Lotus were way ahead of their time and went on to set standards for both low drag and high-speed stability—a combination, as we have seen, that heretofore seemed to be mutually exclusive.

The designs were also pretty radical in appearance, which was all right for an all-out racer but Chapman was concerned that they might be too far out for a road car. And Costin, by his own admission, never did care what his cars looked like, only that they were correct aerodynamically. As a result of this, Chapman did not invite Costin's opinion until he had approved Kirwan-Taylor's final sketches.

When Costin saw the drawings he was pleased. The undertray was completely enclosed (save for drain openings and the radiator exhaust, but more on this in the next chapter), which eliminated turbulence caused by the normal underpinnings. Most important, however, was that the overall body shape was in the right proportions to incorporate Costin's 'reverse chamber principle'. Costin employed this element in all of his car bodies and it simply meant that if a line was drawn through the mean centre of the car's profile, the resulting curve mimicked the cross-section of an aircraft wing. With a negative angle of incidence (the front of the Elite was to be one inch lower than the rear) the body shape behaved like a similarly angled aerofoil. That is, it produced not only a degree of down force but also helped to control the car's centre of pressure which translated to increased stability in the pitch and yaw situations that would be encountered during heavy braking and fast cornering.

In order to get this precisely curved centre line on the Elite's profile, Costin raised the front wing lines slightly. He then increased the rake of the windscreen and moved the roof further back. He also decreased the rear screen's rearward extension, and he eliminated the fins which had been made redundant by the reverse camber line and newly raised rear deck.

The curvature of the Elite's side windows can be seen in this picture. (Author)

Costin then suggested that the back of the car be cut off 'Kamm' fashion. This technique was an aerodynamically correct solution to the back end of a car which, to be perfect, would have to taper to a point like a tear drop. A side benefit of a Kamm type of tail was the flat surface for the rear number plate. Kirwan-Taylor recalled wondering at this stage if 'we weren't copying Coopers with a Manx tail, but Chapman approved so we went with it'.

Costin made the Elite's leading edge more parabolic in curvature (less drag-inducing than other profiles) and he increased the radii of the curves which joined the wings with the bonnet. This facilitated the air flow around the cabin which, as we will see in the next chapter, was so devoid of turbulence that it created a visibility problem in foul weather. Typical of Costin's attention to detail was his specification that the rain gutters were to be curved in section, and thus less drag-inducing than the normal square variety.

The boys from Ford

Colin Chapman knew from his first thoughts on the Elite that his crew at Hornsey could never hope to take the car from prototype to production. He also intended to build more Elites than any Lotus to date; in

The Elite's tapered body shape was abbreviated by the Kamm style rear-end treatment, as here on Mike Ostrov/Hank Mauel's No 95 racing Elite. (Author)

fact, ten cars a week was projected. Chapman obviously needed help and began to visit the industry giants to see how they managed. On a visit to Ford's styling department at Dagenham he found three very receptive enthusiasts. They were John Frayling (a New Zealander), Ron Hickman (from South Africa) and Peter Cambridge. They were at once fascinated with the Elite project, and after taking a course in fibreglass at Wolverhampton they commenced to moonlight at Hornsey.

John Frayling

John Frayling was the first to join Lotus full time, and with a cut in pay! Of course, all three men were in their twenties and the romance of working for Lotus was a heady attraction. Also, the Elite was a whole car whereas at Ford their focus had been limited to the design of hub caps and trim moulding.

Frayling's particular expertise was in clay modelling and his first job was to sculpt Kirwan-Taylor's design in $\frac{1}{5}$ scale. Interestingly the special heat-setting clay he used had to be imported from Ford's styling department in Detroit, USA. Frayling's contribution to the ultimate look of the Elite was enormous because he alone transformed the flat images into three dimensions which were harmonious from all visual angles.

Ron Hickman and Peter Cambridge

Both men's major contribution to the Elite came at the prototype stage. Hickman was skilled at production engineering and handled the leap from the full-size plaster model to the prototype and then on to the production line. He was involved in the scale model phase for a time, and convinced everyone that the partially covered front wheels had to go despite the fact that the Eleven had them and they were effective in reducing turbulence. The problem was that the steering lock was limited by the bodywork (unless a narrower track was used or the wings were flared). The Eleven, for example, took some 40 feet to turn round which was unacceptable on a road car.

Peter Cambridge handled interior design which was sorted out after the full-scale model was built. He was responsible for the Elite's cockpit including, as we will examine later, the design of the unusually high-backed seats.

After dinner at Monken Hadley

If all this sounds like the Elite was designed in neat, compartmentalized little episodes, it wasn't. There were numerous meetings at Chapman's house (at Monken Hadley, near Barnet in Hertfordshire) with Kirwan-Taylor, Costin, Frayling, Hickman and Cambridge, that usually began after dinner and lasted sometimes until two or three in the morning. These discussions were always emphatic, often heated and only occasionally humorous and consisted of each man arguing from his point of expertise. Chapman wanted a saleable race winner, Kirwan-Taylor an elegant Grand Turismo, Costin an aerodynamic *tour de force*, Hickman practicality, especially in terms of production, Cambridge ergonomics and Frayling visual harmony.

That the Elite ended up as beautiful as it did was a credit to the team's desire for excellence and their willingness to explore ideas outside the norm. Of course, Frank Costin had his own theory which was that 'neither Peter nor John were professional stylists and as a result had not managed to achieve the level of sin necessary in that profession'.

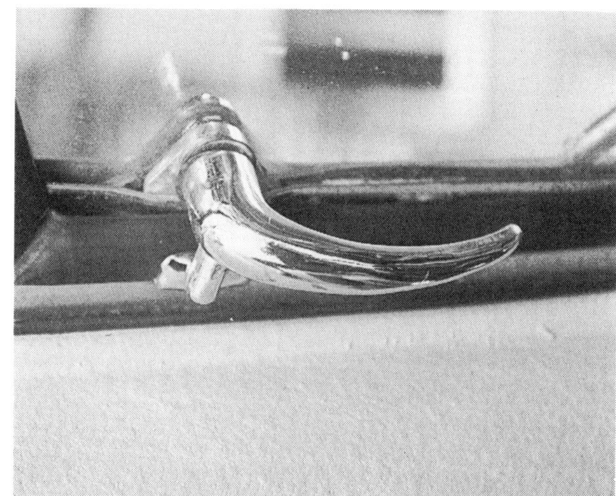

The Elite's latches and handles were a perfect illustration of the design team's philosophy that 'more was less'. (Author)

Above *Outside door handle*

Above right *Quarter window latch*

Right *Inside door handle*

Below right *Side window latch*

Below *Boot latch*

Chapter 2

The prototypes

When he first conjured up the idea for the Elite, Chapman considered a spaceframe chassis clothed in alloy bodywork. After all, this was standard Lotus practice. As discussed in the previous chapter, the trouble with this was how one would get into the car over high chassis sides (a necessary feature of a spaceframe) and through what kind of doors? Chapman liked the Mercedes Benz 300SL and felt that the German car's solutions were quite satisfactory, but to do something similar he would be faced with the enormous cost of tooling up for a production run that he envisaged could go as high as 5,000 cars. Recall that the Eleven was the most prolific Lotus to date, yet only 300 of these were built. And, as always, Chapman was concerned about strength versus weight and, by Lotus standards, the Mercedes was quite heavy.

Why fibreglass?

Instead, Chapman wanted to use a material that, at the time, was being hailed as the construction medium of the future, glass-reinforced plastic (GRP)—fibreglass. From his first notion, Chapman wondered if plastic could not be formed in such a way as to incorporate both the body and chassis. He was familiar with the first commercial uses of fibreglass, boats and a few car body kits which consisted of an unstressed shell mounted on a proprietary chassis. The features that Chapman found irresistible were the low cost of both the material and its fabrication. In fact, if it came to that, fibreglass could be formed using an unskilled workforce. Another advantage, perhaps more to the stylists than to the engineers, was that one's imagination was the only limitation to the complexity of the shapes possible in fibreglass. In Chapman's mind, however, it was GRP's primary characteristic, that of resin bonding, that lent itself beautifully to his ideas about a monocoque body/chassis structure.

Because he sought to break completely new ground with his monocoque, Chapman needed to learn as much about the nature of GRP as he could. He read everything he could get his hands on, magazines, books and technical papers. He listened to the representatives of various fibreglass manufacturers and he examined the boats (including some built by Maximar which would eventually get the contract for the first 250 body/chassis units) and car bodies that were made of the material. The most significant information came, however, from the de Havilland Aircraft Company. Its engineers told Chapman that modern epoxy resins had enormous strengths and were used, for example, in the wing of the de Havilland Comet.

Chapman also learned that fibreglass had excellent strength (especially in tension) and, depending on thickness, was even comparable to steel. An unexpected advantage which made the material superior to steel (other than the fact that it did not rust) was that on impact the resulting damage was localized. That is, all distortion occurred at the point of impact and was not telegraphed to adjacent panels. In a steel-bodied car, for example, doors often refused to open after a frontal impact. Chapman appreciated the safety aspect of a material that dissipated energy before it reached the driver and passenger. As we will see in later chapters, the Elite was superbly constructed and completely safe, and racing drivers survived some of the most fearsome of crashes with either minor injuries or none at all.

Fibreglass also had the potential for thermal insulation which was no small advantage in the British Isles. Alas, Chapman also learned, after production had begun, that it also served to encapsulate and magnify sound. But the more Chapman learned, the more enthusiastic he became. Small-scale experiments led to the conclusion that fibreglass could also handle the stress of suspension and drive train loads as long as the attachment points were widely separated and isolated from the material by rubber bushings. Chapman finally became convinced that fibreglass was precisely the material he was after.

The body/chassis

Colin Chapman was trained as a structural engineer at London University and had no trouble in picturing load paths on stressed sheet material. In order to dissipate these potentially destructive forces on a fibreglass structure, he had to feed these stresses into as many different planes as possible. The method he arrived at to accomplish this was to incorporate bulkheads and enclosed torsion boxes within the body/chassis. This technique had a secondary benefit of providing rigidity despite long panel lengths. The thickness of each panel varied with the expected load, and ranged, for example, from about $\frac{1}{4}$ to $\frac{3}{8}$ in for the undertray to $\frac{1}{8}$ in for the sides of the engine bay.

There were eight major torsion boxes in Chapman's design. Each front wing aft of the wheel was sectioned with bulkheads, as was the air intake. In the latter instance the box was open at each end to allow air to flow to the radiator. The fourth torsion box was also open at both ends and was formed by the transmission tunnel. The differential mount was the fifth torsion box and was a right angle in cross-section. Strength here was maintained by a double wall construction and the use of thick section fibreglass. The roof (also double wall) made up the sixth box and the door sills the seventh and eighth.

One of the exceptionally clever aspects of the Elite's body/chassis was that nowhere, on panels normally open to view, was visible the 'shredded wheat' texture common to fibreglass. This was because each of the panels was constructed in halves so that when bonded together only the finished, or smooth side was open to view. Examples of this technique were the bonnet and boot lids and even the wheel wells. Interestingly, it was not Chapman who thought of it but John Frayling while he was sorting out production at Chapman's first Elite body/chassis subcontractor, Maximar Mouldings Ltd. What pleased Chapman, besides the fact that there was nothing in the Elite's appearance to give away its fibreglass construction, was that Frayling's double skinning provided strength and rigidity to large pieces of glass and a good heft and feel as well.

Metal reinforcement

Chapman decided to use steel reinforcement in only two places in the body/chassis. This was done in the interests of long-term reliability rather than to shore up any inability of the structure to accept point loads, although the addition of metal did simplify the problem of jacking points. Chapman designed a tubular steel hoop that was imbedded in the fibreglass around the windscreen and beneath the dashboard,

This picture shows where the front subframe is positioned in the chassis and how it is concealed within the radiator ducting. (A.N.E. Bates)

Len Pritchard in 1988, in front of the building in Edmonton where the Earls Court prototype was constructed. The building was loaned to Chapman by the owners, Williams and Pritchard panel beaters. Later, it became the first workshop for Cosworth Engineering Co. (David Morgan)

John Frayling's 1/5 scale clay model in front of the Earls Court prototype which is under construction. (Lotus)

and which was welded to a pair of vertical posts that anchored the door hinges. As we will see later in this chapter, the design of these hinges turned out to be a major undertaking. The vertical posts extended slightly out the bottom of the undertray and served as jacking points which could raise one side of the car.

The other metal reinforcement was a steel subframe, partially embedded in the forward part of the chassis, which incorporated pickups for the engine mounts, radiator, electric fan, horns and front suspension. Interestingly, small metal reinforcers were used later in production to correct weaknesses in the car, although this was done due to a fault in the manufacture and not in the original design. These will be discussed in detail in Chapter 5.

The first Elite

With a design in hand and a team to build it at the ready, all Chapman needed was space. The workshops at Hornsey were fairly bursting at the seams and there was also the need for secrecy. Chapman wisely did not want prying eyes during the Elite's prototype phase because there were bound to be problems and delays. With a concept as radical as that of the Elite, he did not want any adverse publicity to spoil its début. With all the coming and going at Hornsey caused by production of the Eleven and the single-seat Type 12, there was no hope of keeping anything confidential.

Chapman's solution was to rent a building from Len Pritchard (of Williams and Pritchard) in Edmonton. There was no sign on the door, and nothing to indicate that Lotus was doing business inside. When word finally did leak that something was going on, the team simply replied that they were working on a replacement for the Lotus Mark 6. As it happened, this was close to the truth because the Mark 7 was designed concurrent with the Elite and its prototype received its début at the same time.

The first person to go to work at Edmonton was John Frayling. His job was to sculpt a full-size mock-up, in plaster, which would serve as the master for the production moulds. He began by constructing a plywood buck of transverse and longitudinal sections, which, when fitted together, mimicked the shape of the car. This he overlaid with wire mesh which supported a layer of plaster of Paris that was sculpted into the final contours.

The process was agonizingly slow and laborious because Frayling worked with home-made tools and his helpers were both occasional and few. Also, as he worked, Frayling was confronted with problems like how individual sections would fit together and how to accommodate the shrinkage that occurred as fibreglass cured. He did a masterful job with these calculations because Lotus did not have the resources to purchase an accurate surface table to obtain base-line measurements.

Chapman became impatient. He wanted to début the Elite with a three-car team at the 1957 Le Mans in June and his good friend in Paris, 'Jabby' Crombac, had even secured entries. Unfortunately, as summer approached it became obvious that one complete car was out of the question, let alone a team. With luck, and all-out effort, perhaps they could have the first Elite ready by the London Motor Show at Earls Court in October.

Like a child's model car kit

Frayling completed the full-size mock-up in early summer. From it he made four moulds, one for the top of the car down to the door sills, another for the undertray and two for the doors. Interestingly, the Earls Court prototype had a chrome strip running along the lower edge of the car from wheel well to wheel well which covered the seam between the top and bottom sections. This was the only Elite to have both this decoration and this mould configuration. Frayling would alter the moulds many times before the car was ready for production.

After hand-finishing the surface of the moulds to eliminate as many imperfections as possible, Frayling mounted them in rigid supports to eliminate any flexing or distortion in the lay-up process. One can only

The Earls Court prototype under construction at the workshop in Edmonton. The fixtures in the foreground are the moulds taken from the full-scale plaster model. (Lotus)

imagine his elation when this was finally done. Frayling was now ready to cast the first Lotus Elite shell, and on a Saturday in early August 1957, he and Peter Kirwan-Taylor laid in the glass fibre cloth and brushed in the mixture of polyester resin and catalyst. Hobbyists, boat builders and DIY Lotus owners the world over would have recognized the aroma and, as Frank Costin called it, the mixture of 'shredded wheat' and golden honey.

The next morning, Kirwan-Taylor and Frayling pulled the sections out of the moulds and put them together like a child's model car kit. An excited telephone call brought Chapman out to have a look. He was delighted, of course, and the rest of the morning was spent admiring the translucent shell. Chapman finally brought everyone back to reality with the shattering reminder that Earls Court was less than two months away!

The Earls Court Elite

In what amounted to a near superhuman effort, the plastic shell was filled in with most of the bits to make up a car just in the nick of time. It took Frayling, Hickman, Cambridge and a Hornsey foreman by the name of Graham Hill to pull it off, and then only by putting in 10- to 12-hour days. Several others, including Peter Kirwan-Taylor, dropped in for evenings and weekends to lend a hand.

At first, Frayling attempted to fabricate moulds for easy assembly as he built up the Elite's interior panels and bulkheads. He had made about 60 of them before he realized that, at the rate he was doing both operations, time would run out before the car could be readied for the show. To speed things up he finished several of the torsion boxes and panels in light alloy and covered them in fibreglass for effect. He also realized that so many moulds would make production a nightmare; his first priority after Earls Court would be to simplify the moulding process.

The week before the show was a flurry of activity with all of the normal disasters. These began with news from Coventry that a new 1216cc FWE would not be ready in time, so an old 1098cc FWA was pinched from the Eleven shops and installed. Time ran out before the prop shaft and radiator could be built up, so the first Elite was actually a non-runner.

The car was painted with its two-tone silver-grey finish the weekend before the Tuesday press showing. The interior, including seats and carpets, was installed as the paint cured on Monday morning. That night, the paint was rubbed down and the windscreen broke as it was locked in place. A very sympathetic glazier was roused from his bed to make another.

By 6 am on Tuesday the windscreen was in place, a coat of wax was on the car and all was ready to trailer the Elite to Alexandra Palace for photographs. Another new Lotus, the Seven, accompanied the Elite. At the time, no one could have predicted how the humbler of the two would very nearly save Lotus from bankruptcy, but more on this in Chapter 9.

The 42nd International Motor Show at Earls Court, London, opened at 10 am on 16 October 1957 with the Elite in its appointed place. The rest, as they say, is history. Press and spectator alike marvelled at the car's fluid shape and novel construction; never mind how few understood it, the Elite was the hit of the show. Chapman had succeed-

Above *The Earls Court prototype on its trailer bound for Alexandra Palace for picture taking. The chaps in overalls were from the works at Hornsey and were seeing the Elite for the first time.* (Lotus)

The Earls Court prototype during its photo session at Alexandra Palace. Notice the boot support, absent on production cars, and the rectangular tail-lights which, in production, were changed for a pair of Lucas lenses. (Lotus)

Rear view of the Earls Court prototype. Notice the chrome strip along the rocker panel. (Lotus)

The Earls Court prototype in position at the show. The large photograph behind shows the Lotus Eleven sweep at Le Mans the previous June. Notice the Elite's chrome wire wheels. (Lotus)

ed in pulling off a complete surprise because, despite persistent rumours about a new Lotus for road use, nothing substantial had leaked to the press.

This was all according to plan because by then Chapman had no doubts that his new Elite was going to take a long time to develop before any real production could get under way. With so radical a design, any public exposure to problems would only hurt the car's potential in the marketplace. As we will see in later chapters, the world's first plastic monocoque automobile was going to be a hard sell anyway.

Meanwhile, the team from Edmonton enjoyed the ten days of the show and basked in the attention. The only real drama occurred when both doors locked and refused to respond to the key. This proved more than a little bothersome when Princess Margaret and Lord Snowdon asked Peter Kirwan-Taylor if they could sit in the car. Thankfully, a little good-natured lock picking and fiddling on the part of Lord Snowdon and Kirwan-Taylor enabled the Royal couple to get in.

Special features of the Earls Court Elite

A casual observer might conclude that the Earls Court Elite was identical to the rest of its progeny. This was, however, not the case because there were numerous detail elements which, in the interests of economy, practicality or ease of manufacture, were changed in the production cars. Several of these features are visible in the R.H. Hodge cut-away drawing, first published in the 18 October 1957 edition of *Autosport*.

The Earls Court Elite had headlights, incorporating sidelights, which could be adjusted by means of a control inside the car. This was simply a wire attached to the upper adjustment screw which extended back to a knob on the dashboard, and twisting this knob moved the headlight up or down. The side windows were fixed in place with ventilation provided by hinged quarter windows and slots in the bodywork above the rear window. In production, the slots disappeared and the side windows became removable perspex panels formed with a compound curvature.

Two features found in the Lotus Eleven were tried on the Earls Court Elite and these were a tubular steel subframe which supported the differential and a radiator air outlet through a duct in the floor ahead of the engine bay. However, tests on the car after the show proved that a fibreglass box could handle differential loads without the need of steel reinforcement.

The separate undertray duct for the radiator (also visible in the Hodge cut-away) was abandoned because it was thought that too little cool airflow would find its way into the engine bay to feed the carb intakes. A related problem, discovered in later prototypes, was that the inboard rear disc brakes were operating at higher than normal temperatures. By closing the bottom duct and allowing the top half of the radiator to exhaust into the engine bay (the lower half was fed into the wheel wells which were low-pressure sites), the carbs got air, albeit pre-heated, and there was a constant flow of air down the fully enclosed transmission tunnel to cool the rear brakes. Because the diff box exhausted downwards, in another low-pressure region, a degree of suck was built into the system as well.

As we have already seen, the Earls Court car was the only Elite with the rocker panel chrome strip. It also had rectangular tail-lights which were changed in production to a pair of round Lucas lenses. The exterior door handles were simple push-buttons that were later traded for a finger pull with a push-button attached. These last items, interestingly enough, came straight from the Hillman Husky parts bin.

There were several other running changes made to the prototypes that followed the Earls Court car and these will be detailed in the next section. Meanwhile, the show Elite was returned to the works and after a series of stress evaluations was placed in the tiny showroom that faced Tottenham Lane. These evaluations, incidentally, yielded a figure of 3,000 foot pounds of force per degree of chassis twist which was superior to any conventional GT then on the roads! After several months on display, Chapman ordered that the car be taken back to Ed-

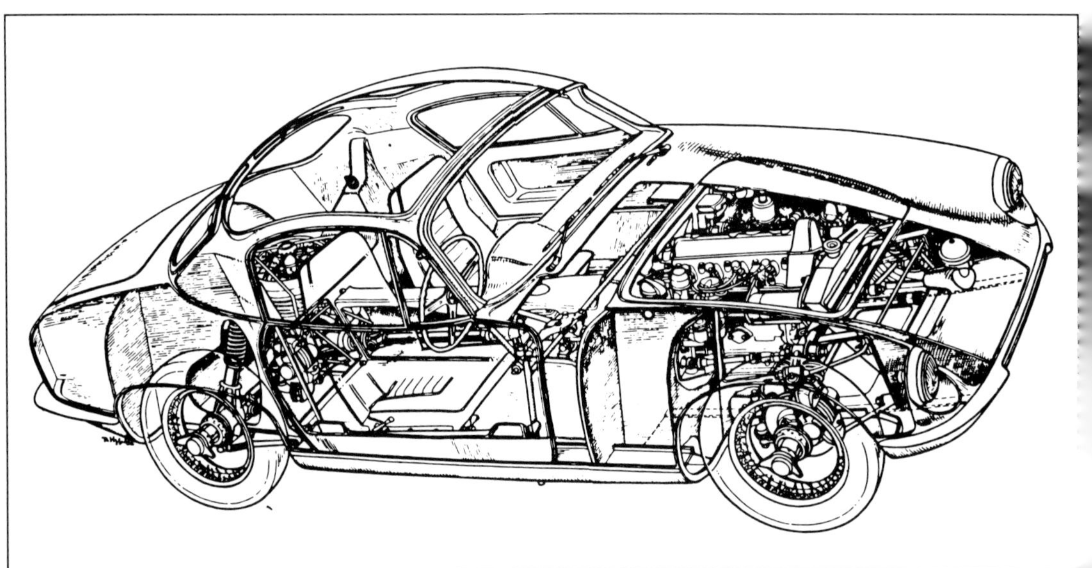

Cutaway drawing of the Earls Court car illustrating the myriad details that differed with the production cars, like the undertray radiator ducting, ventilation slots above the rear windscreen and the steel subframe for the differential. (Richard Spelberg collection)

After Earls Court, the show Elite was displayed in the tiny ground floor showroom at Hornsey. (Lotus)

monton to be broken up. Despite several offers to buy the car, Chapman wisely chose to destroy what was in reality only a mock-up of the real car yet to come.

The pre-production prototypes

Although Chapman would have liked to have seen the Elite get into production at once, it was obvious, as the Earls Court car was put together, that too many questions still needed answers. After all, the car was intended as much for road use as it was for racing and a touring customer's expectations were quite different from those of a racer. Also, until Frayling could streamline the body/chassis construction process, an assembly line was out of the question.

Chapman's plan was to build a handful of cars and get them to the racers as quickly as possible. In this way the production process could be worked out simultaneously with testing and development. At the hands of racers, design weaknesses would appear at once and the cars could be rushed back to the works for modifications or repair. Running changes could therefore be incorporated quickly and easily well before cars were subjected to the rigours of the road.

The vagaries of early Lotus record-keeping make it impossible to determine just how many of the first Elites were considered developmental prototypes, but it is likely the initial 10 to 15 served this purpose. Fortunately, a member of the Elite production team at Hornsey, Tony Caldersmith, not only took special notice of the early cars, but also took notes! Tony recalled that chassis numbers 1001 and 1002 (the Earls Court Elite was not given a chassis number) were constructed at Edmonton, the next batch were assembled at Tottenham Lane (1003–1006) and then back again to Edmonton to chassis number 1015. The rest of Elite production took place at Chapman's new factory at Cheshunt, but more of that in Chapter 5. Maximar Mouldings Ltd began moulding Elites with the third chassis number.

The Elite production staff at Hornsey and later at Edmonton consisted of Tony Caldersmith, Production Manager Graham Lewis, Len Laverock and Peter Lean (the son of movie director David Lean). Mal Simpson (Rob Walker's mechanic) and David Lazenby also spent short periods on Elite assembly. Caldersmith remembered that besides the fellows on the payroll, there was also a steady stream of volunteers who would drift in and out of the works, lending a hand as they passed through, all for the thrill of being a part of what was going on at Lotus.

The Caldersmith Chronicles

Chapman originally designed the Elite with its primary fuel tank in the right front wing, a Kirwan-Taylor idea which allowed the car's weight distribution to remain the same as the tank emptied. The Earls Court car had the filler inside the engine bay, but the rest of the cars with this feature had the fillers mounted on the exterior top surface of the wing. The tanks used the inside of the torsion box aft of the wheel well, and a problem which occurred right away was one of leaks that usually found their way into the cockpit. Instead of placing a metal tank inside the box, the interior was coated with a sealer that did not always seal. Most of the pre-production prototypes had these wing tanks, and a few early production cars had them as well. Kirwan-Taylor recalled that unfortunately there was also a negative public reaction to fuel tanks located in this place, and eventually almost all of the original cars were converted to a steel tank ($6\frac{1}{2}$ gallons) in the boot.

Caldersmith remembered that another problem arose with the prototypes when they were driven at high speed in particularly foul weather, which was the obstruction of vision out of the side windows. It seems that the airflow was so well attached to the cabin that rain water was transformed into a translucent sheet that made sighting out of the sides of the car extremely difficult. Costin solved the problem by designing a diagonal strip of stainless steel which was fixed to the outside surface of the quarter window. The trailing edge of this strip was raised to create a degree of turbulence which prevented water from forming a boundary layer. Who but Costin would have thought of it?

Most of the prototypes had a triangular-shaped rear shock absorber tower in the cabin that left the top of the shock mounting exposed. Caldersmith also recalled that several cars were delivered without rain gutters, and that the battery location moved from the centre of the boot, when a wing tank was fitted, to a shelf with a cover on the left-hand side of the boot when the conventional tank was used. Oddly enough, the Earls Court Elite had its battery on the left-hand side of the boot even though a wing tank was fitted. An irritating weakness on the early prototypes was that the doors drooped on their hinges, but from chassis 1004 the hinges and their mounting uprights were made of thicker steel which cured the problem.

1001 and 1002

According to Tony Caldersmith's records, the first two pre-production prototypes were built, essentially side by side, at Edmonton. Both were completed some six months after the Earls Court Show, and both were finished in yellow. From his first thoughts on a fibreglass monocoque, Chapman believed that a paint job was redundant on a GRP structure and that colour should be incorporated in the gel coat, the thin layer of resin that forms the smooth surface on top of a fibreglass mat or cloth. Chassis 1001 and 1002 consequently had yellow pigment added to this exterior surface resin.

Production and quality of finish problems prevented Chapman from incorporating this technique in the Elite process, but he never let go of the idea. In fact, he worked on it for 20 years until it finally gelled (pun

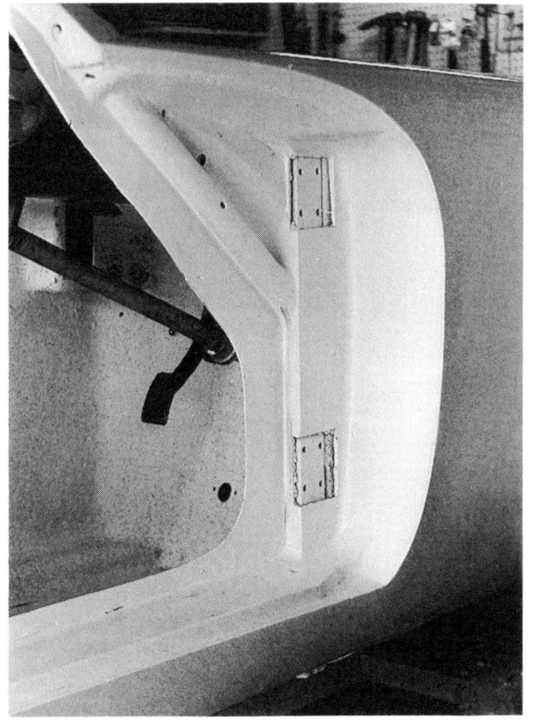

Above *Late production door hinge attachment detail.* (Author)

Above right *The cover of* Road & Track *magazine showing chassis 1001 which eventually went to Ian Walker.* (Road & Track)

intended) in the Resinsukt Process which was perfected by Technocraft at the Lotus works at Hethel for both cars and boats.

Chassis 1001 was meant to have its début at the Geneva Motor Show and so was built to a left-hand-drive specification. As it happened, the car was not completed in time, but its finish was so good that the car was transported around London and photographed for use in future publicity and sales brochures. The August 1958 issue of *Road & Track* magazine featured this spectacular car on its cover.

Posing done, the car was converted to RHD and painted a pale green, undoubtedly a ruse to convince the press that Elites were beginning to roll off the production line, for by then a few journalists were beginning to ask what was happening. In any case, it was given the registration number EL 5 and loaned to Ian Walker for one year on the condition that he race the car as often and on as many different circuits as he could. Chapter 4 will detail this tough assignment.

Meanwhile, chassis 1002 was loaned, in the same manner and with the same instructions, to John Lawry. Caldersmith's notes show that it was registered 923 FPJ and was repainted in British Racing Green. Lawry spent the year chasing Walker but, nonetheless, finishing well up at the chequered flag.

Lawry was so taken with his Elite he bought it after the season was over and apparently retired the car from competition despite records showing that he submitted an entry for the 1959 Le Mans 24 Hours. In 1988 chassis 1002 was owned by Horst Auer in Germany, and has been treated to a ground-up restoration; the accompanying photographs illustrate several details that disappeared in later production. Interestingly, Tony's records show that both of these cars had upgraded FWA engines as the production FWEs were still not available from Coventry Climax.

In the restoration of chassis 1002, the wing tank has been fitted with a stainless steel container. Chassis number 1002 differed from production Elites in numerous details including the transmission tunnel **middle**, *the housing for the Chapman strut* **bottom** *and the boot configuration* **far right**. (Horst Auer)

1003

Chassis 1003, according to Ron Hickman, was the first to be built at Maximar although the actual labour was supplied by a team of Lotus men which included Hickman, Frayling and, occasionally, John Standen. Standen was a purchasing agent from Ford who had also been pirated by Chapman. He became a close personal friend and one of the original shareholders of Lotus Cars; eventually he took charge of all purchasing for the works.

This third chassis came to be known as 'the doorless wonder' because it was driven on the roads, for a time, without them. Eventually it was completed, however, and was painted BRG and sold to Peter Lumsden who registered the car WUU 2. This was one of the most famous Elites of all time because Lumsden took the car to a class win at Le Mans in 1959. In 1988 this Elite was owned by Matt Carroll in Australia.

1004

According to Tony Caldersmith's notes, this car was also used by the works for development and testing of close ratio gears and cast iron front brake calipers (as opposed to light alloy) before being sold to Jonathan Williams, when it was painted dark blue and given the registration number JPW 24. Williams raced the car in club events with good success in 1959. Today this Elite is owned by Tony Mantle, the proprietor of Climax Engine Services.

1005

This light blue Elite was prepared for the Paris Auto Show in 1958. It was subsequently purchased by Sir John Whitmore and raced in England and Europe, but unfortunately was destroyed in a spectacular crash at Monza in Italy. Luckily, Whitmore was unhurt and went on to take a second in class at Le Mans in the Border Reivers Elite, with Jim Clark co-driving.

1006

This car was sold to Graham Warner and became one of the most famous Elites in racing, LOV 1. Warner's exploits in English club racing

The ex-Lumsden Elite is still being raced in historic events in Australia. Here is the car in 1988. (Photographer unknown)

(along with Les Leston's DAD 10) reached almost legendary status and the whole story will be told in Chapter 7.

1007

Tony had no records for this car but it was probably the red Elite, registered 6 SME, that went to the Rome Auto Show. On its return, the car posed for photos for publicity and sales brochures. It may also have been the rumoured ultra-lightweight chassis which was raced several times by Colin Chapman.

1008 and 1009

Both of these cars were prepared for the 1958 Earls Court Show. Chassis 1008 was painted light blue (more on Elite colours in Chapter 9) and was sold to Keith Hall after the show. Hall was a works Eleven driver who scored a Le Mans class win in 1957. Interestingly, there is no record that Hall raced his Elite, which means that this may have been the first pre-production prototype to be used exclusively on the road.

Chassis 1009 was painted lime green and delivered to Chris Barber, then, as now, a popular Dixieland jazz band leader. Barber registered his car CB 23 and put it on the street with the occasional club race just to explore the possibilities. He obviously enjoyed himself because as time progressed his Elite was transformed into an all-out racer which, by then, rarely saw road use.

1010

Lotus records show that this chassis was delivered on 31 December 1958, the same date given to Chris Barber's car, and these Elites have the earliest delivery dates of the production run, prototype or otherwise. Even though the cars that went to Williams, Whitmore, Warner and Hall were built earlier they were first used, for a time, by the works and did not go to their owners until February and March 1959—at least, so said Lotus records which were not always entirely accurate. For example, chassis 1010, invoiced on New Year's Eve to Ian Scott-Watson of the Scottish Border Reivers racing team for Jim Clark to drive, was actually raced by Clark the day after Christmas at Brands Hatch!

1011

This Elite was first painted BRG and was also used as a works development car. It crashed heavily on London Bridge and required the grafting of a new front end.

1012

There were no Caldersmith notes for this car.

1013 and 1015

These numbers were assigned to the light blue and BRG Elites that went to Sebring for the 1959 race.

1014

This chassis was a dark blue Elite sold to Lt Merle Roberson, an American serviceman stationed in Berlin. The car was involved in a head-on crash on the Autobahn but, fortunately, the lieutenant survived.

Although development certainly continued after the 15th car was delivered, most experts agree that further refinements were relatively minor until the change to the Series II and body/chassis manufacture by the Bristol Aircraft Company. Chapman was satisfied that his concept was not only sound but was also winning races. Surely, all appeared ready for full-scale production. All he needed was a new factory which, as we will see later, his friend Peter Kirwan-Taylor helped to arrange. Meanwhile, Maximar Mouldings Ltd, of Pulborough, Sussex, under the guidance of Frayling and Hickman, was writing the book on fibreglass construction.

Chapter 3

The engine, suspension and drive line

The engine

Fire pump origins

In 1954, a fire pump and fork-lift manufacturer by the name of Coventry Climax started building racing engines. When they quit motor sport 11 years later, their power plants had accounted for four World Championships in Formula 1 Grand Prix racing (Cooper in 1959–1960, and Lotus in 1963 and 1965), countless Formula 2 and sports car victories and the definition of entry level club racing in Great Britain in the mid 1950s. And it all began with the design and production of a new petrol engine to power fire-fighters' water pumps.

Coventry Climax was one of the major suppliers of portable fire pumps during the Second World War and the high output and reliability of their product helped England survive the Blitz. Stories were widely told of Climax fire pumps in action for weeks at a time, without the need for service or adjustment.

The engines were small displacement, side-valve, four-cylinder units which, interestingly, were developed from a line of automotive power plants supplied by Climax to the car industry in the 1920s and '30s. In fire pump use, the engines were coupled to a water pump which could be carried by two or three men.

After the war, Coventry Climax continued to build self-contained fire pumps in addition to serving industry with the manufacture of fork-lift trucks. By 1950 its old line of automobile engines seemed all but forgotten and probably would have remained so had it not been for the outbreak of new hostilities.

The Korean 'police action' had erupted into a full-scale shooting war and the British Civil Defence moved to modernize its equipment. Part of the programme was to put out a call, backed by the promise of a large contract, for a new and improved fire pump. The requirements included greater mobility and increased power in order to deliver water to modern high-rise buildings; specifically, a fire pump with twice the output and half the weight of existing equipment was needed. This meant a pump driven by a petrol engine contained within some kind of carriage weighing no more than 350 pounds but with a power output of not less than 35 bhp. To ensure reliability, the engine must also be able to rev from dead cold to at least 4,000 rpm and maintain that performance without significant wear.

The assignment was given to two men at Coventry Climax, Wally Hassan and Harry Mundy. Prophetically, both men had racing backgrounds; Hassan had worked for Bentley in its Le Mans-winning years and then for ERA, Bristol and Jaguar where he played a major role in the development of the XK engine, while Mundy had come from BRM where he specialized in modern alloys. Together, the two men laid out the design of a petrol engine which they hoped would win the Government contract for Coventry Climax. Management accepted the design in September 1950, and saw a running prototype in April 1951.

The FWP

The engine was a single overhead cam, four-cylinder unit that displaced 1020cc. The block was an aluminium casting that utilized cast iron cylinder liners. Both the crank- and camshafts ran in three bearings, the latter driven by a duplex roller chain. A jackshaft drove the oil pump, magneto and fuel pump, and the weight of the engine was a mere 180 pounds. Coventry Climax named the engine 'FWP', featherweight pump.

Although, at first glance, the specifications sounded suspiciously exotic for an industrial engine, everything made good sense. The use of alloy was for weight saving and the SOHC design allowed for both ample revs and a large safety margin. Valve clearances were set by means

Magazine advert for Coventry Climax. (Coventry Climax)

of shims, as in the Jaguar XK engine, which meant that there could be extremely long intervals between adjustments. Clearances were generous throughout the engine which allowed for peak revs from a cold start. Unfortunately, this design element also contributed to one of the Elite engine's most maligned characteristics, but more of that later.

When the Government came to see the new fire pump, Coventry Climax put on a convincing demonstration. The engine developed 40 bhp and was red-lined at 6,000 rpm. Water output was 30 gallons per minute and the entire unit, packaged in a neat tubular steel carriage, could be carried easily by two men. The contract was won, with the first order for 15,000 units!

The featherweight racing engine

Of course, Hassan and Mundy were anxious to get into motor racing and they convinced Coventry Climax management that such an endeavour would promote the company's industrial products. As unlikely as this sounds, an advertising campaign was mounted with the slogan 'The Fire Pump that Wins Races'. Oddly enough it worked, and the Godiva emblem (depicting the young lady who took her breezy horse-back ride through the streets of Coventry in the 11th century) became a familiar trademark.

At the London Motor Show of 1953, Coventry Climax displayed a prototype light alloy V-8, intended for Formula 1, and a fire pump engine bored out to 1098cc and named the FWA (Featherweight Series 'A'—for automobile) to attract builders of sports cars in the 1100cc class. One of the show-goers was Colin Chapman who not only took a keen interest, but also ordered an engine to test for the 1954 season.

The FWA

At that time, Lotus specialized in small-bore racing cars, and Chapman's first FWA was installed in a Lotus Mark 9. The engine was ideally suited to the Lotus with its high power output and light weight, but an unexpected and soon to be realized attribute would be its extraordinary reliability. In Stage I form the FWA had a compression ratio of 9.8 to 1 and was rated at 76 bhp at 6,200 rpm. A blow to the knitted gloves and tweed cap fraternity was that the transition from pump to racing car required few changes.

The castings were cleaned up so that the block took on a slightly more finished look, a steel crankshaft was substituted for the cast iron version, the bore was increased to a displacement of 1098cc, which required new pistons, and the compression ratio was increased. Larger valves and up-rated springs were fitted together with a four-branch, free-flow exhaust system and an alloy intake manifold for the twin SU carburettors. A distributor with centrifugal advance replaced the magneto and a splash pan was installed below the crank throws.

The ultimate development of the FWA was a degree of tune called the Stage III. This took brake horsepower to 96 at about 7,500 rpm. The upgrade required the skimming of 40 thou off the head for a 10.5 to 1 compression ratio, fitting a five-bearing cam with .360 inches of lift (Stage I had a three-bearing with .310 inches of lift) and oversize valve springs. Twin Webers in either 38 or 40 DCOE (side draft) configuration could be used in place of the SUs. The three-bearing camshaft, incidentally, was safe to 7,200 rpm, while the five-bearing could

Two FWEs with Weber carbs; one has early rod and lever linkage and the other has a throttle cable. Both employ apparently complex throttle actuators. (Author)

Twin SU installation. Notice the in-line coolant thermostat, upper left. (Author)

be twisted to 7,900 with absolute reliability.

By 1955 the Coventry Climax FWA had become the dominant engine in the 1100cc class in England and Europe. In that year alone, Great Britain witnessed 69 firsts, 49 seconds and 42 third places. By 1958 the Lotus Eleven with its FWA had become the most successful small-bore sports racer of all time!

The FWB

Buoyed by the success of the FWA, Coventry Climax decided to bring out the Series 'B' at 1460cc to compete in the 1½-litre racing class. The conversion necessitated boring the cylinders to a 3-inch diameter (from 2.85) and stroking the crankshaft to provide a throw of 3.15 inches (from 2.625). The result was a satisfying engine with abundant torque and a brake horsepower figure of 100 at 6,400 rpm. Unfortunately, the crankshaft was prone to breakage at peak revs so a strict red-line of 6,000 had to be maintained regardless of the type of lift of the camshaft.

FWA + FWB = FWE

By the time Chapman and Kirwan-Taylor began discussing plans for the Elite, the friendship between Lotus and Coventry Climax had grown strong. When Chapman needed a favour Coventry Climax responded, so the company listened intently when Chapman inquired about a special engine for his new monocoque GT. Chapman told them he wanted an FW engine to contest the 1300cc class.

Climax agreed and assembled the FWE (Featherweight Elite) which combined the FWA's crankshaft with the FWB's bore. The result was a 1216cc (74.25 cubic inches) engine that weighed 210 pounds, complete with ancillaries. Despite popular myth, this was the only engine Lotus ever offered for the Elite. There were instances of works-installed engines other than the FWE, but these were done for racing purposes or experimentation and will be discussed later in this chapter.

Interestingly, Coventry Climax tested a prototype FWE by fitting one in a company MG Magnette ZA saloon. The engine weighed 112 pounds less than the MG unit and, with twin SUs and a fire pump camshaft, it managed 100 miles per hour in top gear and 0 to 50 in around 10 seconds, all with a fuel consumption of 29 miles per gallon! Coventry Climax originally planned on building a cheaper version of the FWE using a cast iron block, but none were ever built.

Stage I

The FWE, like the 'A', was eventually offered in three stages of tune. In Stage I guise the compression ratio was 10.0 to 1, intake was via a single SU carburettor and exhaust by a cast iron manifold. The camshaft was carried in three bearings and was ground to .310 inches of lift. The power output was about 75 bhp at 6,100 rpm.

All three engines ('A', 'B' and 'E'), incidentally, used the same head, valve train and ancillaries. Ostensibly the blocks were identical but in reality the FWA used a different casting and was identified by two separate oil fittings on either end of its lower left flank to route oil, by flexible lines, to a remote filter. The FWB and FWE shared the same casting which had its oil galleries exit at a boss located at the centre of its lower left flank. A standard Tecalemit filter assembly was bolted to this boss.

Single SU intake manifold. (Author)

The Stage I FWE powered the lion's share of Elites and in this application was sublimely understressed. Because of the Elite's light weight and superb aerodynamics it took, for example, only 24 bhp to maintain 60 mph on level ground! Unfortunately, the engine required much more than light use to bed in the piston rings, and the Elite acquired the reputation of being an oil burner. A Lotus dealer in California tried to turn this adversity into an attribute by claiming that the car's high performance required a quart every 300 miles, but even in perfect order 500 miles was about all the mileage one could expect.

As we have seen, in fire pump use the engine had to have wide tolerances to prevent galling and seizing, and these specifications were unchanged in the transition to automotive engine. Also, the valve train ran awash in oil, no problem in a stationary engine but once under way much of this fluid was lost down the guides. Happily, the FWE was not a leaker by nature and proper attention to gaskets and seals yielded a spotless garage floor.

The Stage I FWE had one other weakness, and that was a tendency to burn exhaust valves, which was due exclusively to excessively lean fuel mixtures. Otherwise, the engine delivered everything a Gran Turismo promised and a full examination of its road performance will be found in Chapter 11.

Stage II

In 1960 a Special Equipment Elite was offered which featured, among other equipment to be discussed in Chapter 5, a Stage II FWE. This specification included dual 1½-inch SU carburettors, a four-branch, free-flow exhaust manifold, and a three-bearing camshaft with .360 inches of lift. Coventry Climax markings were not always clear or consistent but the low-lift three-bearing had FWA 3020 on its shaft and the high-lift five-bearing was identified by either FWA 3060 or FWA 3001. The Stage II engine had a 10.0 to 1 compression ratio and was rated at 85 to 90 horsepower at 7,000 rpm.

Stage III

Of course, competition Elites, whether prepared by the works, Team

Elite or privateers, generally had 'full race' or Stage III engines. Late in production the touring customer was offered this engine in the 'Super' series, but more on that in a later chapter. The hot set-up consisted of a 10.5 to 1 compression ratio (40 thou off the head and some machine work inside the ports to facilitate gas flow), a four-branch exhaust, twin SUs or Webers and the five-bearing, high-lift (.360 inch) camshaft. Maximum brake horsepower was achieved at 7,000 rpm and ranged (according to the works) from 95 to 105. In reality, the maximum actual horsepower for a Stage III FWE was probably around 100 which, nonetheless, was considerable for 1216cc!

High revs

Regardless of stage, the FWE was completely tractable and ticked over at about 1,000 rpm. Not much happened below 4,000, so a lot of revs were necessary to get into the engine's performance band. Unfortunately, high revs led to two more problems.

The FWE was equipped with a fibre timing gear to help quieten an otherwise busy-sounding engine. The life expectancy of this gear was about 40,000 miles, and it was prone to loose its teeth if taken much beyond that distance. The results of a stripped timing gear were eight bent valves, but happily a steel gear was supplied in the Stage III engines and could be retrofitted to the other engines as well.

Another problem relating to the high-revving nature of the FWE was engine vibration due to clutch imbalance. The standard pressure plate was an MG item (as was the disc) designed for a maximum of about 5,000 rpm. When taken to 7,000 and beyond the springs shifted in their seats due to centrifugal forces and threw the engine out of balance. The solution was to locate the springs by welding, or better by installing a diaphragm clutch which does not use radial springs to exert pressure on the driven disc and is therefore unaffected by extremely high revolutions.

The FWE was otherwise an extremely reliable engine and would run perfectly for very long intervals with little or no attention. The problem was in servicing, because the engine required expert care which it rarely received, even at the hands of many of the Lotus dealers. These nightmares and others will be covered in detail in Chapter 9, but con-

The 744cc FWM (Featherweight Marine) engine. (Photographer unknown)

sider, for example, the single operation of setting valve clearances. A good man, familiar with Coventry Climax and in possession of a wide assortment of shims, might take half a day to set up a head. A lesser mechanic might never get it right.

The FWE was a distinctive and, to some eyes, a good-looking engine. The cam cover, head, block, sump and water pump case were light alloy castings and, although rough in finish, exposed maximum surface area for cooling. Coventry Climax liked to paint its FWEs light grey although Elite engines had yellow cam covers for a nice contrast. Lotus borrowed a page from Ferrari by painting the cam covers red on some of the 'Super' series (Stage III) cars.

In all, 1,355 FWEs were built by Coventry Climax (from a total of 1,988 featherweights of all types, excluding, of course, the fire pumps). Lotus took about 1,000 for the Elite with the remainder going to TVR, Fairthorpe, Turner and Jack Brabham for his Sprite and Triumph Herald conversions.

The 2-litre

The Le Mans 24 Hours race was the biggest spectacle in racing in the 'fifties and 'sixties and, for reasons which will be discussed in a later chapter, it took on enormous importance to racing car builders. Chapman had always been mesmerized by this race, and in 1957 his Lotus Elevens took not only 1st and 2nd in the 1100cc Class with FWA-powered cars, but another fitted with an FWC (a short-stroke FWA which displaced 744cc) was placed 1st in the 750cc Class, 1st in the Index of Performance and also won the Biennial Cup!

When the Elite of Peter Lumsden and Peter Riley took 1st in Class in 1959 and 8th overall, Chapman began to wonder about an overall win with a larger engine. For the 1960 endurance classic he ordered an Elite to be fitted with a 2-litre Coventry Climax FPF. This was a twin-cam that displaced 1960cc and produced about 180 bhp. The engine was in current use in sports racers and in Formula 1, and Chapman had high hopes. Unfortunately, the car never turned a wheel in the race but the reason for that and other intrigues will have to wait until Chapter 8.

The 750

Apparently Coventry Climax never much cared for their FWC (despite the Eleven's Le Mans win) because it was not developed fully and it did not relate to their newer line of twin-cam engines. When Chapman asked for a 750 for the 1958 Le Mans, they immediately produced the FWM (Featherweight marine) which was, essentially, half of their new 1½-litre Formula 1 V-8. The engine displaced 744cc and featured a twin-cam head. With dual Webers it produced an amazing 81 bhp at 8,000 rpm.

The reason why Chapman was so taken with the 750 Class at Le Mans was because this was DB Panhard territory, and the thought of snatching a win away from a French car at a French race was simply irresistible. Also, the prize money and prestige for a class or index win were substantial. The 750 Elite did turn a wheel in anger at Le Mans, but was not around at the finish. Turn to Chapter 8 to find out why.

The Ford twin-cams

Because so much has been made over the years of the two or three Elites fitted at the works with Ford twin-cam engines (as used in the

The Elan twin-cam Ford engine installation in the Lazenby Elite. (Brian Stutz)

The ex-Lazenby Elite in Switzerland in 1989. (Brian Stutz)

Lotus Elan), they will be discussed briefly here even though the cars were produced long after the Elite officially ceased production. There were persistent rumours, fed no doubt by the wishful thinking of Lotus enthusiasts who wanted to see the Elite revived, that Lotus's Financial Director, Fred Bushell, had convinced Chapman to dispose of 30 to 40 left-over Elite body/chassis by fitting them with Elan engines and gearboxes.

What really happened was that in July 1967, David Lazenby, who was General Manager of Lotus Components, asked Chapman's permission to build a twin-cam Elite for use as a company car. Chapman obliged and an Elite body/chassis went through the Elan line where it picked up an engine, transmission and interior trim. The conversion worked pretty well and the car was even used on Lazenby's honeymoon to the south of Italy without, incidentally, any problem.

Several enthusiasts' magazines of the time tested the car and one loudly proclaimed on its cover 'Return of the Elite'. The car survived and, in 1989, resided in superb condition in Switzerland.

There is some evidence that one or two others were built at the works. One car may have pre-dated the Lazenby effort as an experiment to see if a twin-cam-engined Elite might generate some cash flow in advance of the Lotus Cortina project. Chris Rawlinson, who was in charge of vehicle build at the time, recalled that the car was a nightmare and was dismantled. As it happened, Rawlinson himself built a twin-cam Elite in 1964 and gave his drawings to a friend, Vic Grimwood, who assembled another in 1966. No doubt there were others, with some passed off as works conversions to further confuse the situation. Suffice to say that there was only one official works-built Elan-engined Elite with the rest being no more than well-intentioned efforts to get another Lotus 14 on the road.

The suspension

If Chapman was a genius at chassis design, then he was an absolute marvel at conjuring up suspension systems. His sports racers, especially the Eleven, had earned reputations for being able to corner like they were on a tether. The beauty of it all, besides the elegant simplicity of the components themselves, was that Chapman's cars were relatively softly sprung. Yet, at the time, the accepted standard was to set up a car as stiff and unrelenting as a coal cart. Of course, Chapman's method lessened the effects of shock into the chassis, to say nothing of the driver, which made long-distance racing a much less stressful proposition.

The state of the art in 1957 was Colin Chapman's first single-seat racing car—the type 12 Formula 2. All independent by means of wishbones in front and a new element, called the Chapman strut, at the rear, the car went around corners as if it was on rails, and drivers reported a ride akin to a family saloon. The Lotus 12 was softly sprung but firmly damped, and a controlled degree of camber change was built into the rear suspension so that the handling remained unchanged as the fuel load decreased. The components, both front and rear, were of light weight and superbly simple and they used widely spaced chassis attachment points to dissipate loads into the structure. The Elite got all of it—not a nut or a bolt was changed, save for an increase in wheel travel and a softening of the spring rates.

In front

The front suspension was a double wishbone design with a lower member constructed of $\frac{7}{8}$ inch diameter mild steel tubing. The ends of this wishbone were attached to pickups in the front subframe by bolts fed through Metalastik rubber bushings. The 'point', or wheel end, of the wishbone picked up both the bottom of the coil over an Armstrong shock absorber and the brass steering trunnion. Threaded into the top of this trunnion was the ubiquitous Triumph upright (for a time it seemed every builder in the UK from Formula 1 to Formula 2, from sports racers to specialist road cars, used this marvellously adaptable piece of equipment) which carried the steering arm, stub axle, brake disc bracket and ball joint for the upper wishbone.

The wishbone was an example of Chapman's technique of designing a multiplicity of functions in what other men might visualize as a single component. The Elite's top member was thus a wishbone formed by intersecting the $\frac{5}{8}$ inch diameter anti-roll bar with an arm that carried the ball joint (to the upright) and picked up the chassis (front subframe)

Series I front suspension with cast iron brake caliper. The 'Aeroquip' brake line allows for a harder pedal. (Author)

Early style knock-offs featured square ears and lettering. (Author)

Later production round-ear knock-off, with no markings. This Elite is fitted with 14-inch double-laced chrome wire wheels. (Author)

adjacent to the top of the shock absorber. The anti-roll bar was clamped to the subframe in the Elite's nose by means of light alloy blocks which were equipped with grease nipples for lubrication. The roll bar to top arm and top arm to chassis were also isolated by Metalastik bushings. Total travel for the front suspension was 6 inches.

Front brakes

The front suspension weighed only 54 pounds per side, and this included the 9½-inch diameter brake disc and a cast iron brake caliper. A few of the prototypes and all Elites intended for serious competition work were fitted with the ultra-lightweight Girling-type AR calipers which reduced the unsprung weight even further. Stopping power was also greater with the alloy calipers because they utilized a 2-inch piston (the cast iron unit used a 1½-inch item) with a correspondingly larger pad for a greater swept area.

Both types of calipers were mounted on the leading edge of the brake disc which, at the time, was thought to reduce wheel bearing loads. It probably did on a heavy car, but the theory was academic in an automobile as light as the Elite. A complete discussion of how the car handled and stopped will be saved for a later chapter, but for now suffice it to say that nothing in the front suspension suffered from unusual wear and the car could be brought down from high speeds very quickly indeed.

Tread pattern of the Pirelli Cinturato. (Author)

Tread pattern of the Michelin X. (Author)

Wheels and tyres

The Elite was fitted with Dunlop single-laced (48 spoke), centre lock wire wheels, 15 inches in diameter and 4 inches in width. Most were supplied painted silver, but chrome could be ordered as well. Knock-offs were two-eared; early versions were squared off with 'do' and 'undo' markings, while later cars came with rounded ears and no lettering.

Before the Earls Court prototype was built, Chapman went to great lengths looking for a suitable road tyre. He reckoned nothing available was perfectly suited to a car as light as the Elite, and was telling the tyre companies that his new car would weigh under 1,500 pounds! Firestone was the first to respond by offering to mould a tyre designed expressly for the Elite.

The result was a tyre with a special nylon carcass and a new tread design called the 'P300'. Despite the fanfare, Chapman was a little chagrined to learn that the tyre was not a radial, and unfortunately the situation got worse. Owners reported poor adhesion in the wet, horrific noise on almost any surface and treads that peeled off at speed! Len Street, service manager at Hornsey (before he opened a Lotus centre in London), recalled, 'I used to go down to Firestone twice a month with a load of tyres with the tread thrown off!'

Happily, Michelin came to the rescue with its famous brand 'X' radials. Their tyres were inexpensive, stuck well in all conditions, were designed for light cars and had an added bonus of extremely long wear. They were supplied to Lotus in size 135 × 15 and became the standard fitment. The only disadvantage of the Michelin X was a somewhat 'dead' feel and a sudden loss of grip when ultimate cornering angles had been achieved.

The premium tyre for the Elite was the Pirelli Cintura which became standard on the Special Equipment version of the car. This tyre was a fabric radial (the Michelin was steel) supplied to Lotus in size

155 × 15. It was long-wearing, had excellent wet weather grip and very high cornering limits. It also had a more gradual 'breakaway' than the Michelin and was better at transmitting this information to the driver. The Cintura, incidentally, was a close relative to the Pirelli Cinturato which was often fitted as an alternative.

Steering

The Elite's steering was an extremely quick rack and pinion manufactured by Alford and Alder which required only 2½ turns, lock to lock, and employed an unusual geometry called the negative Ackerman effect. This meant that in cornering attitudes, the outer wheel turned through a greater arc than the inner one. The results were tenacious high speed cornering and accurate placement, but also a marked sensitivity in straight-line running. Happily, the feel was superb and the effort 'finger-tip' light.

At the rear—the Chapman Strut

The Elite's rear suspension was fully independent also, but by means of the Chapman Strut. This device was yet another example of Chapman's uncanny ability at combining functions. In this case, the coil spring was placed over an Armstrong shock absorber whose lower end was a shrink fit in a light alloy hub carrier.

The upper end of the strut (the shock absorber rod) attached to the body/chassis within the humps or metacones which were the prominent features in the rear of the passenger compartment. This attachment point was isolated from the fibreglass by a hefty rubber bushing.

The bottom end of the strut was the hub carrier which located the wheel hub and its two large tapered roller bearings by means of an interference fit. The hub was driven by a double articulated halfshaft which was attached to the differential by a stub axle. To triangulate this system, a dog-legged radius arm picked up the bottom of the hub carrier and extended forward into the wheel well. Attachment to the

The Series I rear suspension featured a dog-legged radius arm and finned hub carrier. (Author)

body/chassis was via a ball and socket arrangement again isolated by rubber.

Suspension travel at the rear was a generous 7 inches and, at rest, the rear wheels exhibited about 2 degrees of negative (outward at the bottom) camber. The entire rear suspension weighed only 53 pounds per side, helped considerably by the inboard location of the brakes. As it happened, the dog-legged radius arm gave some problems in extended hard use, leading to a revision which defined the Series II version of the Elite. This change and others will be covered in Chapter 5. For a time Chapman considered a less expensive 'Club' version of the Elite with a rigid back axle, but nothing ever came of the idea.

Rear brakes

The Elite featured disc brakes at the rear as well, but mounted inboard, adjacent to the differential. The discs were $9\frac{1}{2}$ inches in diameter and until just after the change to Series II, or around chassis number 1565, the calipers were Girling alloy type NR. With the change to an under-dash umbrella-pull handbrake (from a tunnel-mounted fly-off type) came cast iron calipers. In both cases the handbrake pulled a cable that actuated a separate set of small pads on both discs. Oddly enough, round pads were used with the alloy calipers and square ones on the cast iron type.

Final drive

The differential was bolted to the body/chassis and isolated by Metalastik half-bushes. Its cover was a specially cast Lotus item made of aluminium alloy, and integral with the casting were substantial brackets which picked up the brake calipers.

The nosepiece of the Elite diff was also light alloy, although this was a standard BMC part which, as can be seen from the accompanying table, was used on a surprising variety of automobiles. Equally curious was the array of ratios available as optional equipment on the Elite,

The intricate light alloy casting for the differential case incorporated cooling fins, pick-ups for the brake calipers and four bosses which carried the bolts to the chassis. (Author)

which included 5.375, 5.125, 4.875, 4.55, 4.22, 3.89 and 3.73 to 1! Depending on stage of tune and the diff ratio, an Elite could do 95 mph in the quarter mile (in about 14 seconds) or reach 130 mph in top gear.

Elite differential ratios

Ratio	No of teeth (crown & ring gear)	Original application
3.73	11/41	early Riley 1.5
3.89	10/39	unknown
4.22	9/38	early Sprite/Midget and Riley 1.5
4.55	9/41	Morris $\frac{1}{4}$ ton van
4.875	8/39	A35 van
5.375	8/43	Morris GPO van

The gearboxes: BMC and ZF

The standard gearbox for the Elite was the BMC 'B' series, similar in pattern and ratios to that fitted to the MG Magnette saloon. The case was light alloy and incorporated a special bell housing that matched the back plate on the Climax engine. Sadly, the gearbox was one of the few proprietary pieces used on the Elite that proved to be out of keeping with the rest of the car, at least as standard, but more on that in a moment.

The 'B' series box had a non-synchro first gear that groaned the same whether new or well used. Worse than that, the ratios were widely spaced and ill suited to the FWE's torque and horsepower characteristics. The gears were 3.67:1 for first, 2.20:1 for second, 1.32:1 for third and 1:1 for fourth. The good news was that close ratio gear sets were available that completely transformed the 'B' series box into a real delight. First gear remained non-synchro but the ratio became eminently more usable. The numbers for these gears were 2.45:1 first, 1.62:1 second, 1.27:1 third and 1:1 top.

Concurrent with other projects, Chapman had developed close ties with a German firm called Zahnradfabrik Friedrichshafen AG, or ZF for short. On several occasions they had built special gears for Chapman but were also well known for precision transaxles, differentials and gearboxes.

In 1959 Chapman asked ZF to design a gearbox for the Elite. He had in mind a Special Equipment version of the car that would feature, among other extras, an all-synchro, close ratio transmission. ZF agreed and built the S4-12. It was compact and light in weight (despite a cast iron gear case, although the bell housing was of magnesium), and was a sheer pleasure to use.

The lever had a short and positive throw and was topped with an oddly slender knob in white or black bakelite, inscribed with the ZF initials. Ratios were closely spaced (2.53 for first, 1.71 for second, 1.23 for third and 1:1 for top gear) and, like the BMC close ratio, it was totally in concert with the FWE's power band. If the ZF had any disadvantage it was a high noise level in all gears, but in keeping with the company's reputation, the S4-12 proved to be robust and utterly reliable.

In a short while this transmission became the first choice among Elite racers and in later production was offered as standard equipment on the 'Super' series cars as well as the SE version. Interestingly, ZF found other customers for its gearbox which included Sabra, Lola and OSCA.

Chapter 4

Ian Walker and the second Elite

Even as Colin Chapman and his team of Elite designers and builders basked in the spotlight at the Earls Court exhibition hall, workmen were back at Hornsey cleaning up the moulds in preparation for laying up the second Elite. This one was to be a rolling test bed for the monocoque concept for, as we have already seen, Chapman's intent was to perform the testing in full view of the public. Consequently, chassis number 1001 was headed for the race track at the hands of one of Chapman's neighbours, Ian Walker.

Chapman's plan was somewhat understandable considering that Lotus had built nothing but racing cars until the Elite, but public reaction to any failure would be likely to upset any confidence in so radical a design. The stakes were, therefore, enormous, yet the mood at Hornsey was one of haste and the lads were told to get on with it.

Everyone involved with the project believed the developmental problems would be minor. This was not simple arrogance but a belief in their abilities and confidence that if the engineering was up to standards, the finished product would be likewise.

The man—Ian Walker

In 1958 Ian Walker was a successful 32-year-old businessman with a passion for motorsport. He had met Chapman two years earlier at Hornsey when he stopped by to see if the Lotus Engineering Company Ltd could improve the traction of his Ford Prefect. This normally staid saloon had been developed into a very quick race and rally car and Walker was having difficulty in getting the power to the ground. Chap-

Chassis number 1001, still in yellow and left-hand drive, pauses for pictures outside the Hornsey works. Notice the wing tank fitted with a flip-up cover. (Photographer unknown)

man designed an anti-tramp bar which prevented the rear axle from 'winding up', the cause of the loss of adhesion.

At the time, Chapman and Walker were also neighbours and, now and again, the two would get together for a chat which, Walker remembered, was not always about cars. During the course of one of these conversations Chapman took a keen interest in Walker's mention that one of his family's businesses produced the formers for the plywood fuselage of the de Havilland Mosquito. It was also developing the moulds for the wing and engine panels for the de Havilland Comet. Chapman arranged a visit to see these moulds and formers and, although he never let on as to why, Walker believed that he was already formulating his ideas for a GRP monocoque body/chassis.

In 1957 Walker had decided that he wanted to concentrate on circuit racing (although he remained a member of the Ford works rally team) and bought a Lotus Eleven. The car, nicknamed 'The Yellow Peril', had quite an interesting history, having been campaigned in the 1956 season by Graham Hill while he was a foreman at Lotus. The Eleven was a 'Sports' model powered by an 1172cc Ford side-valve engine.

Walker recalled that the Lotus was his first proper racing car and it took him a few races to get the feel of things. The Eleven seemed to handle a little skittishly and Walker found himself doing a lot of sideways motoring. Nonetheless, he entered the Autosport Production Sports Car series where, incidentally, competitors had to drive their cars to the circuits—no trailers allowed! Chapman came around during one of the early races to offer advice on tyre pressures and other hints on how to set the car up, and Walker responded by winning the next 11 races and capturing the Championship!

Chapman was impressed with Walker's skill behind the wheel and the fact that he listened to advice, so he invited him to look over Peter Kirwan-Taylor's drawings of the Elite. Chapman wanted to do some international level rallying with the Elite and asked Walker's opinion. Unfortunately, the number of cars that needed to be built for homologation put paid to the notion, but when Walker suggested he contest the Autosport Championship in an Elite, Chapman agreed. Walker wanted to do the driving, of course, so Chapman offered to loan him the first running prototype for the 1958 racing session.

The car—EL 5

Walker took delivery of his Elite at 3.30am on 10 May 1958 at the shop at Edmonton after what he described as 'superhuman efforts by the small Lotus crew supervised by the legendary Willie Griffiths to get the car roadworthy'. Unknown to Walker at the time was the fact that chassis 1001 had originally been built to a left-hand drive specification for the Geneva Motor Show held in March of '58. It was also originally yellow but was re-sprayed pale green as part of its transformation to right-hand drive. At some point before it was delivered to Walker, chassis 1001 was also taken to Brands Hatch for a shake-down run.

Walker's Elite was registered EL 5 (the works desperately wanted EL 1 but it was unavailable) and the last-minute flurry of activity was because the car had been entered for a race at Silverstone which just happened to be later that morning! On the way home, just before dawn, Walker stopped at an all-night service station to fill up with petrol and the pump attendant completely deflated his pride by saying,

Ian Walker's second outing at Mallory Park resulted in another win. Here Walker is out distancing an MGA. (Autosport)

'That's a nice little car—did you build it yourself?'

After a few hours' sleep, Walker met up with Mike Costin, who was then Lotus Production Engineer, and the two convoyed toward Silverstone. A minor drama occurred near Hockliffe on the A5 road when the steering failed. Walker managed to stop the Elite without hitting anything and Costin quickly diagnosed the problem—a taper pin which located the steering wheel hub to its shaft had fallen out.

As luck would have it, the Elite had stopped in front of a smithy and Costin immediately disappeared inside to the clang of horseshoes and wrought iron. He reappeared holding a horseshoe nail and as he hammered it into the steering column, Costin recited a modified version of the well-known saying: 'For want of a horseshoe nail a race was lost'. Walker went on to win the qualifying heat and the race that day, and he set fastest lap in the process. Years later it occurred to him that the nail might never have been replaced!

The Elite's instant success was satisfying, but Walker could not rest on his laurels. The next day (11 May 1958) he drove EL 5 to Mallory Park with Colin Chapman tagging along and Mike Costin again acting as engineer and mechanic. The car put up the fastest lap and won the 1600cc class going away. Walker remembered one magazine report describing the win as having been accomplished 'with insolent ease'.

Driving impressions

By the end of his first week with the Elite, Walker had accumulated enough road and racing miles to form an impression of its handling characteristics. At the time, his daily transportation was a Lancia Aurelia B20 GT which was considered the current standard of excellence in road holding. Walker felt the Elite surpassed the Lancia with ease although, he admitted, the Lotus was a little short on creature comforts and somewhat excessive in noise level.

During EL 5's first outing at Silverstone, Mike Costin offered some advice on how to extract the most cornering power out of the car. 'Mike told me that owing to the strut type of rear suspension, the car might prove to be a handful on slow corners. He explained that the trick was to settle the car prior to the corner and then to use power, progressively, all the way through. During the first meeting I did have some trouble at Becketts Corner in practice and the next time around I did as Mike suggested and the car went through the corner on the proverbial rails.

'The technique improved with each lap and the lap times, already good, progressed to excellent. As I recall, this feature of the road holding, which I suspect would have never shown up on the road, was its only vice. I remember thinking how beautifully responsive it was with such precise steering which, with the power to weight available, made it possible to adjust slide or drift quite easily. At the time, disc brakes all around were a novelty to me and I was impressed how deep into a corner their efficiency permitted. During the entire season they never gave any trouble—the same cannot be said for the handbrake which was never really effective.'

The Elite handbrake

The Elite's handbrake was originally designed as an 'umbrella pull' under the dash, and a dome-shaped protrusion under the pedals (which exists on all Elites) was to be one of the mounting points. Unfortunately, the leverage was insufficient to fully actuate the separate handbrake pads on the rear alloy calipers, so later prototypes traded the umbrella pull for a 'fly-off' handle mounted on the transmission tunnel. This worked much better, but holding power was never very high. Late in Series II production, with the change to cast iron rear calipers and a revised actuating system for the handbrake pads, the umbrella pull was tried again. This time the results were much improved and the Elite ended its days with the handbrake it was supposed to have had originally.

The Autosport *editorial*

On 16 May 1958, *Autosport* magazine paid tribute to the Elite with the following editorial:

'The first appearance of the unconventional Lotus Elite at the Silverstone and Mallory Park events was most auspicious—2 victories in 2 successive races. Competing in qualifying heats for the Autosport Championship, Ian Walker's pretty little car was outstanding, delighting all who saw it in action with its superb road holding,

Ian Walker and John Lawry carve up the field at Crystal Palace in July. (Charles Dunn)

Ian and his wife Mavis enjoy a summer sprint meeting. Walker had to tape the wing filler door to keep it from flying open. (Photographer unknown)

flashing performance and the effortless look of a genuine race-bred machine. From drawing board to racing circuit, within the space of a few months, is an effort worthy of Ferrari, particularly when one realizes that the Elite is going into quantity production as a Grand Touring machine. Eventually, the cars will be seen in international races and rallies, in which they will receive the most severe testing. The more conservative designers viewed with mixed emotions the method of construction, but one recalls the criticism that was accorded the Volkswagen-inspired Porsche when it first appeared. Colin Chapman and his men have shown clearly that initiative is not lacking in the British motor industry; their latest product may well revolutionize construction methods, employing, as it does, the best principles of aeronautical design allied to the invaluable experiences gained on racing circuits.'

Walker's next outing with EL 5 was on 26 May at Mallory Park where he again led the race from start to finish and posted the fastest lap. John Lawry showed up with chassis 1002 but did not start. Lawry had an agreement with Chapman which was similar to that with Walker. He had known Chapman for several years by then, having won the Autosport Championship in 1956 in an 1172cc Lotus Mark 6. He later ran an Eleven Sports, although not as successfully as Walker, and handled the pit signals for Team Lotus at Le Mans in 1957. The 1958 season was spent chasing Walker and often picking up a second in his BRG (originally yellow) Elite which was registered 923 FPJ. Lawry must have really enjoyed the experience because at the end of the season he bought the car and took it home for good.

Win after win

On 1 June Walker took EL 5 to Snetterton where he won his class (1600cc) but took second to Dick Protheroe in an Austin Healey 100S. 'I did not consider that a disgrace because Dickie was a very good and forceful driver and the 100S had over twice the engine capacity.' Walker returned to Snetterton again on 29 June and he and John Lawry took first and second with Ian scoring another fastest lap. Crystal Palace was next on 5 July and despite a 360-degree spin when overtaking a back marker who was not watching his mirrors, Walker won the race by 12 seconds and set fastest lap yet again.

Interestingly, a number of people approached Walker during the season asking to buy EL 5. One of the most persistent was Chris Barber, the jazz musician, who approached Walker at race meetings, at home—just about everywhere. Walker remembered that during one of his phone calls he asked if he could just drive the car. Unfortunately, Walker had to decline because that particular week the car was on display at the Coventry Climax showrooms in Piccadilly.

'Undeterred, Chris talked or bribed the caretaker at about 2am into opening the massive plate glass windows. He then drove the Elite up and down Piccadilly. It did not have a production silencing system, nor was it road taxed or insured, and I think he was lucky to return it to the showroom without falling foul of the law.'

In all, Ian Walker entered EL 5 in 12 races, of which he won 10 and put up the same number of fastest laps. Despite this fantastic record, the Autosport Championship was not decided until the last race at Snetterton. This was a three-hour event which began in twilight at

Pit stop at the Snetterton Three Hour. The Autosport *championship hinged on this race. A young Graham Hill is on the extreme left.* (Autosport)

EL 5 being pushed off after a pit stop to fix a minor electrical fault at the Autosport *finale at Snetterton. Several laps later the left rear suspension collapsed.* (Photographer unknown)

After 1001 was sold through the David Buxton dealership, the works used its registration number on a company car which challenged LOV 1 at Silverstone in 1959. (Charles Dunn)

4pm and ended in darkness at 7pm. Walker had a 5 point lead in the standings over Protheroe and was looking forward to winning the Championship for the second year running. He figured he could finish the race as far back as third place and still take the title, so his race strategy was to lay back in second and take no chances.

As darkness fell, Walker was a secure second place, some 30 seconds behind Protheroe. His only bother had been some minor electrical problems that required a pit stop to put right. Then, 'At about three-quarters distance and when braking hard for the sharp right hander at the end of the straight, the car went out of control, spinning into the in-field and narrowly missing a telegraph pole.

'A quick investigation indicated that the left rear suspension had collapsed, but fortunately the depth of the wheel arch was retaining the wheel. I still had drive and slowly made my way back to the pits where Colin Chapman diagnosed the problem which was that the radius arm had pulled out of its location in the glass fibre chassis. Chapman obviously did not want this known or reported in the press so the car was immediately retired and wheeled away.'

Snetterton was, of course, a disappointment to Walker who was so close to his second racing championship. Still, he mused in 1989, 'The results we achieved and the editorial publicity which was generated in 1958 maintained public interest in the Elite whilst the factory was slowly getting to grips with series production.'

After Snetterton, EL 5 was returned to the works at Hornsey. Walker was told that the body/chassis was stripped of all useful components and broken up, but according to the works chassis list 1001 was invoiced to David Buxton (who later became one of the major Elite dealers in the UK) in September 1959. One can only wonder if the buyer was told of the car's history.

Years later Willie Griffiths paused to reflect on 1001 and said that the car should have been scrapped although he couldn't remember if it was. 'It was a real dog. There was no jigging to speak of and it was a nightmare to build in the time available. The top suspension pickups, which were moulded in the GRP chassis, were so far out that I had to make a longer top arm on one side to maintain the correct track. I never did have the time to find out how this affected the camber change on bump.' It obviously made no difference to Ian Walker who by his exploits not only proved the concept of a fibreglass monocoque was feasible, but also showed that it was going to be marvellously successful. Chapman could not have asked for more.

Chapter 5

The assembly line

Simplifying the body/chassis process

When the Elite design team got back to Hornsey after the Earls Court show they agreed that their number one priority had to be to simplify construction of the body/chassis. This was because, as we have seen, the Earls Court prototype had required 60 separate moulds, and even then some interior finishing panels were omitted in the rush to make the show. To further expedite construction, some parts of the monocoque had been formed in aluminium sheet and covered with fibreglass for appearance's sake. There were far too many bits which required separate operations to be economically feasible, and worse there were too many bonded joints to be traversed by chassis loads which compromised torsional strength.

While chassis 1001 and 1002 were pieced together at Edmonton for Walker and Lawry, the first 'simplified Elite' was taking shape at Maximar Mouldings Ltd in Pulborough, Sussex, a boat-building company which had achieved a very good reputation for the construction of superb fibreglass hulls. Colin Chapman was so taken with their product that he considered moving into the boatbuilding business himself, and although the idea was set aside it obviously was not forgotten. In 1972 Chapman bought two boatbuilding companies, Moonraker Boats Ltd and JCL Marine, to explore the possibilities.

Ron Hickman, John Frayling and John Standen all but took up residence in Pulborough in order to spend their days in the Maximar workshops. While the three sought to incorporate ever more sections into fewer major moulds, Maximar offered advice on materials and lay-up techniques and prepared the jigs and tools that would hold the large sections as they were bonded together. In large measure Maximar subsidized the development of the Elite monocoque even though its contract was for a flat rate to build 250 of them. In the end, Maximar actually put together a total of 280.

Because of the need to get prototypes into the hands of the racers as fast as possible, several more cars were built using partially simplified moulds and individually laid-up sections. The process of simplification was extremely laborious and time-consuming and much of it was trial and error. When they finally stepped back to admire their work, all agreed that the new moulds were fantastic. Their extraordinary effort had reduced the number of body/chassis moulds from over 60 to three!

The major moulds

The mouldings were constructed of random mat cloth and polyester resin. The first assembly consisted of the undertray, which included the front and rear wheel wells, the differential box and rear suspension mounts, as well as the front subframe and the gearbox mount. The next moulding fitted on top of the first and consisted of the spare tyre shelf, the cockpit floor, the interior covers for the rear suspension pickups and the radiator ducting. This middle component also included the steel windshield hoop and the door hinge uprights.

The third major moulding was made up of the entire upper body surface including the roof, headlight recesses, door openings and the like. After this large piece was lowered on to the middle and undertray sections, a liner was bonded to the underside of the roof panel for added rigidity.

The three large pieces were glued together using epoxy resin and 'micro balloons' which consisted of phenolic resin spheres that spread their adhesives when subjected to clamping pressure. This force was applied by the mating of jigs, spring clamps and, in the case of the undertray contacting the cockpit floor, by means of rivets. When bonding was done, the only discernible seams were cleverly hidden by the front and rear bumpers.

Additional moulds were used to form the doors, engine and boot lids, boot floor and bulkhead. Most Elites, of both Maximar and Bristol manufacture, had epoxy doors. This was because epoxy had superior strength to polyester and was less brittle into the bargain. Both of these qualities were thought advantageous considering that doors were subject to significant abuses like being slammed shut, leaned on and left open for long periods of time. Interestingly, most of the Elite's bonnet and boot lids were made of epoxy as well, but there were inexplicable lapses from both of the body/chassis suppliers where the lids were done in polyester resin like the rest of the car!

The finished monocoque, devoid of accessories, weighed about 200 pounds, appreciably less than the 300–335 pounds of the last of the Bristol bodies (the final contractor for Elite body/chassis). The reasons for this weight gain will be discussed later in this chapter.

Lotus moves to Cheshunt

As convenient to Londoners as No 7 Tottenham Lane may have been, there was simply no room to expand. Hemmed in by a builder's yard

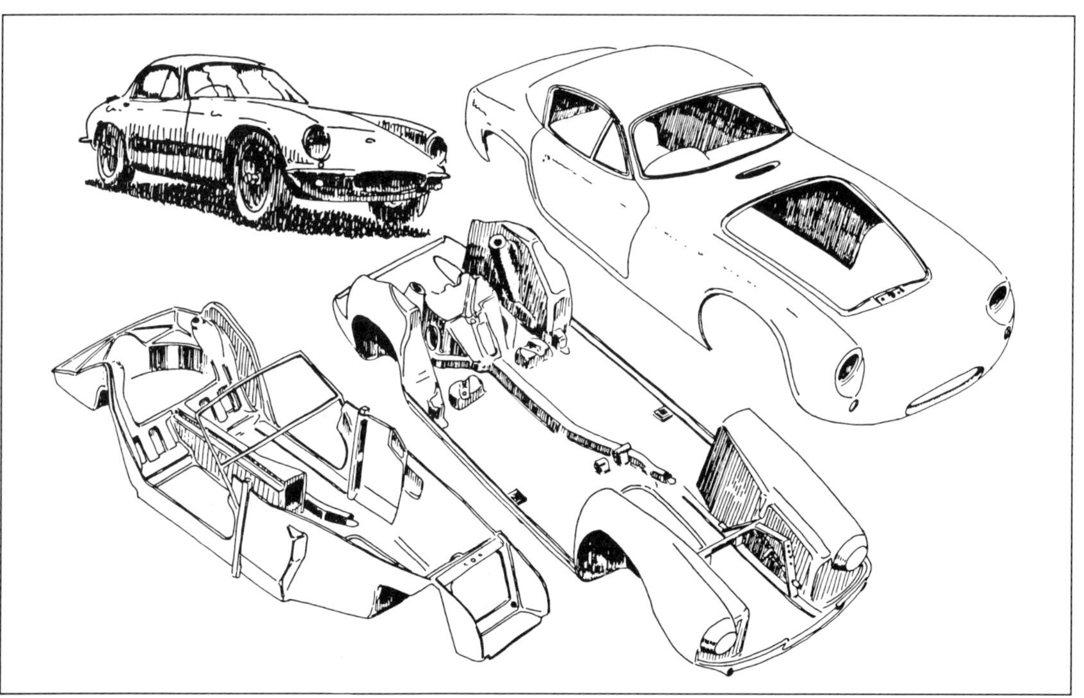

The three major mouldings in the construction of the Elite's body/chassis. (Richard Spelberg Jr collection)

and a main British Railways line, Chapman's rented premises were all but used up with the manufacture of the Lotus sports racers. He wanted a new and modern facility and his old friend, Peter Kirwan-Taylor, helped him to get it. At the time, Kirwan-Taylor was a member of the prestigious accounting firm of Peat, Marwick, Mitchell and was involved with the business dealings of many substantial companies. As a result of this he knew of several who wished to invest their profits in diversified fields. One of these was the Eagle Star Insurance Company, who put up some £280,000 ($1m) for Lotus Engineering Company to build a modest factory in a newly formed industrial park in Delamare Road, Cheshunt, Hertfordshire.

Meanwhile, Chapman reorganized his company. At Hornsey it had been the Lotus Engineering Company Ltd with a small staff of permanent employees. As we have seen, incredibly Lotus relied on a steady stream of volunteers who would drop in to work on the racing cars in the evenings and at weekends; these people were college students, apprentices and enthusiasts who wanted to be part of Lotus.

The situation was markedly different at Cheshunt. Chapman split Lotus into three separate companies. Lotus Components built the sports racing cars, Lotus Cars was formed to produce the Elite, and Lotus Developments was set up to design and develop new cars. Team Lotus became an independent operation with facilities to prepare and maintain the works' racing cars. All of the personnel were full-time paid employees—the days of working for a beer and a sandwich were over.

Although having been in operation for nearly four months, the new factory opened officially on 14 October 1959 with a ceremony and a grand celebration attended by members of the press, racing drivers, local government officials and friends of Lotus. It appeared to everyone that Lotus had come of age; the buildings were modern and spacious and a line of brand new Lotus Elites was seen gleaming in the car park.

According to the Elite chassis list and the invoice dates, production

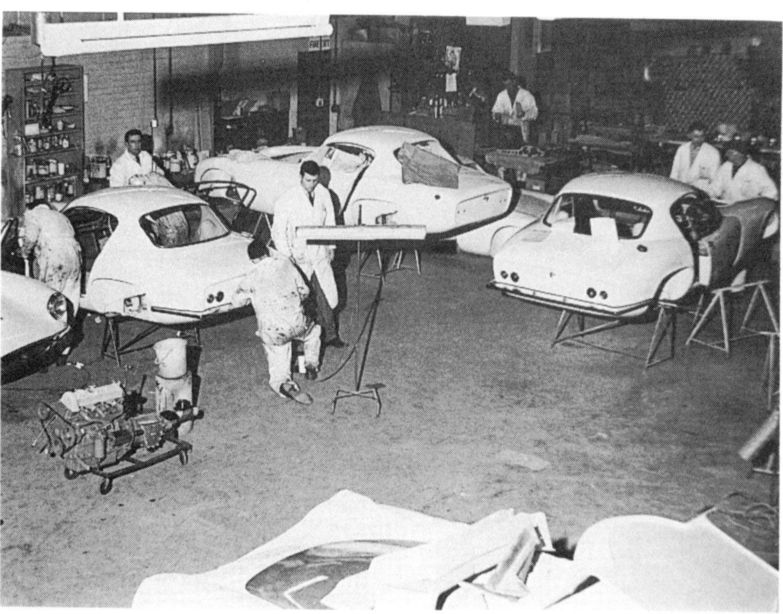

Elite assembly at Cheshunt. A Stage I engine awaits installation at the left. (Lotus)

Assembly line at Cheshunt. The man in the centre of the picture is fitting a rear windscreen. The shelves hold carpet pieces. (Lotus)

ranged from 8 to 36 cars per month. Six body/chassis were delivered by special truck from Pulborough to Cheshunt, fully painted and with doors and lids attached. The monocoque was then mounted on a dolly, covered with a protective blanket and fitted with trim, electrics, suspension, engine and drive train. Interestingly, Colin Chapman and Works Manager Len Street test drove every Elite after it was detailed prior to delivery. Time demands eventually prevented Chapman from continuing this practice, but it is significant that he wanted every car to be just right.

Noise suppression

As soon as the Elite hit the road the first obvious problem was the level of noise in the cockpit. It was positively shattering, despite the original belief that fibreglass would be both a terrific thermal and sound insulator. The prototypes demonstrated that negligible heat found its way into the cabin but, on the other hand, every sound seemed to be amplified. One could even hear the soft 'whoosh' of the clutch engaging the driven disc!

At first, various means of sound insulation were tried including different types of headliners. It was quickly discovered that insulating the roof panel made little difference, so in production it was left as bare fibreglass. In some early cars this panel was smooth but it was eventually changed to a pebble-grain finish. Interestingly, early roof panels alternated in paint colour from white to black to grey, with the last finally being applied as standard.

Eventually it became clear that the thicker the panel the better the sound insulation, but to thicken the Elite's monocoque also meant to add weight which was against fundamental Lotus doctrine. As we will see later in this chapter, the Elite did gain weight late in production and became a quieter car as a result, but the Maximar product relied on alternating layers of natural 20 ounce jute and 15 pound felt or tar paper on the floor panels and transmission tunnel to deaden the noise. At best, however, the early Elites were pretty raucous.

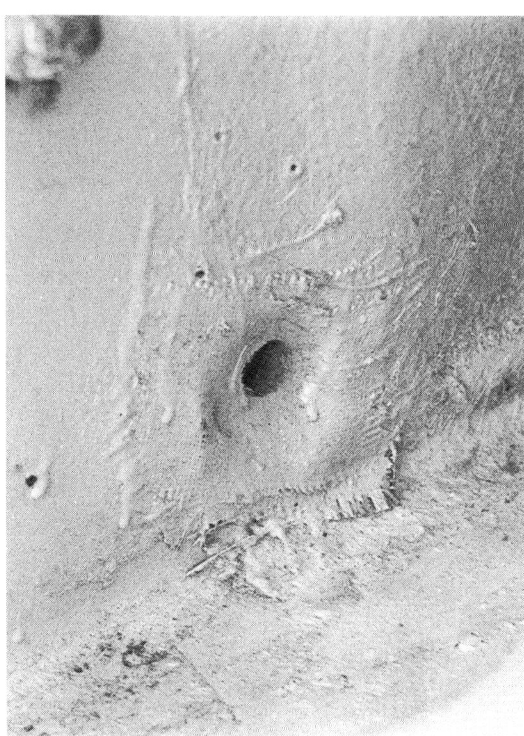

Above *Typical Maximar reinforcement —a woven cloth patch over a transmission mounting bobbin.* (Author)

Maximar quality

Much has been made over the years of the marginal quality of some of the Maximar-built Elites. As it happened, this was probably an unfair assessment. When the Elite was new, early failures 'made the headlines' because there was so much public scrutiny—and, as we will see in later chapters, scepticism—of the GRP monocoque.

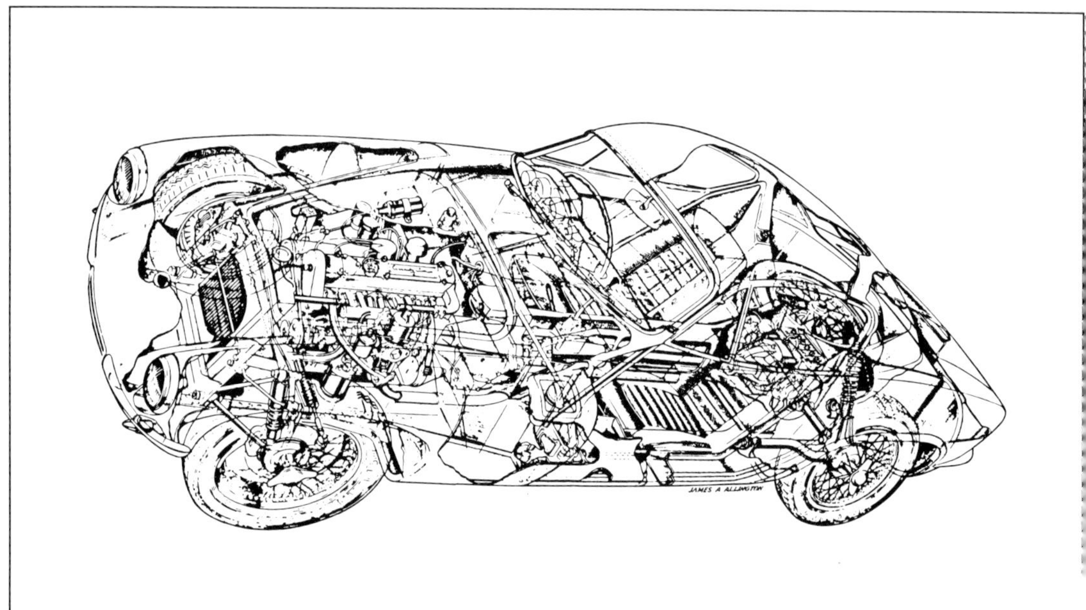

Left *The Series I floor is completely flat up to the rear bulk head. The nuts and metal plate lower right secure the radius arm mount.* (Author)

Indeed, there were examples of differentials breaking loose and seams delaminating. In addition to this, the workforce at Maximar did not seem all that concerned about surface finish and paint quality. But then, Chapman had driven a hard bargain and as the stream of criticism from Lotus worsened, so did Maximar's willingness to put in the extra man-hours to perfect their product.

What is clear from the thousands of racing miles on so many Maximar-built Elites and the number of high mileage examples that survive, is that once the structural flaws were corrected, usually by increasing the thickness and the extent of overlap in the lay-ups, the failures stopped. On the plus side, Maximar body/chassis were the lightest Elites of all by a significant margin and at about 1,200 pounds (less fluids) came nearest to Chapman's target weight of 10 hundredweight (1,120 pounds), a fact not lost on the racers which explained why, for a long time, they preferred the Maximar body/chassis.

Series I Elites

Although provision was built into the moulds for fitting the controls in a left-hand drive configuration, there were very few (perhaps only one or two) built in this way by Maximar despite nearly 150 of their body/chassis going to the States. There were details, however, that were common to all but the very last Maximar bodies, which came to be known as the Series I specification. These detail fitments included the dog-legged rear radius arms, front wishbones with double grease nipples at the trunnion end, shorter shock absorbers, stiffer front (150 pounds per inch) and rear (96 pounds per inch) springs and a throttle linkage comprised of rods and levers. Most Series I Elites stored their side windows in a cloth envelope which was placed in the boot, and all SIs sold for road use were fitted with a single SU carburettor and a cast iron exhaust manifold.

To add a little confusion to the story, at the very end of Maximar's run of body/chassis as many as 20–30 cars were built with Series II

Left *James Allington cutaway of the Series I Elite.* (Lotus Cars Ltd)

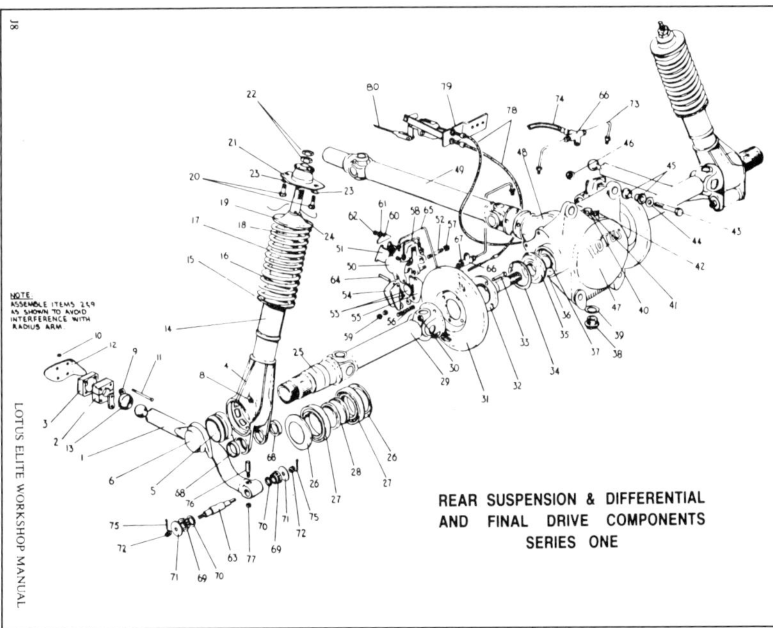

Right *A James Allington drawing of the Series I rear suspension.* (Lotus Elite Workshop Manual)

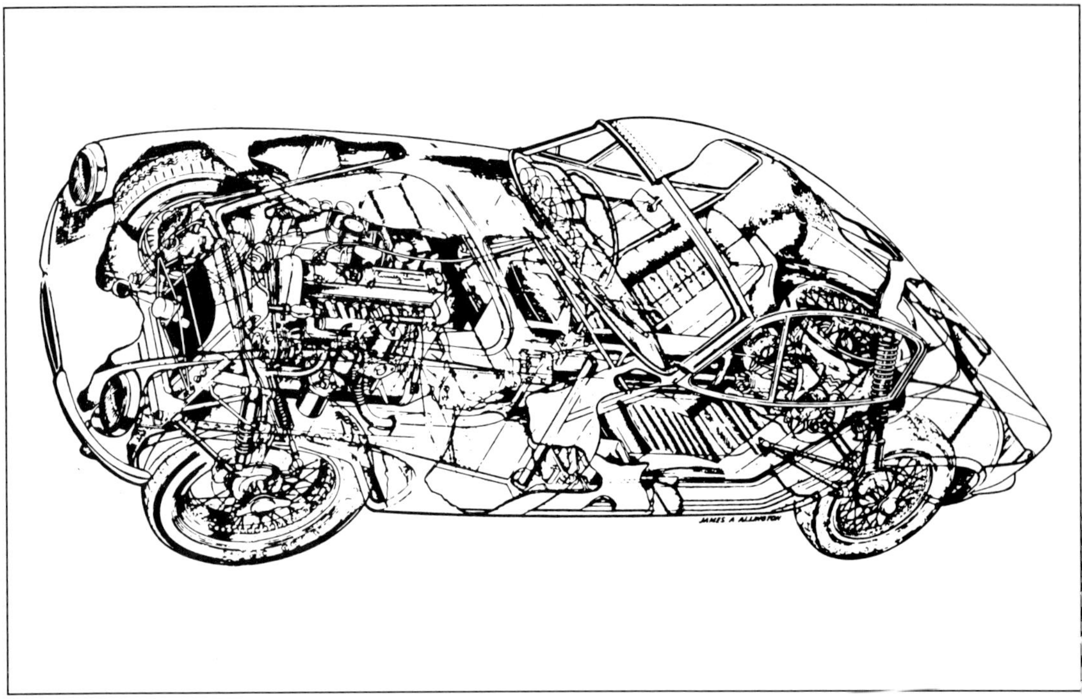

Above *James Allington cutaway of the Series II Elite.* (Lotus Cars Ltd)

suspensions! In the end, Maximar ended its association with Lotus with chassis 1280. Max Johnson, the owner of Maximar, was more than relieved to see the end of the production run. The effort had drained the resources of his company, perhaps terminally because a few years later the boatbuilder quit the business. In 1965 George Clay purchased Maximar and formed a company called Riverside Concrete on the old Maximar grounds, supplying concrete products to the building trade.

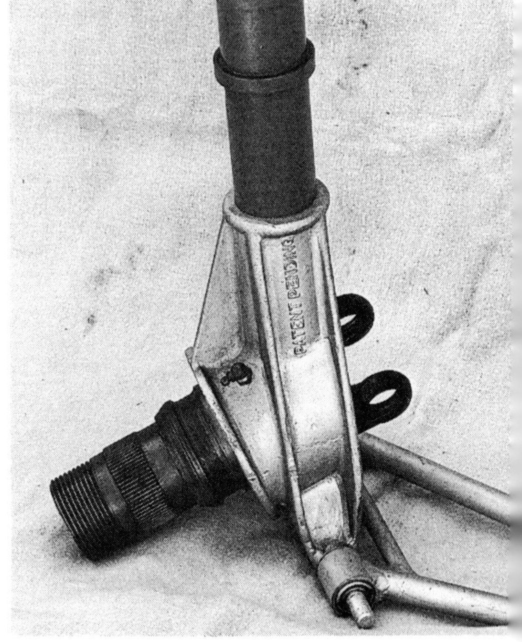

A comparison of Series I (left) and Series II lower front wishbones and their trunnions. (Author)

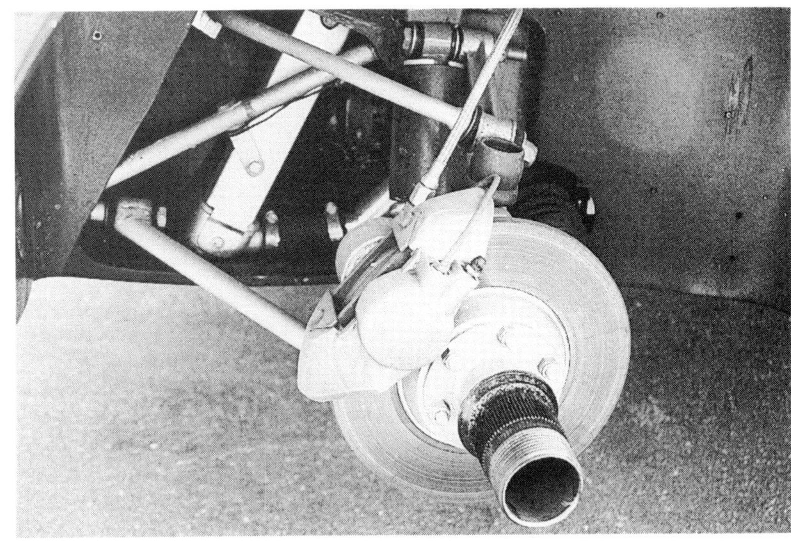

Series II front suspension with a Girling AR light alloy brake caliper fitted. Both the piston diameter and the swept area of the pads were greater than the cast iron calipers. (Author)

Far left *This intricate undertray moulding on a Series II Elite was necessary to accommodate the wishbone suspension. This example has been undercoated for sound damping.* (Author)

Left *The transition hub carrier featured the Series II wishbone and Series I finned housing.* (Barry Swackhamer)

Series II Elites

In long-term hard use (usually on a race track), the Series I Elite developed a problem with rear wheel steering. The dog-legged radius arm was prone to bending, which cranked in a few degrees of oversteer. In addition to this, the arm moved through an arc of about 15 degrees on the hub carrier by means of a pair of tapered roller bearings. Pre-load had to be set exactly on these bearings because too much yielded binding in movement, and too little resulted in sloppiness and even more oversteer.

Chapman corrected this problem by designing a wishbone to replace the radius arm. It was quite long (21 inches) which required a revised pickup point on the body/chassis. This necessitated a revision on both the undertray and the middle moulds. The wishbone terminated in a ball, the same as the SI dog-leg, and was isolated from its pickup in the same manner, which was by means of a hollow rubber ball slipped over its end. The pickup consisted of a dome-shaped metal cover which clamped the ball into a recess in the fibreglass. The metal cover was bolted in place through a pair of bobbins which were laid up in the undertray moulding. The middle moulding required clearance for these bobbins, so the cockpit floor was raised on both sides of the car to cover them. This modification appeared as a 'step' on the floor behind the seats.

LOTUS ELITE WORKSHOP MANUAL

REAR SUSPENSION & DIFFERENTIAL AND FINAL DRIVE COMPONENTS

A James Allington drawing of the Series II rear suspension. (Lotus Elite Workshop Manual)

Series II rear suspension showing the smooth hub carrier and the wishbone. The grease nipple for wheel bearing lubrication is at the bottom of the hub carrier. (Author)

The wishbone was attached to the hub carrier through widely spaced sleeves (isolated by Metalastik bushings) and pivoted on a steel rod which was threaded at both ends to accept self-locking nuts. Initially the SI hub carrier, identified by a ribbed casting, was modified to suit the new wishbone. Only a few of these 'transitional' hub carriers were produced before a completely new design appeared. This was a smooth alloy casting, somewhat wider in section than the Series I style, and was produced until the end of Elite production.

The front suspension was also changed on the Series II, but in this instance the modification was relatively minor and consisted of switching to a newer trunnion (and altering the wishbone end accordingly) with a single grease nipple. A significant change at both ends of the car was the switch to shock absorbers with a longer travel, and softer springs, 112 pounds per inch in front and 69 pounds at the back (Len

Street believed that they were closer to 80 pounds). This change was in deference to the touring customer who complained that the early Elites were too stiff.

Besides the wishbone rear suspension and the softer ride, there were two other changes made to the Series II Elites. These included an eventual change to a throttle cable instead of the previous arms and levers, and the addition of pockets in the seat backs to store the side windows.

Bristol Plastics Ltd

When Chapman designed the improved rear suspension he also began looking for a new supplier to build the body/chassis. Maximar had been increasingly difficult to work with, due primarily to their reluctance to improve fit and finish. In a way this was understandable, as payment from Lotus was often slow in coming and many body/chassis were delivered on a credit basis. With every penny committed to the new factory at Cheshunt, cash flow to Lotus's suppliers was sporadic at best.

Nonetheless, the people at Bristol Plastics, a division of the Bristol Aircraft Ltd, were very excited over the prospect of building the Elite monocoque. As it happened they had had some automotive experience already, having produced the body shells for the Noble

ON THE ROAD

Large order from Lotus Cars Limited endorses outstanding quality of glass-fibre car bodies

otus Cars Limited have just placed an order with Bristol eroplane Plastics Limited for a very large number of plastic ar bodies for their new Lotus Elite grand touring car. This der, one of the largest ever awarded to a plastics anufacturer by a British car firm, is a striking endorsement the outstanding quality of Bristol plastic car bodies.

The most roadworthy car body EVER BUILT

he Lotus Elite car body consists of a shell made of glass-inforced epoxide and polyester resin. The chassis and body re fused together into a highly sophisticated, integral moulding which forms the most advanced car body ever built.

The structure, which is corrosion-proof, is exceptionally gid with a good resistance to impact damage. In addition,

provide a shell which embodies all the most desirable qualitie of roadworthiness.

Bristol Aeroplane Plastics Limited are among the leader of plastics technology in Europe and have perfected a number of new techniques. These new techniques, whic include developments in foaming polyurethane, could b used for further major advances in car body design.

Bristol Plastics advert from Sport Car *magazine. (Sports Car* magazine*)*

miniature car. Being aircraft oriented, they were also very proud of the quality of their work and when Chapman showed them some examples of Maximar's problems the hook was baited. Bristol not only agreed to produce the fibreglass monocoque, but also agreed to refinish the moulds and build new jigs and tools as well.

Chapman's original order for 500 (Bristol went on to build a total of about 750) was one of the largest contracts ever awarded by a British car builder to a British plastics company and was hailed in the trade papers as something of a landmark. In September 1959, a month before Cheshunt's official opening celebration, the papers were signed and Bristol went to work. All of their body/chassis, incidentally, were built to the Series II specification, although the SI dog-leg attachment recess was left in the moulds. Production began at Bristol's Southmead Road factory on Hurn airfield near Bournemouth, on the South Coast, but was eventually moved to Filton, Bristol.

How an Elite monocoque was built

Bristol Plastics collected a set of master moulds from Hornsey. These were first-generation mouldings taken from Frayling's full-scale plaster mock-up. From these masters six complete sets of moulds were constructed, painstaking care being taken with their finish. Bristol wanted as near perfect a surface as possible prior to applying paint, so several weeks were spent by Bristol technicians in filling low spots, sanding imperfections and polishing surfaces.

The moulds were made of fibreglass and were mounted on rigid supports so that no distortion occurred in the lay-up process. The first step in the lay-up procedure required the application of wax to the mould surfaces. Next, a thin film of catalysed polyester resin was sprayed into the mould; this formed the 'gel coat', or outer surface, of the finished piece. Once the gel coat had set, successive layers of glass mat were applied, each thickness being wetted with catalysed polyester resin. Of interest to fibreglass DIY'ers, the Bristol technicians carried their resin in buckets and applied it with paint brushes. In order to ensure consistent lay-ups, the technicians worked to charts which specified the number of layers of mat and the amount of resin to be applied. Too much resin tended to embrittle the panel while too little failed to saturate which meant that it would never completely harden.

After the finished pieces (which were translucent and whitish in colour) were pulled from their moulds, they were placed in large jigs. These specially made fixtures were precision aligned so that the fit of one to another, in the bonding, for example, of the three major monocoque sections, was held to aircraft tolerances. To further ensure exact fit, the front subframe and the windscreen hoop were bolted to the moulds.

To speed the production of the Elite's large body/chassis sections, Bristol used ovens heated to 40 degrees Centigrade to hasten set-up time. Even so, six hours were required for these pieces and when they were glued together they had to be held in compression jigs for an additional 12 hours at room temperature! The slow cure was necessary for as perfect a bond as possible.

Pieces fresh from the moulds were trimmed using Desoutter oscillating saws which were originally designed for surgical use. Precise trimming was facilitated by incorporating scribe lines in the moulds which were, of course, transferred to the mouldings.

Quality control, at least in terms of aesthetics, was quite good. Gary Weston worked on the Elite line at Bristol for almost three years, and his job was to laminate the body seam under the door sills and then to fit the doors to their openings. He cut the gap with a sanding disc and the inspector used a penny coin to check the clearance all around. This explains, incidentally, why doors from one Elite rarely fit well on another. Weston recalled that one person was assigned to cut all the holes in the body/chassis which was accomplished using jigs and templates. Another technician fitted nothing but boot and bonnet lids and so on. In this way Bristol personnel became expert at specialized tasks and could maintain consistently high quality—or so it appeared.

Disaster

The first Bristol 'bodies' that were trucked to Cheshunt were superb. Fit and finish rivalled that of metal-bodied cars, paint work was deep and lustrous and detailing was exceptional. Then disaster struck.

Telephones started ringing at Cheshunt to report that Elite differentials were pulling out of the body/chassis! Worse than that was news that the Government had heard of the trouble and was holding up a shipment of Elites at Dover which was bound for Europe. A quick round of the works, with the time-honoured long screwdriver testing equipment, proved everyone's worst fears—the diff boxes were being laid up incorrectly and were flexing and breaking up under load. If this was not enough, Chapman got word from an Elite racer that a rear wishbone on his Bristol-bodied car had pulled out of the fibreglass during a club event.

Mike Costin remembered the problem well. 'The lay-up system was fully defined when the job went to Bristol and was intended to be exactly as Maximar bodies had ended up through the development stage. The problem was that the Bristol people made the first few and then put the job on to piecework. The operators took the short way out and instead of doing it the time-consuming way as specified in the lay-up schemes, they just used all the pieces of glass and rovings as they saw fit.' Diff boxes ended up too thin or not overlapped at the edges.

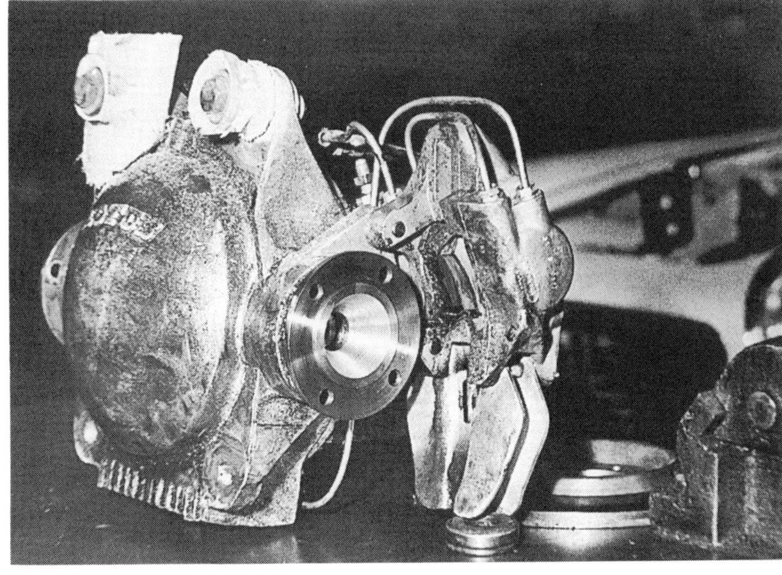

This differential has broken away from an early Bristol body/chassis; the upper bobbins have pulled completely free. (Photographer unknown)

Wishbone bobbins were held in place by resin or, again, cloth that was not overlapped.

Diff straps

Ron White of Lotus Developments recalled what happened next. 'Chapman came down and said he wanted something done quick. I came up with the diff straps, two pieces of strip steel about 2 inches wide with a bend at the end to pick up the top differential bolts. A quick blacksmith job.

'Chapman took the car out to the road in front of the works, revved to 6,000 and dropped the clutch. He stopped 200 yards down the road, revved to six grand and dropped the clutch again. He did this again and again until there was a big crunch noise and the car came to a

The differential reinforcing straps are visible on the top surface of this diff box which has been removed from a Bristol body/chassis. The ends of these straps pick up the top differential mounting bolts before they enter the bosses on the diff case. (Author)

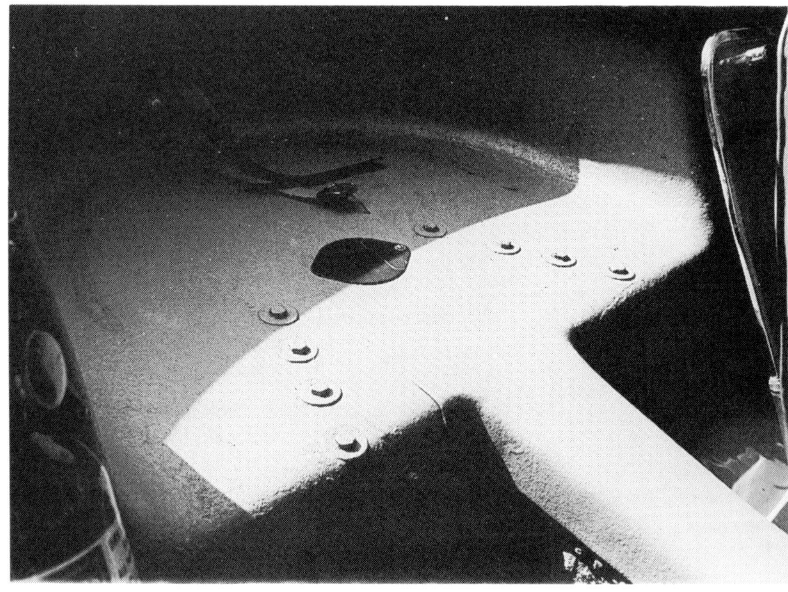

The 'V' pattern of bolt heads on the spare tyre well identifies an Elite fitted with diff straps. The oval cover in the centre is the diff oil dipstick access. (Author)

stop. We brought it in, pulled the diff and found the teeth had sheared off the crown wheel.' Chapman was obviously pleased and said, 'If we can strip the teeth off the crown wheel without the diff pulling out we should be all right'.

The next problem was what to do about the Elites at Dover and the cars already shipped overseas. Lotus outfitted a Ford Anglia van for fibreglass work and sent one of their 'glass men' to Dover with a fistful of diff straps. Once the Dover cars were 'strapped' he accompanied them across the Channel. The plan was to track down all the Bristol bodies at the Lotus dealers and cut out the old diff boxes or, if they looked all right, to install straps as insurance. The replacement diff boxes were specially built sections which had been custom made by Bristol. Len Street recalled that, besides France, the little Anglia van travelled as far away as Holland and Italy to 'glass in' the new diff boxes.

Back at Cheshunt, the steel straps were added to the normal assembly line and were fitted as necessary. Some cars were so bad, however, that completely new boxes were installed, while others came through strong enough to require no work at all. Probably close to half of the Bristol-bodied cars, however, ended up being fitted with the steel strap differential reinforcement.

The step repair

Meanwhile, examination of the wishbone cups in the undertray showed some bobbins supported by mostly resin with very little fibreglass cloth. Because of normal road shocks and the fact that the bobbins were torqued frequently (to replace the rubber isolation balls), the resin tended to break up and the bobbins loosened or, worse, pulled out entirely. Since the Elite utilized a three-point attachment system, this meant instant suspension collapse!

Lotus Developments took a look at this problem also and came up with the so-called 'step repair'. A 5 to 6 inch oval hole was cut into the floorboard 'step' behind the seats which exposed the top of the bobbins. A steel strap was drilled to accept two short bolts, and was then placed over the bobbin tops and bolted in place. A thick mush of resin and chopped fibreglass cloth was then spooned into the hole to cover both the bobbins and their strap. Finally, a layer of cloth was placed over the opening to finish off the repair, but no attempt was made to smooth the surface because it was covered by carpeting and would be unseen.

A survey of some 50 Elites ranging from chassis 1370 to 1953 was made as part of the research for this book, and the results showed that there was no relationship at all between diff straps and step repairs. While fully half of the cars had the differential modification, only about a third showed evidence of the bobbin reinforcement. Some cars had no modifications at all, a few had both but some had only one or the other! There was only one car that had evidence of a new diff box having been grafted into place.

Of course, no one was more concerned over the failures and the repairs than Bristol Plastics Ltd. Their dilemma was that they were already feeling a financial pinch over the Elite body/chassis. Bristol had underestimated the time necessary to build the monocoque and had quickly arrived at the conclusion that hand lay-ups coupled with long curing times, despite the use of multiple moulds, was eating away at

This Series II Elite bears many scars but the sunken oval in the centre of the picture, on the 'step' behind the floor board, identifies a bobbin reinforced Bristol body/chassis. (Author)

their profit margin. Also, Lotus simply was not able to sell all the Elites they were building, and the fields next to the Cheshunt works were sprouting unfinished cars like weeds. Hundreds had already left the Bristol shops and no one knew how much it would take, if anything, to put each one right.

Double dimples

In their methodical, aircraft-inspired method, Bristol took another look at the Elite body/chassis, only this time they considered its structure more than its appearance. The diff straps and the step repairs were working, so the urgency, if not the gravity, of the situation had lessened. Bristol had gained some time but they already knew that they would have to absorb the cost of further development.

A return to the 'lay-up specifications' for the diff box and wishbone bobbins was easy enough, but Bristol decided to reinforce these areas with thicker-section fibreglass. They also looked at the floor panel and transmission tunnel and increased the thickness of those areas as well. Each change in operation increased their costs, so Bristol engineers also considered ways to economize.

Len Street recalled that they began to build doors using polyester instead of epoxy resin. They also investigated using a lighter gauge steel in the windscreen hoop, but dismissed this notion as too risky in terms of cabin rigidity—they did not want the windscreens popping out when the car was cornered hard!

In order to identify a reinforced chassis, Bristol placed a small (approximately $\frac{1}{2}$ inch diameter by $\frac{1}{8}$ inch thick) disc on the centreline of the undertray mould between the silencer recesses. The result was a circular depression or dimple in the finished undertray that was easily felt by hand from the back of the car but would normally be unseen so as not to spoil the car's appearance. Only a handful of these 'single dimple' cars were built, but Cheshunt chose to ignore the mark anyway and installed diff straps and bobbin reinforcements as before. Chapman was not convinced and his decision to continue the works' modifications led to an increasingly strained relationship.

Finally Bristol, no doubt in exasperation, told Chapman that he no longer needed to reinforce their product. They were building 'double dimpled' body/chassis, the state of the art in fibreglass monocoques. Identified by two circular depressions, one about $\frac{1}{2}$ inch in diameter and the other $\frac{3}{16}$ inch, again on the centreline between the muffler depressions, these Elites were the strongest and heaviest (about 1,420 pounds less fluids) ever. Interestingly, they were also the quietest by a significant margin. Diff boxes, bobbin mouldings, doors (back to epoxy), transmission tunnels and floors were substantially heavier lay-ups than even the maximum tolerances shown on the original Bristol charts.

Bristol had really put their pride on the line with the double dimpled cars, so they made sure every other detail was perfect as well. Exposed edges were rounded off, holes were sanded to remove any trace of 'spider-webbing', lids and door radiuses were more carefully matched and even the door hinge bobbins were laid-up in heavier section. Alas, the double dimpled Elite was rather short-lived; it appeared at around chassis number 1900 and continued to the end of production at about 2050. Tony Bates, Elite restorer *extraordinaire* (see Chapter 13), observed that the very last cars may have slipped slightly in quality again because he had seen 'some very thin prop shaft tunnels. Hardly any fibre at all, only gel coat.'

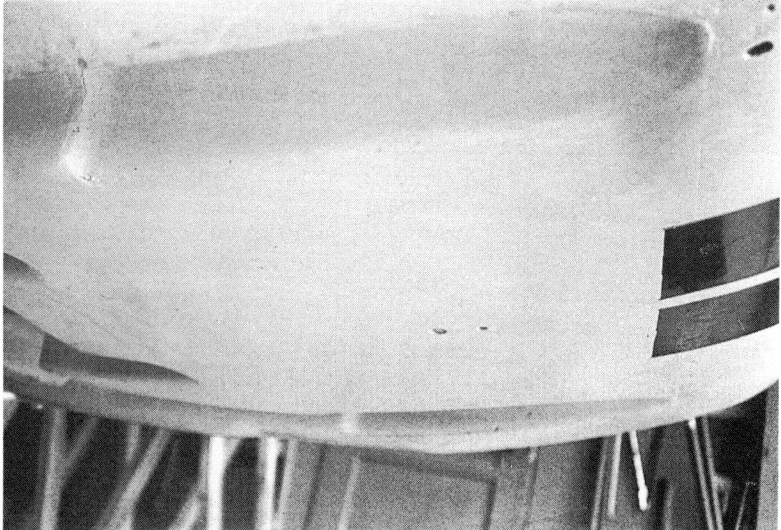

Double dimples were located on the rear underbody centreline, between the silencer recesses. In this picture the bands on the right are the ends of racing stripes. (Author)

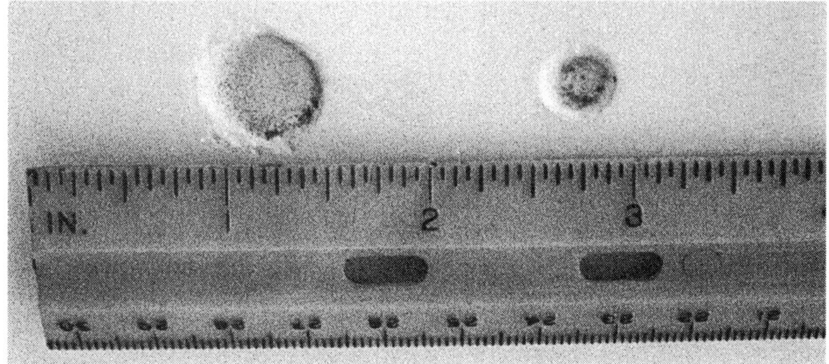

The two depressions that identify a 'double dimpled' Bristol body/ chassis. (Author)

The end of the line

The Elite had been a difficult lesson in economics for both Lotus and Bristol Plastics and they breathed a collective sigh of relief when the Lotus Elan made its début in 1962, because this meant the end of production for Chapman's monocoque GT. According to the works chassis list, Elite production officially ended in September 1963, although there remained 30–40 body/chassis at Cheshunt. Bristol ended up with a few as well, perhaps as many as half-a-dozen that Lotus refused to pay for. 'Rejected on the basis of quality,' they said. Bristol also ended up keeping the moulds because Lotus did not want to buy them even though their own set, which had been used to make repair sections for damaged cars, were getting (according to Len Street) 'pretty knackered'.

Tony Bates discovered years later that the remaining bodies at Filton were eventually used in Bristol's fire-fighters training programme. They were burned for fire extinguishing drills! Fortunately some of the moulds still existed and Bates was able to purchase them. Oddly, the undertray mould showed no evidence of ever having been dimpled.

Chassis numbers

By now, sharp-eyed readers will have figured out that there were about 1070 Elites built. The exact number remains unknown because numerous body/chassis were sold to restore accident or racing write-offs. In some cases those monocoques were assigned the chassis number of the damaged car, while in others the car was given a new number. Interestingly, there was an error in the Bristol numbering scheme because they began their production at chassis number 1251 while Maximar ended theirs at 1280. Therefore there were 29 Elites with identical chassis numbers but different origins! Bristol, incidentally, put a small alloy tag next to the Lotus chassis plate which exclaimed in red and silver, 'Body moulded by Bristol Aircraft'.

Another curiosity of the works chassis list shows a series of a dozen scattered entries beginning with 1337 and ending with 1524 for a customer called 'Ecurie Shirlee'. As will be discussed in Chapter 10, this was the name of the Western United States distributor for Lotus after Jay Chamberlain was ousted. What is peculiar is that the Ecurie Shirlee entries were written over the names of other customers and were dated one to two years after the date of the original invoice. On inspection, several of these cars had all the fitments of a later manufacture than their chassis numbers would indicate. For example, chassis number 1483 (Larry Darwin, USA) has an umbrella handbrake and Royalite interior (more on Royalite in a moment) despite the fact that it was much too early to be so equipped. To compound the mystery, the original invoice for Larry's car was dated April 1961, but the Ecurie Shirlee entry showed January 1963!

The bare bodies/chassis that remained at Cheshunt after regular production stopped were eventually finished off over the next few years and sold. By then, some items like the stainless steel bumpers and oval were no longer obtainable so fibreglass replicas were fabricated and installed.

Besides being scribed on the chassis plate, which was fixed inside the engine bay, both Maximar and Bristol recorded numbers in several other places on the car, although not always consistently. Maximar and Bristol liked to write the chassis number, in pencil (or chalk!), on the

Chassis number chalked on the inner door panel. (Author)

inside of the doors under the upholstery. They occasionally stencilled the number at the back of the spare tyre well, again under the upholstery. Several Series Is had numbers punched on the diagonal tube of the front subframe while others had them pencilled on the underside of boot and bonnet lid hinge plates.

Bristol also marked hinge plates and doors. They stamped or scribed the numbers into the metal and scratched them into the fibreglass between the hinge plate bobbins. Bristol also liked to paint or write chassis numbers on slips of paper which were stuffed into the hollow panel at the back of the boot and in various places under the upholstery or sound-deadening material. Occasionally, Bristol scratched numbers on the front subframe and in the fibreglass inside the wheel wells, frequently the right rear!

The Special Equipment Elite

Colin Chapman used the occasion of the 1960 Earls Court Motor Show to announce the Special Equipment (SE) Elite. This model was produced in answer to requests by owners for a bit more performance and a better gearbox. To accommodate them the SE was equipped with twin SUs, a four-branch exhaust system, Stage II camshaft (.360 inches of lift) and a ZF gearbox. Power output was about 85 bhp as opposed to 75 for the standard Elite with a single carburettor and the cast iron exhaust manifold. A 4.2 differential was usually fitted and to identify the SE version to passers-by, all had a dual tone paint job with the roof done in silver. The SE also came with the visually interesting Lucas PL700 headlamps, Pirelli Cintura tyres and ashtrays fitted into the door panels.

The Royalite interior

Shortly after the Special Equipment version was introduced Lotus began supplying the standard model with twin SUs, although the cast iron exhaust manifold was retained. This change increased bhp to around 80.

Coincidental with the carburettor change came a redesigned in-

The so-called 'soft' interior was standard until the introduction of Royalite. (Adrien Schagen)

Royalite transmission tunnel cover and door panel. (Author)

Early style, large diameter 'thin rim' steering wheel. (Author)

Late production, reduced diameter 'thick rim' steering wheel. (Author)

terior. The so-called 'soft' interior with its floppy door pockets and upholstered transmission tunnel arm rest was replaced with a semi-rigid plastic called Royalite. The door pockets became small rigid bins which also incorporated convenient arm rests. The transmission tunnel cover was a single piece that extended from the spare tyre well to the dash panel. Royalite, incidentally, was a trade name for thermo (heat)-formed plastics and its addition to the Elite certainly made the inside look more contemporary compared to the earlier style. Industrial artists thought so too because the Royalite interior went on to win a British design award for its functional elegance.

An umbrella pull handbrake returned with the Royalite interior, and with it came cast iron rear calipers (the earlier cars were fitted with alloy rear brakes). A new, small diameter (15 inches as opposed to the earlier 16) steering wheel was fitted as well. This wheel had the same handsome wood rim with alloy spokes and a black accent stripe set into its face, but was made with a significantly thicker section than the earlier style. The 'thin rim', incidentally, had also gone through a change from very early examples which had a reddish hue to the wood to those supplied later which were 'blond' in colour.

Several other running changes were made during the early production of the Series II Elite and these included a rounded radiator tank instead of a square design, a larger diameter clutch slave cylinder and thicker gauge stainless steel for the front and rear bumpers.

The Super series

With so many Elites finding their way on to racing circuits, it occurred to Chapman that a market might exist for cars already set up for competition. In 1961 he announced the Super 95 which was quickly followed by the Super 100 and finally the Super 105. The numbers referred to brake horsepower outputs and were identified by a chrome script on the right rear edge of the boot lid. Power increases over the Stage III tune were accomplished first, by careful selection of the engines. As in any manufacturing line, some engines, for no apparent reason, produce more power than others, and these were identified at Coventry when they were run in on the bench.

Further increases in output were the result of careful preparation of the cylinder head. Blending of combustion chamber radii was followed by the usual porting and polishing. Although the Super Elites could be supplied fully trimmed for road use, they were normally delivered stripped and ready to race. The following is the specification list originally written by Mike Costin for the Super 100:

1. 100 bhp engine specifications.
2. Four-branch specially tuned exhaust system.
3. Heat shields over starter motor and attached to side of engine by exhaust pipe.
4. SU electric fuel pump to be fitted in boot.
5. Fuel tank to our latest large capacity pattern.
6. Large Le Mans fuel cap with a $3\frac{1}{2}$ inch diameter neck.
7. 5 Dunlop Red Spot racing wheels.
8. ZF four-speed, all-synchromesh close ratio gearbox.
9. Racing suspension front and rear of the hard ride type.
10. NACA duct in bonnet over carburettors.
11. Light calipers to suit new specifications.
12. Oil cooler and air duct to be fitted to cars for racing use only.
13. Oil filter to be fitted to cars for racing use only (this was a remote filter).
14. Special Lucas starter motor.
    'Unless otherwise specified, Super 100s will be supplied less front and rear bumpers; interior trim and the normal Elite seats will be removed and replaced by adjustable Formula Junior seats.'

Exact production figures for the Super Elites remain unknown although Appendix II offers some clues.

After five years of production at Hornsey, Edmonton and Cheshunt, the Elite assembly line was finally shut down in September 1963. The enthusiasts' press took notice but none was more dramatic than *Road & Track* magazine's full-page obituary which was published in June 1964. Never mind that they got the span of production wrong and that by stating that the factory was at Luton they confused Lotus with Speedex (later Marcos), it was still quite something to read:

'After six years of production, the Lotus Elite is no more. Gone it is, the way of the Allard J-2, the L-29 Cord, the Mercedes SSK and other designs of sacred memory.

Super series Elites were identified by chrome script on the boot lid. Notice also the large diameter fuel filler. (George Rance)

Lucas PL 700 headlamps were standard on Special Equipment and Super series Elites. They threw a more powerful beam than standard lamps. (George Rance)

'A beautiful design was the Elite, one of the great designs of the post WW-II era, one that seems certain to be looked back upon as a landmark of some sort in automobile design. Without question it was the best, if not the very best looking Grand Touring car ever built. The body, all fiberglass, was designed entirely in the Lotus works at Luton, England, and was not only an immediate and lasting success but also an example, perhaps the only example, of the fluid plasticity of speed/motion to be captured in that glass fiber and resin medium.

'Admittedly, the Elite had its problems. The monocoque type construction created a drumming that was extremely annoying to most passengers, the body had minimal (if that) protection from the expected hazards of normal driving, and the average mechanic went into shock when asked to work on it.

'The car was also plagued by other problems—a high initial price that scared off all but the most sanguine, a marketing situation during its introduction that could only be described as impossible and a long period (before Bob Challman of Ecurie Shirlee Corp. stepped in to give the American Lotus plan a respectability and dependability it never had before) when the buyer of an Elite didn't know whether he'd ever see his dealer again.

'So, think well of the Elite. It will be remembered as one of the outstanding designs.'

Chapter 6

Team Elite

Chapman's dilemma

As hard as it was for Colin Chapman to accept being stalemated, he came to the realization at the beginning of 1959 that he had spread himself too thinly. The tiny factory at Hornsey was fairly bursting at the seams with production of not only a few Elites and Sevens, but also the Fifteen and Seventeen sports racers, an occasional Eleven and the Sixteen formula car! If this was not enough, Chapman's financial reserves were all but gone with the beginning of construction of his new factory at Cheshunt.

Then came the news in June of Peter Lumsden and Peter Riley's class win at Le Mans. Of course, this was the very race Chapman so much wanted for himself. He was obviously delighted that the Elite had fulfilled its design criteria, but the victory would have been all the sweeter had Team Lotus run the car.

At first, Chapman was simply frustrated at not having the resources to field a team of Elites at Le Mans. But soon his emotion turned to that of annoyance when a few reporters in the motoring press implied that the win in France was something of a fluke. After all, nothing as radical as a fibreglass monocoque, and one so delicate in appearance at that, could compete on equal terms with established marques such as Porsche and Alfa Romeo. To dispel the sceptics, Chapman wanted desperately to repeat the victory in 1960, but as soon as his thoughts returned to how he might accomplish the goal, another crisis arose in some other corner of the works to divert his attention.

Enter David Buxton

Fortunately, someone else was thinking about a team of Elites. His name was David Buxton, the irrepressible Lotus dealer from Derbyshire (see Chapter 9). Buxton not only loved racing but also understood what it took to win, and he believed that the Elite could be unbeatable in the European long-distance events. His idea was to enter three British Racing Green Elites in all national and international endurance races.

Buxton approached Chapman, who was at once delighted and relieved to hear of the plan. A deal was struck which consisted of permission to call the group Team Elite (which sounded like a works team), unlimited technical assistance, entry under the Lotus Engineering banner—although Team Elite paid all entry fees—and an agreement to provide special, ultra-lightweight body/chassis should any of Buxton's cars be written off in racing accidents. As we will see, the latter clause came back to haunt Chapman, although there never were any special body/chassis delivered. All preparation and maintenance of the cars and their transportation was to be carried out by Buxton's staff.

Buxton designed the team's insignia which consisted of $1\frac{1}{4}$ inch lettering on the doors which spelled out 'TEAM ELITE'. Not unlike other racing teams of the period, Buxton's group was very private and intensely personal and a far cry from the blare of modern commercialism. As it happened, Team Elite was born in the twilight of the gentlemen's racing team and before its last race was run it would feel the impact of a new age in racing.

The nature of the team

Sponsorship existed in those days, of course, but consisted mainly of free products and technical advice, although a few companies did offer cash incentives. Team Elite had contracts with Dunlop, Ferodo, Champion, Girling, Esso and Lucas. The last two gave fuel and electrical supplies and enough money to about cover the maintenance of a season's engines.

It was New Year 1960 by the time the Team cars were prepped and ready for their assault on the European endurance events. Two of the cars came off Buxton's showroom floor and were driven by the proprietor himself and Bill Allen. The third Elite was owned and driven by John Wagstaff and wore his personal FP 98 registration number. The three men had successfully raced small bore racing cars together and were fiercely competitive. The fact that they were friends and lived close to one another characterized the nature of the Team. When co-drivers were needed, as at Le Mans for example, candidates were selected as much on the basis of how well they got along with the other members of the group as to how fast they motored.

First go at Le Mans

In June, the Lotus Engineering entries for Team Elite were accepted by the Le Mans organizers and Buxton selected the drivers. He and Allen would pair up in a company car while Wagstaff and Tony Marsh would co-drive in John's Elite. The manager was Colin's father, Stanley, with additional help given by Keith Duckworth who, at the time, was a Lotus employee. Technical support was the responsibility of Dennis Coundrey who was a director of David Buxton Racing. Together with the independent entries of Masson/Laurent and Baillie/Parkes, the Lotus camp was confident of duplicating Lumsden/Riley's class win of the year before.

Their confidence was rewarded with Masson/Laurent taking a 1st in Class and a 13th overall. The Team Elite car of Wagstaff and Marsh took a second in Class and won the Index of Thermal Efficiency to the tune of 30,000 francs. This and most other prize money, incidentally, went to the mechanics. The original Team Elite drivers were the old-style sportsmen who thought it reward enough just to be there.

The five-minute board goes up before the start of a club race starring Team Elite (car no 138) and Roger Nathan who is nestled between the Jag and the dark-coloured Elite, fitted with 'wobbly web' mag wheels. (Roger Nathan collection)

The Team's next outing at the Spa circuit in Belgium ended in disaster. On the very last lap both Wagstaff and Allen passed the class-leading Abarth Porsche only to have Wagstaff spin off into a ditch. A back marker, who had slowed to avoid John, was 'T-boned' by Allen. The impact launched his Elite which rolled several times. Miraculously, Allen was ejected through the roof and escaped with minor bruises. Years later while relating his memories, Buxton recalled that under his leadership Team Elite lost three cars, much to Chapman's chagrin as he had to replace them with brand new body/chassis units. With a typical Buxton chuckle he also remembererd that after Clive Hunt took over the Team in 1962 Chapman had to replace four more!

The Team mechanics dutifully cleaned up the hardware and hurriedly put together another car for Wagstaff and Alan Stacey to drive at the Nürburgring in Germany for the 1,000 kilometre race. Despite a steering rack coming adrift in the race's final stages, the Team Elite car held together long enough to capture a 1st in Class.

In all, Chapman was quite pleased with Team Elite's results in the 1960 season. Its tally sheet was most impressive with an Index win at Le Mans, a victory at the 'Ring and the 1,000 Kilometres at Montlhery (Wagstaff 1st, Buxton 2nd) and numerous victories in national races. The press also acknowledged the Elite's superiority and praised the efforts of the team.

New Team colours and trouble for Buxton

The New Year brought some changes for Team Elite. David Buxton was forced to spend more of his time unravelling the mysteries of his sales contracts. It seems that the tax man was looking into allegations of several imaginative ways of new car financing and the practice of rebuilding race cars and registering them as new road vehicles. In the end, Buxton had to leave England for a time to sort out the difficulties.

Meanwhile, to relieve some of the pressure in Buxton's workshops, then back-logged with normal customer service, the Team's Climax

David Buxton leads John Wagstaff, and a hard-working MGA, at Mallory Park in 1961. The following year Team Elite abandoned the NACA duct in favour of a 4-inch diameter hose which led from the frontal air intake to the forward carburettor. (Ron Hunt)

Still in Le Mans trim, the Wagstaff Elite displays its body material disc, forward of the door opening, and its number light. Notice also the two ventilation openings in the side window. (Wagstaff collection)

engines were sent out to Cosworth for rebuilds and tuning. A new colour scheme was chosen for the cars which consisted of green racing stripes over a white body. The Team picked this arrangement to better spot the cars (for pit signals) during races run under bad visibility. Besides, the lads wanted something distinctive (the Elite seemed to lend itself to racing stripes) and everyone thought that this combination looked quite smart. The shade of green, by the way, matched the colour of the self-adhesive Scotchlite Le Mans identification diamond affixed to the rear of the body work. These geometric markings, by their colour and shape, identified a car's speed potential which was a great help in overtaking manoeuvres. The body material was also marked on the car, in the Elite's case by a Scotchlite disc, yellow in colour, placed on both sides of the body just forward of the windscreen pillar. This identification was intended to help the safety personnel in the event of a crash.

The Team's second run at Le Mans

The 1961 Le Mans entry included two Team Elite cars, one for Bill Allen and Trevor Taylor and the other for Clive Hunt and an American Lotus enthusiast, Doc Wyllie. The latter pair, incidentally, drove Buxton's old car. At the end of 24 hours it was Allen/Taylor 1st in Class and 12th overall. Hunt and Wyllie had gone out in the ninth hour with a split fuel tank but the Team was ecstatic. There were now three consecutive years of Le Mans victories and the Team had scored two of them.

Clive Hunt to the rescue

Clive Hunt had expressed particular enthusiasm for the Team, and so was invited to drive at Monza and Montlhery and, although let down by mechanical problems, he showed great talent. Of equal importance at the time was the fact that Hunt was a man of means and all breathed a sigh of relief when he offered to assume the financial and organizational support of the Team.

John Thornburn and the transporter Clive Hunt purchased for Team Elite when he took over primary sponsorship. The colour scheme was green and white, even down to the racing stripes on the cab. (Team Elite)

Hunt ran a successful contracting company in Derbyshire which meant that he could set up a racing shop in the same locale as the previous headquarters. This also meant there would be minimal disruption of the Team's support personnel and Hunt endeavoured to keep as many of the old hands as he could. Ron Bennet came along as Chief Mechanic with Malcolm Malone as his number two. Cyril Embrey was first entrusted with engine preparation but later took on the job of Team Manager. Hunt even looked after Rhoddy Harvey-Bailey, the Team's tireless 'gopher'. To mark his takeover, Hunt added the designation '62' to the TEAM ELITE insignia; he also purchased a new transporter and had its cab painted in the Team's livery.

When Hunt contacted the old sponsors to advise of the change in directors he was surprised at some of the conditions in their new contracts. He had not known that Esso, for example, had nominated their own drivers for specific races. Besides Team Elite's mainstays of Hunt, Wagstaff and Allen, Esso would add Trevor Taylor, Alan Stacey, Peter Arundell, Doc Wyllie, David Hobbs, Frank Gardner, Dennis Hulme and John Coundley! Taylor became a close friend of the Team, incidentally, and stayed on as No 1 while most of the others contributed good finishing positions. Sadly, Arundell drove only once, at the 'Ring, and crashed his Elite in practice; but the conditions imposed by Esso signalled the beginnings of the influence sponsors were to have on the look and the content of today's motor sport.

A full calendar was planned for 1962 with the first outing at Snetterton where Wagstaff finished 2nd in Class. The next race was at Oulton Park which saw both Hunt and Taylor on the first row of the starting grid. Hunt dropped back with a persistent misfire but Trevor Taylor won the Class and set a new lap record in the process.

Then followed a 2nd and a 3rd at Mallory Park with Hunt and Wagstaff driving, the latter setting a new lap record. Yet another class win and lap record fell to Taylor during the next round at Silverstone.

The same weekend Hunt paired with David Hobbs and Wagstaff with Pat Ferguson at the Nürburgring. The boss dropped out after a brake disc broke, but Wagstaff and Ferguson took a 2nd in Class.

The Team's third Le Mans

With such an auspicious beginning to the new season, hopes were high for another Team Elite victory at Le Mans. Alfa Romeo had other ideas, however, and entered two of their new Zagato coupés. Simca Abarth had a similar notion and showed up with no fewer than four of their indecently fast rear-engined bolides. Le Mans observers reckoned the small GT class was the one to watch, but when Team Elite, which consisted of David Hobbs and Frank Gardner and Hunt/Wyllie, took off as if it was a sprint race, most thought it was going to be over early.

Not to worry, the Hobbs/Gardner Elite was never caught and took 1st in Class, 1st in the Index of Thermal Efficiency and 8th overall. It averaged 99.6 mph for the 24 hours and achieved a top speed down the Mulsanne straight of 135 mph, all the while averaging nearly 20 miles per gallon of fuel. Not bad for a fragile-looking fibreglass car with an ex-fire pump engine! The Hunt/Wyllie car, by the way, took a 3rd in Class and a 2nd in the Index.

The Team's final days

Despite a strong showing during the rest of the season with Hunt taking a second at Brands Hatch, a first in the Tourist Trophy and Wagstaff taking seconds at the Snetterton Three Hours and at the Montlhery 1,000 Kilometres, it seemed to the young men from Derbyshire that the final days of Team Elite were at hand. After five years the Elite was nearing the end of its production run and presumably its competition career. Although the Team was fiercely loyal to Colin Chapman and Lotus, the news of the Elan being more road car than racer was met with disappointment. With no successor to the Elite, Hunt considered packing it in and very nearly did so when the Team Manager, Cyril Embrey, had to give up his position due to the press of family business. Wagstaff convinced him to continue, for a while anyway, and offered to do double duty until John Thornburn joined the Team as the new manager.

Any concern over the Elite losing its competitive edge proved unfounded and the 1963 season looked like a carbon copy of the previous year. Hunt took 2nd at Snetterton. Taylor won at Oulton Park, breaking the class record he had set the year before. Sir John Whitmore, standing in for Hobbs, won at Goodwood and set a new lap record, while Hunt trailed him for 2nd. Taylor won again at Silverstone, Ferguson at Spa (with a new lap record) and Hobbs with Taylor at the 'Ring.

Their fourth Le Mans

But could they pull it off at Le Mans? Two cars were entered, one for Gardner/Coundley and the other for Wagstaff/Ferguson. Despite 'Fergie' sliding off into the sandbank at the end of the Mulsanne straight on the very first lap, he and Wagstaff finished 1st in Class and came in 10th overall. The Gardner/Coundley Elite burst its engine but the Team was extremely happy and justifiably proud. They had accomplished the Elite's fifth victory at the Sarthe, a fitting tribute to a car that would cease production in three months' time.

One of Wagstaff's last outings in his Le Mans winner was at Silverstone in 1964. Here he is, not only getting the inside wheel up, but also dragging the exhaust system on the ground. The frontal air intake is partially blanked off to keep the engine temperature up in cold weather. No thermostat was ever used. (Harold Barker)

The last season

The 1964 racing season witnessed greater sponsor influence and more works-supported teams, and while all this resulted in faster and more sophisticated cars it also contributed to ever-escalating costs. Even though Hunt, Allen and Wagstaff took no money, the Team's resources were getting thin. Worse than that, Hunt's business had taken a nose-dive due to his frequent absences, so he let everyone know that 1964 would be the last season. Typical of the Team's friendship, Hunt made the announcement early enough to allow everyone to begin looking for other arrangements.

As one last favour to Chapman, Hunt agreed to prepare a Lotus Elan to race at Le Mans. He also accepted a contract from Jack Brabham to prepare a B18 sports racer for Dennis Hulme to campaign in the European Championship Series. Both cars were painted in the Team Elite colours. One Elite was kept, primarily for John Wagstaff, to contest those races where reliability was likely to be a factor in a good finishing order.

By June and the 1964 24 Hours of Le Mans, only the Brabham had done reasonably well, a compliment to both Hulme's driving and the level of preparation afforded by Team Elite. The Elan suffered mechanical failure in almost every outing and the Elite was occasionally trailered out. Hunt nonetheless decided to bring both cars to France, the Elite for himself and Wagstaff and the Elan for two French drivers, Gele and Richard. The Elan went out in the second hour with overheating but Hunt and Wagstaff brought the Elite home to another class win. This made an amazing six consecutive victories at Le Mans, and Team Elite had accounted for four of them.

In the months that followed Le Vingt Quatre du Mans, the Team gradually withdrew from competition and was disbanded. Wagstaff acquired the Elite he had raced the previous two years and ran it occasionally in local club events. Because most of the Team members still lived around Derbyshire they kept in contact, usually at race meetings, and every now and again would get together for a reunion.

The Team revived

When the Lotus 47 (the twin-cam racing version of the Europa) was introduced, Wagstaff thought it might be fun to go racing again in what looked to be a good long-distance car. He asked an old friend (who also happened to be best man at his wedding) by the name of David Preston to join him in the adventure, the idea being that the two would co-drive, with Wagstaff using his experience to set up the team and arrange for race entries. Preston, by the way, was an accomplished driver and an excellent engineer.

But what team? Of course, Wagstaff immediately thought of reforming Team Elite. On checking with the authorities they were amazed to learn that the name had never been registered. The first order of business was to copyright the title, Team Elite, in both their names and then send out presentations to the old sponsors. Most returned to contribute their support including a new one, Goodyear. They were so impressed with the Team's prior record that they designed a tyre expressly for the 47 and gave the team 160 of them! A member of the original Team Elite support crew by the name of John Thornburn came aboard to look after the car.

Wagstaff broke his back in a bob-sled accident in St Moritz but was able to drive the 47 at the Le Mans test day, albeit held rigid in a plaster cast. Although the cast was removed before the actual race, he thought it best not to continue and signed Trevor Taylor to co-drive with Preston; the car blew a head gasket in the fourth hour and retired. The colour scheme, incidentally, was green stripes over a white body.

The Team Elite Lotus 47 was easily the most successful non-works car, but by the season's end a pair of factory 47s with the new removable bodies were eclipsing everybody. Preston and Wagstaff decided to sell the car and buy a Lola T-70 for 1968. Trevor Taylor was retained to drive the car (no small-bore racer this!) and it was raced in its stock blue colour. He scored numerous wins including the Tourist Trophy at Oulton Park.

Before the season was over, Team Elite was approached by John

John Wagstaff (left) and Ron Bennett plan the next step in the restoration of John's Le Mans-winning Team Elite car. John's Team Elite replica is the car on the right with the roll bar. (Wagstaff collection)

Surtees, who had his hands full developing a Formula 1 car, with a request to campaign his Formula 5000 TS5 in the 1969 F5000 Championship Series. Full support was given by Esso Petroleum and, again, Trevor Taylor did the driving, but this time the car appeared in the Team colours. They finished the season 2nd in points, a good effort indeed.

At the ready

Running the Team had been great fun for Wagstaff, but the accounts showed that it had also been frightfully expensive. Unfortunately, too much so for Wagstaff and Preston to continue, so after a decade in existence the Team was once again retired. In retrospect, it was one of the most successful, if not the most publicized, teams in England in the 'sixties. Of course, much of the credit goes to its namesake, which brings us around to Wagstaff's last Elite. Sold in 1966, the Le Mans class winner turned up 13 years later in America. John bought his old racer, which is the only satisfactorily documented Team car in existence, and brought it home to England. Today it sits in his garage, ready to go just in case the lads feel like trying it again.

Far right *Team Elite cars were fitted with full Perspex side windows fitted with vent openings. A flow-through ventilation was accomplished by exhausting air through a slot cut in the roof above the rear window. Recall that the Earls Court prototype utilized a similar feature.* (Wagstaff collection)

Team Elite replicas

With the value of historic racing cars growing seemingly by quantum leaps every year, it is no surprise that a few of them are misrepresented

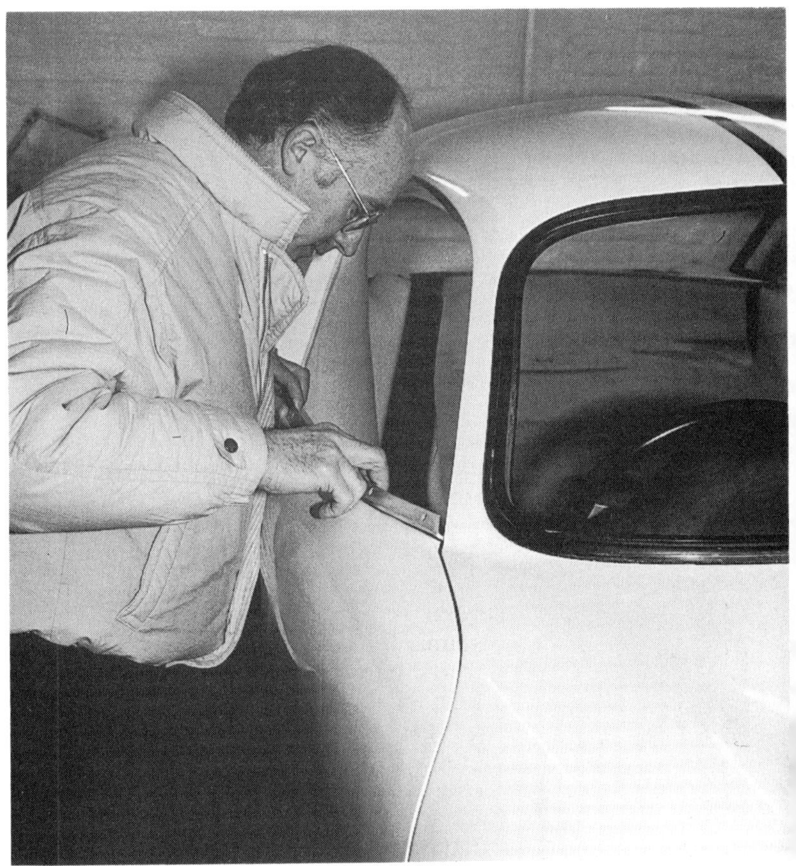

Ron Bennett, ex-Team Elite mechanic, fits the light alloy 'L'-section rail to the Wagstaff Le Mans winner, to which the full Perspex side windows were bolted. The rear window was also plastic and was attached directly to the fibreglass with screws and cup washers. (Wagstaff collection)

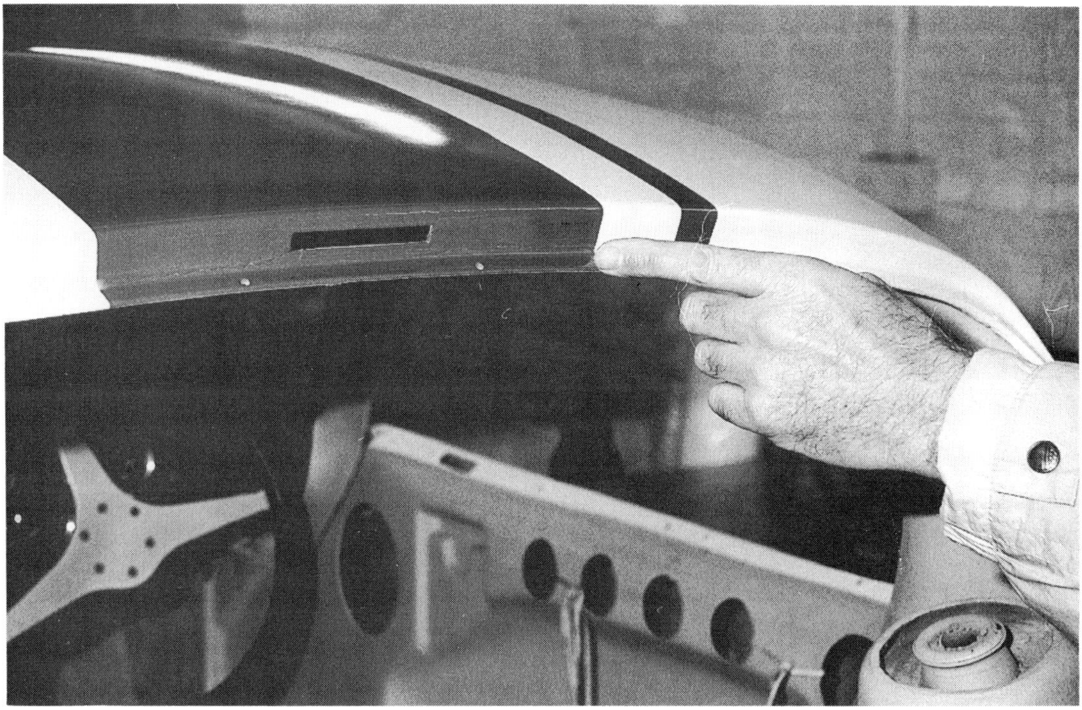

Below *In order to fit 7-inch wide tyres at the rear of Team Elite cars, the lower spring perch was off set to gain clearance.* (Wagstaff collection)

to increase their worth all the more. Unfortunately, Team Elite has been the target of several counterfeiters. In the main, the extent of their 'fakery' has been a green over white paint job, but in at least one instance a car had several genuine Team Elite fittings. Wagstaff remarked that it is probably only a matter of time before somebody appears with Graham Warner's original LOV 1, 'Which I can clearly remember exploding in a thousand pieces at Snetterton.'

Team Elite mods

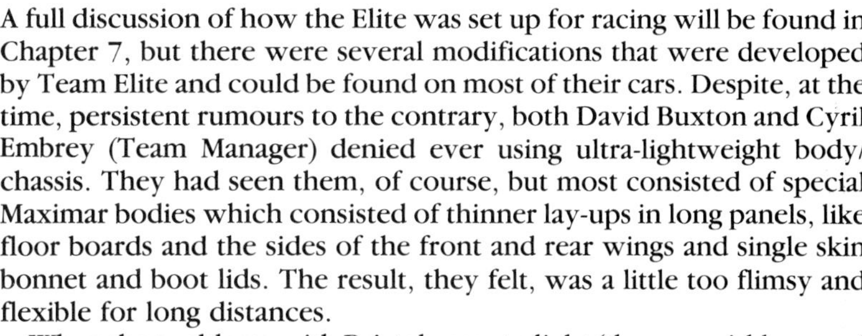

A full discussion of how the Elite was set up for racing will be found in Chapter 7, but there were several modifications that were developed by Team Elite and could be found on most of their cars. Despite, at the time, persistent rumours to the contrary, both David Buxton and Cyril Embrey (Team Manager) denied ever using ultra-lightweight body/chassis. They had seen them, of course, but most consisted of special Maximar bodies which consisted of thinner lay-ups in long panels, like floor boards and the sides of the front and rear wings and single skin bonnet and boot lids. The result, they felt, was a little too flimsy and flexible for long distances.

When the problems with Bristol came to light (the rear wishbones of several Team Elite cars had pulled loose), the Team purchased only Maximar bodies, which they quickly realized were also much lighter into the bargain. They also had the so-called 'hard ride' suspension which the racers preferred. When Team Elite finally returned to buying Bristol-bodied cars, they incorporated their own hard ride spring and shock absorber combination and specified double dimpled cars for strength. In order to pare off some weight the Team resorted to cutting holes in the inner panels of the doors, boot and bonnet lids. They also fitted plexiglass rear windscreens and single pane plexi side windows

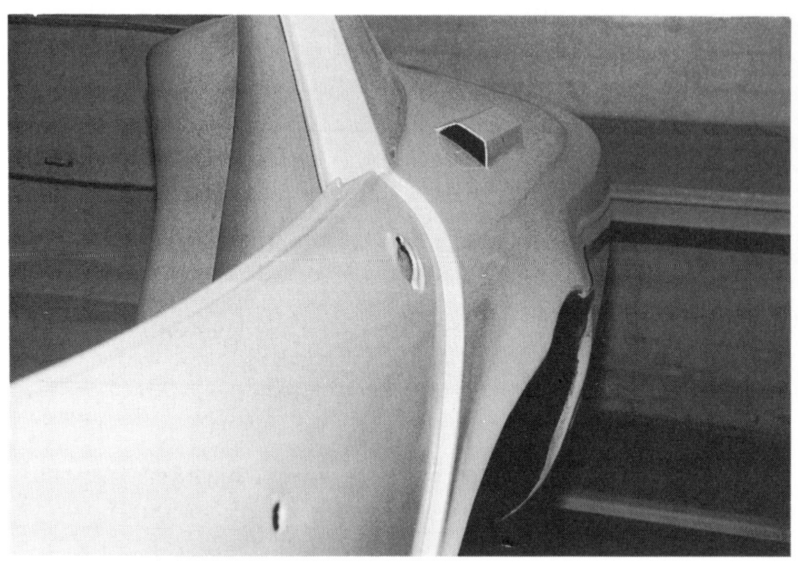

What looked like air scoops at the rear of Wagstaff's car were actually fender bulges, fashioned from a one-gallon oil drum and fibreglassed in place. These bulges covered the area where the wide racing tyres touched the inside of the wheel well at full bump. Notice also how the well has been flared outward for clearance. (Wagstaff collection)

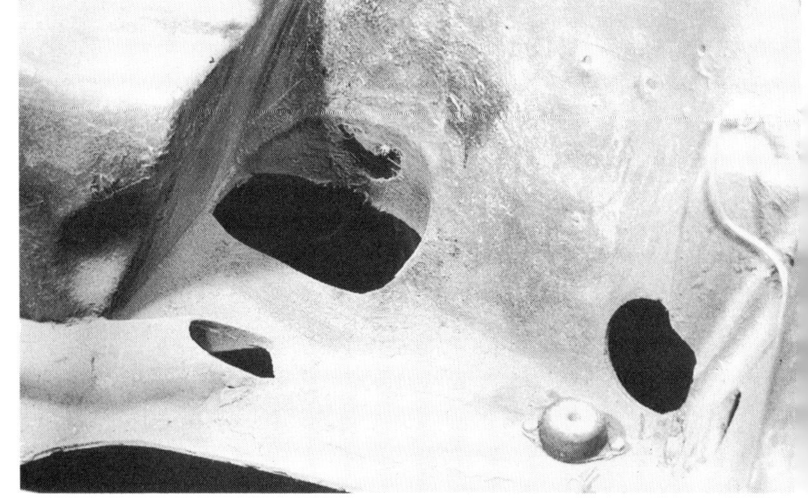

The large opening in the centre of the picture is where the specially fabricated exhaust system exited the Team Elite cars. The opening at the lower right is for the steering arm. (The Wagstaff collection)

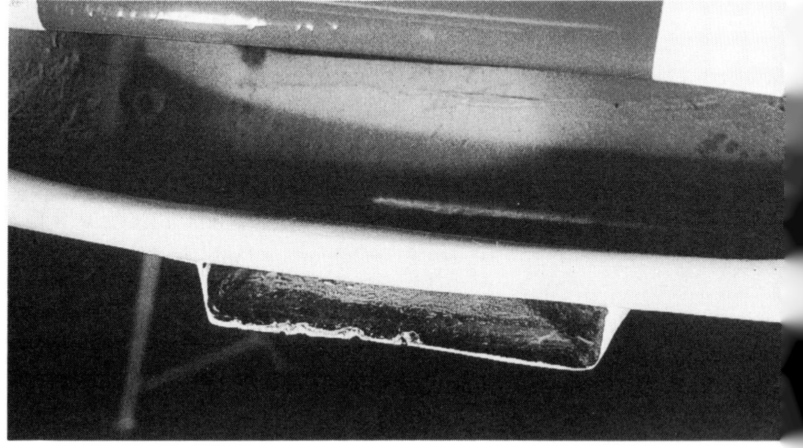

The oil cooler scoop was fashioned on Team Elite cars by cutting a flap under the radiator air intake and wedging it open while the sides were 'glassed' in place. (Wagstaff collection)

Above *A single, high-speed windscreen wiper was fitted to Team cars, as was a washer nozzle. The heater intake at the base of the windscreen has been covered with fibreglass.* (Wagstaff collection)

Above right *A useful device fitted to Team Elite cars was a wooden block bolted to a hinge under the right-hand side bonnet support. The block was rotated into position under the support to keep the bonnet up during engine service.* (Wagstaff collection)

which did away with the heavy quarter window glass and the chrome-plated, brass window surround. Cyril Embrey recalled asking Bristol if they would make up a couple of lightweight chassis but they declined, replying that it would take too much time. Besides, they had their own problems!

All Team Elite cars ran alloy brakes, front and rear, and, as a result, all used the fly-off handbrakes. During Clive Hunt's tenure the Team cars used $10\frac{1}{2}$-inch front brakes from the Lotus 19; they also used dual master cylinders with a balance bar, and the rear wishbone was fitted with a bronze, rather than rubber, ball. This was clamped in place using a pair of standard metal cups bolted to the existing bobbins.

Several details in the engine bay also identified Team Elite cars. These included the glassing over of the circular heater box opening and the fitting of a hinged wooden block to the bulkhead next to the bonnet bracket. This allowed the block to be swung under the bracket to keep the bonnet up. Another engine bay detail was an exhaust system that exited out of the side of the engine bay to terminate under the body midway between the front and rear wheel wells.

The Team cars also used distinctive air scoops for the front-mounted oil coolers. Cyril Embrey constructed them by making three cuts in the fibreglass under the Elite's nose, wedging the resulting flap open and then 'glassing' in the sides. Oddly, some Team cars raced with door panels in place because some international organizers required interiors in the GT class! Seats in later cars, incidentally, were Lotus Formula Junior items as fitted to the Super Elites. Belts and harnesses were never used.

Team Elite's International Racing Record

Year	Event	Drivers	Results
1960	Montlhery Coupes de Vitesse	Wagstaff	2nd in Class
	Le Mans	Buxton/Allen	DNF (clutch)
		Wagstaff/Marsh	1st in Class 1st Thermal Index
	Aintree International	Wagstaff	1st in Class Lap record
	Nürburgring	Wagstaff/Stacey	1st in Class
	Montlhery Coupe de Salon	Wagstaff	1st in Class
	Spa Grand Prix	Wagstaff	Crash
		Allen	Crash
1961	Oulton Park	Wagstaff	1st in Class Lap record
	Le Mans	Allen/Taylor	1st in Class
		Hunt/Wyllie	DNF (fuel tank)
	Spa Grand Prix	Wagstaff	2nd in Class
1962	Mallory Park	Wagstaff	1st in Class Lap record
	Le Mans	Hobbs/Gardner	1st in Class 1st Thermal Index
		Hunt/Wyllie	3rd in Class 2nd in Index
	Nürburgring	Wagstaff/Ferguson	2nd in Class
		Hunt/Hobbs	DNF (brake disc)
	Montlhery	Wagstaff	2nd in Class
	Snetterton International	Wagstaff	2nd in Class
1963	Le Mans	Gardner/Coundley	DNF (engine)
		Wagstaff/Ferguson	1st in Class 3rd Thermal Index
	Spa Grand Prix	Ferguson	1st in Class
	Nürburgring	Wagstaff/Baird Hobbs/Taylor	Hobbs/Taylor took over from Wagstaff/Baird at halfway mark. All four shared in Class win.
	Nassau Governors Trophy	Wagstaff	1st in Class
1964	Le Mans	Hunt/Wagstaff	1st in Class

Chapter 7

Club racing in the United Kingdom

It was said that occasionally in the trenches during the First World War, British soldiers would suspend a helmet over a camp fire and drip castor oil on the searing metal to catch the aroma while they reminisced on motor racing back home. Nowhere in the world was the urge to compete behind the wheel of fast cars as strong as it was in the British Isles and the passage of time has done nothing to diminish this enthusiasm. A case was made at the beginning of this book that the Elite was born into the Golden Age of sports cars and that its success on the race-track would, to a significant degree, determine its acceptance in the market-place. As evidence of the importance of racing, both as a means of development and marketing, consider again the early exploits of Ian Walker and John Lawry and the fact that five Elites appeared at the Boxing Day meeting (26 December 1958) at Brands Hatch some five days before the earliest sales invoice date on the works' chassis list!

The 'Boxing Day Elites' were driven by Colin Chapman (probably 1007), Jim Clark in the Border Reivers car (chassis 1010 invoiced to Ian Scott-Watson on New Year's Eve 1958), Chris Barber in number 1009 (also invoiced on that day), Lt Merle Roberson in chassis 1014, and Mike Costin in (probably) chassis 1011 which featured a curious air intake slot at the leading edge of the bonnet. This car, incidentally, with its odd intake, was the subject of early works magazine advertisements.

The race itself consisted of everyone going like the hammers with Clark, Chapman and Costin easily out-distancing the rest of the field. Clark led, essentially, for the entire race, with Chapman working as hard as he could to maintain contact. A backmarker got in Clark's way on the last lap which allowed Chapman to narrowly squeeze through for the win; Clark went on to take second with Costin a short distance behind for third.

A clean sweep for the Lotus Elite, this was typical of the level of competition and finishing orders for many seasons to come. Whether the Elite ran in the GT class, sports cars to 1600cc or brashly contested overall honours, spectators could hardly wait for the spectacle to begin. The races frequently became a kind of David and Goliath display with the Elite nipping at the heels of much larger and, theoretically, far superior machinery. At many race meetings the first thing a spectator would do was to check the entry list to see how many Elites were running. The excitement, it seemed, was proportional to their number.

The reason why there were scores of competitors who raced Elites in England in the 'sixties was because the car had good power to weight, it was stable at high speed, it handled and stopped and, when everything was screwed together right, it was sublimely reliable as well. As a result of this, the Elite was competitive for many seasons at everything from a 10-lap class race to a three-hour enduro with the occasional hill climb and sprint thrown in. The car could be counted on to figure in the results whether in the hands of the occasional competitor or the driver who raced every weekend in pursuit of a cham-

The start of a club race at Mallory Park, with David Buxton in the Team Elite entry, Roger Nathan in car 95 and Dick Fores in car 96. (Photographer unknown)

pionship. Before getting into the profiles of a few of the more famous club racers of the early 'sixties, a roster of names is offered below as a tribute to those who contributed to the Elite's reputation in the United Kingdom. Every driver listed scored, at one time or another, in the top three places of their speciality, whether club meeting, endurance, sprint or hill climb. My sincere apologies to any that I have missed.

Roster of Elite racers, 1959–63

Addicott, Dizzy
Alderson, Derek
Allen, Bill
Allison, Cliff
Arundell, Peter

Baillie, Sir Gawaine
Baird, Gil
Barber, Chris
Beckwith, Mike
Bell, W.A.
Bennet, A.D.
Berry, J.
Bowman, A.
Brierley, J.C.
Butterworth, J.T.
Buxton, David

Chambers, Adrien
Chapman, Colin
Clark, Jim
Costin, Mike
Coundley, John

Davies, Maurice
Deathridge, R.M.
Derisley, Jon
Dickson, Tom
Dobson, E.
Duggan, Bob
Dunn, J.S.

Felix, F.J.
Ferguson, Pat
Fores, R.A.

Gardner, Frank
Gaston, John
Greenall, Hon Edward

Harrison-Hansley, Ian
Hawkins, Paul
Haydon, D.
Hegbourne, Tony
Hetreed, Brian
Hobbs, David
Hunt, Clive
Hurrell, Sid

Ivey, P.D.

Jackson, L.
Jennings, R.D.
Johnson, Mike
Jones, E.
Jopp, Peter

Kennerly, J.R.

Lawry, John
Lepp, J.A.
Leston, Les
Lumsden, Peter
Lund, Ted

McCormack, S.
McKee, Bob
MacKinnon, Major
McLellen, Major
McNally, P.
MacQuaker, H.W.
Marsh, Tony
Melville, Richard
Morrison, S.W.

Nathan, Roger
Nicholson, John

Nurse, Austin

Osborne, A.J.

Parkes, Michael
Parkin, H.
Pinkney, Bill
Pollard, H.
Price, Mrs C.A.

Radford, F.
Riley, Peter
Roberson, Merle
Rodgers, J.B.
Rose, R.

Rowcliffe, H.

Sargent, Peter
Shaw, Bill
Sherman, P.
Smallthwaite, Brian
Smart, R.
Stacey, Alan
Stiller, H.
Summers, Chris
Surtees, Norman
Sutton, Julian

Taylor, Henry
Taylor, Norman
Taylor, Sidney
Taylor, Trevor
Thompson, W.A.
Threlfall, Tom

Vincent, Bob

Wagstaff, John
Walker, Ian
Warner, Graham
Wharton, Derek
Whitehouse, B.
Whitmore, Sir John
Whitworth, C.B.
Williams, J.P.

The Flying Scot—Jim Clark

When Ian Scott-Watson purchased a Lotus Elite for Jim Clark to drive under the Border Reivers racing team banner, the young Scot was only in his second year of competition. Nonetheless, he had already entered 54 races and won 27 of them. He finished 2nd 10 times and was 3rd on four occasions, and all this at the wheel of a surprising variety of cars including a DKW, Porsche 1600 Super, TR3 and Jaguar D Type.

Clark first tried an Elite at a special Lotus test session at Brands Hatch arranged by Scott-Watson. The plan was to test the Type 16, but the open-wheeler impressed Clark much less than did the Elite which he thought was fabulous, so his sponsor arranged a purchase. As we know, the car was chassis number 1010, it was white in colour and served as Scott-Watson's personal transportation between races. Also mentioned earlier, Clark's first outing with the car was on Boxing Day 1958 at Brands Hatch where he took second to Chapman. He raced this car only two more times, once at Mallory Park where he took first in class (and the first round of the Autosport Championship), and then at

Jim Clark in the second Border Reivers Elite, chassis no 1038. This car was outfitted for Le Mans, hence the wing and boot petrol tanks. (Photographer unknown)

Oulton Park where he dropped to 10th.

Border Reivers planned to take the Elite to Le Mans but the works neglected to prepare the car. Instead, Chapman offered a new Elite (chassis 1038) which he would set up especially for the 24-hour race and would include long-range tanks, alloy brakes, special lighting and the like. Scott-Watson was understandably annoyed but reluctantly agreed and purchased the BRG car for Clark.

Jim Clark and John Whitmore took the Border Reivers' Elite to 10th overall and 2nd in Class behind Peter Lumsden and Peter Riley, despite being plagued with starter motor troubles which required about two hours of lost time in the pits! In an interview several years later, Clark was asked if he enjoyed the greater speed of the three-litre Aston Martin which he drove the following year at Le Mans. Clark replied that his Elite was timed at 142 miles an hour down Mulsanne while the Aston could do no better than 150.

In 1959 Clark actively campaigned the Le Mans Elite and took it to eight 1sts, two 2nds, one 4th, one 5th and two DNFs in 14 starts. He won the Autosport Production Sports Car Championship (the same series that Ian Walker had won in 1958) and the Mallory Park Production Sports Car Championship as well. He also impressed Colin Chapman and signed to drive Lotus Formula Junior the following year which ultimately led to Lotus F1 and two World Championship titles.

Jim Clark drove an Elite in competition only once more after the 1959 season and that was in the Daytona Inter-Continental GT race in February 1962. He and Peter Berry drove David Hobbs' Mecha-Matic transmissioned car (see Chapter 12) to a fourth place after having to pit, while in the lead, to replace a flat battery. Clark enjoyed the automatic gearbox so much that he ordered his personal Elite fitted with one for road use. In his book (*Jim Clark at the Wheel*, Coward-McCanning, New York, 1965) Clark remarked, 'Those who scorn automatics take note!'

LOV 1

Without question, the two most recognizable Elites in English club racing were LOV 1 and DAD 10. The cars were driven so spiritedly and the drivers were so competitive that their appearance on the grid, either together or separately, guaranteed some of the best racing there was. When the two raced each other the action was almost always door handle to door handle with the pair of Elites simply running away from the rest of the field.

LOV 1, with its white and black paint scheme, was driven by Graham Warner, Managing Director of The Chequered Flag, sports car dealers, in London (see Chapter 9). His car, chassis 1006, was originally driven on the road, but as the GT class gained in popularity Warner saw a way to promote his business and satisfy his competitive goals at the same time.

He re-registered his car (785 VMK became LOV 1), sent it through his workshops, which built the Gemini Formula Junior, for full race preparation and installed one of the recently produced ZF gearboxes. From 1959 to 1962, when the car was destroyed in a major shunt at Snetterton, Warner accumulated an amazing total of over 60 wins! He particularly enjoyed doing battle with Ben Pon in his Porsche Carrera in the World Cup Series. Warner beat Pon, incidentally, in 1960 and '61. Along the way Warner achieved numerous lap records for small

LOV 1 understeering into a corner. (Chequered Flag)

GTs including Brands Hatch and Snetterton, and in 1960 he was named the BRSCC National Series Production Sports Car Champion.

In February, 1961, *Autosport* magazine did a road test of LOV 1 (John Bolster driving) and reported that although the noise level was 'somewhat shattering', the car showed no sign of temperament. It idled without wetting its plugs, started with no hesitation and travelled across London with the ease of a taxi. The car also achieved a maximum speed of 130.4 mph, went from 0 to 60 in 6.6 seconds, did the quarter mile in 15.1 seconds and returned 20 miles to the gallon!

Bolster reported that acceleration from 80 to 100 miles an hour was astonishingly lively, and while cruising at the 'ton' stability was excellent. He ended the test by stating that in a few days LOV 1 'made me the master of the Queen's highway'. At the hands of Graham Warner, the same could be said of the car on most of the circuits in England.

DAD 10

DAD 10 (pronounced 'daddio') came on the scene a little later than LOV 1 but it captured the spectators' interest and loyalty as quickly as had Graham Walker's mount. DAD 10 was driven by Les Leston, the proprietor of a motoring accessory shop in London, and was painted red with white racing stripes. Interestingly enough, Leston purchased chassis number 1533 through The Chequered Flag. Les Leston's shop advertised heavily in *Autosport* magazine and a smiling Leston holding a steering wheel was a familiar trademark, although, oddly enough, the adverts rarely mentioned his racing Elite.

Leston's first season in the Elite was in 1961 and after a few races to settle himself and the car, he began to show well in the results. He quickly ran up an impressive record of class wins and picked up the Peco Trophy as well. When he and Graham Warner met, however, LOV 1 always seemed to be just a little bit faster. The reason for this, at least in part, was the power weight ratio. DAD 10 was a Series II car and heavier than the very early chassis on LOV 1. Leston's car, incidentally, was somewhat unusual in that it had a wing tank in addition to

DAD 10 leaving the pits at the Nürburgring in 1962. (LAT)

the standard item in the boot, with a filler cap slightly recessed in an effort to restore some of the lost aerodynamics.

Not content to chase LOV 1, Leston embarked on a programme of development which continued until he retired the car near the end of the 1962 season. The first order of business was to pare some weight off which his mechanic, Roger Durrant, accomplished by fitting Perspex screens in the side and rear windows. Durrant also installed a set of Borrani light alloy wheels, but this still was not enough.

Then Leston saw pictures of the 'Costin nose' (details later in this chapter) on the Malle/Carnegie Elite at Le Mans, and heard that the modification was good for about a 15 per cent increase in brake horsepower. Frank Costin was immediately commissioned to oversee his aerodynamic improvements incorporated on DAD 10. Durrant also strengthened the front subframe by adding a diagonal tube and a gusset to the diff box by fitting steel bobbins in the diff pickups, and followed Team Elite's example by using a pair of metal cups to hold the rear wishbone rubber balls.

While all of this attention to detail appeared to work, Warner crashed his car before the two could meet enough times to even the score. No matter, DAD 10 and Les Leston with Graham Warner and LOV 1 had assured themselves a place in club racing lore for ever.

When DAD 10 was sold it was repainted, although the fictitious registration number was kept, and the car was raced for several more seasons before slipping into obscurity. In 1978 Malcolm Ricketts found the car in a field next to a repair shop, overgrown with weeds and neglected. A triumvirate was formed, comprising Ricketts, Robin Longdon and Anthony Bates, to purchase the car, restore it and then campaign it in historic racing.

Chapter 13 will discuss how Tony Bates accomplished the restoration and Chapter 14 will detail Robin Longdon's success behind the wheel, but suffice to say for now that they accomplished their goals beautifully. Of course, a great deal of controversy arose when the trio announced that they had found the real DAD 10. Over the years, it seems, several others had claimed the same thing, in places as far away as California, but the documentation for this car was overwhelming. Not only was the front subframe modified as per the sketch in Durrant's notebook, but the car had a genuine 'Costin nose' with the clips to hold the plastic headlight covers still in place under a layer of plastic filler. The filler hole for the wing tank was recessed in the same way and so on. Even Leston himself agreed that it was indeed his old racer.

DAD 10 racing record *(compiled by Robin Longdon)*

Date	Circuit	Result	Remarks
1961			
Date unknown	Snetterton	DNF	Engine trouble
4 April	Goodwood	7th	
7 May	Brands Hatch	2nd	
13 May	Silverstone	?	
28 May	Nürburgring	?	
3 June	Brands Hatch	5th OA	2nd in Class
18 June	Snetterton	1st	
8 July	Silverstone	DNF	electrics
?	Aintree	5th	1st in Class
7 August	Brands Hatch	4th	1st in Class
Costin nose fitted			
19 August	Goodwood	7th	1st in Class
?	Tour de France	DNF	Diff loosened at 4½ hours
30 Sept	Brands Hatch	2nd	1st in Class
22 Oct	Montlhery	DNS	Drivers late!
26 Dec	Brands Hatch		1st in Class, Peco Trophy
1962			
4 April	Oulton Park		4th in Class, new engine
23 April	Goodwood	?	Stopped to check wheels
12 May	Silverstone	8th	3rd in Class
18 May	Spa	DNS	Diff failure in practice
27 May	Nürburgring	16th	
11 June	Mallory Park	6th	In both heats
? July	Silverstone	3rd	1st in Class
15 July	Snetterton	DNF	Misfiring
6 August	Brands Hatch	8th	1st in Class, Peco Trophy
18 August	Goodwood		12th in Class, misfiring
26 August	Brands Hatch		2nd in Class
flush windscreen fitted (?)			
1 Sept	Crystal Palace	DNF	Blew up engine
DAD 10 offered for sale with trailer and spare engine			
26 Dec	Brands Hatch		3rd in Class, driven by Peter Jopp, entered by Leston
1963			
DAD 10 sold			
6 Oct	Montlhery	?	Painted white, driven by K. Lall

DAD 10's restored body/chassis poses for photos in Tony Bates' back garden. (A.N.E. Bates)

8 MPG

What sounds like a fuel mileage figure for a 1960s American sedan was actually the registration number of an Elite that burst upon the racing scene in the hands of a 20-year-old driver named Roger Nathan. He began racing in an Austin Healey 3000 when he was 17 although he was never happy with the car and convinced his father that a Lotus Elite would be a much better ride. In 1961 he got one; a 'bog standard' car which took him to fourth or fifth place in most of his starts.

In 1961 Nathan uprated his white Elite, first to the SE specification and then to full race with a Stage III head, alloy brakes and the like. He recalled that he really started to motor quickly when at Brands Hatch: 'I remember going past the pits during practice with the likes of Graham Warner and Les Leston in their famous Elites when I got a pit signal which indicated that I was third fastest. The next thing I knew I woke up in an ambulance with a big black nurse who was trying to take my pants down to give me an anti-tetanus injection. I took exception to this, being a shy young lad, and leapt out only to wake up in the Dartford Emergency Hospital suffering from concussion.

'I later found out that going into the bend behind the pits the outside rear drive shaft broke at the weld next to the universal joint, which allowed the wheel to steer the car into a spin. I hit the earth bank on the infield, shot up in the air and landed upside down, which broke the car's back on impact. Les Leston was first around and thought I must be dead. He undid my seat belts and pulled me out. The thing that saved my life was the high backs of the seats which prevented the roof from caving in completely.'

Undaunted, Nathan stripped all of the usable bits from the wreck and requested a new shell from Cheshunt. He remembered that a body/chassis was obtained, 'through devious means', from Lotus Developments with the proviso that the damaged remains of his car be returned to the works. The 'new' 8 MPG was made ready during the winter of 1962. A new paint job (Jaguar metallic blue) put the finishing touch to the car.

From his first outing, everything went absolutely right and he won most of his races and captured the Autosport Championship (the third

Nathan's first Elite met its end at Brands Hatch. Note that the doors have parted company with the body, and the broken undertray forward of the sump. (S. Lewis)

Roger Nathan on the shoulders of his crew after winning the Autosport Championship. (Photographer unknown)

8 MPG understeering into a corner. Notice the Costin nose, Le Mans petrol filler and full plexiglass side windows. (E. Selwyn-Smith)

8 MPG chases another Elite with a Costin nose at Silverstone in 1963. Notice the ducts for the front brakes and the Perspex covers for the headlights. (Harold Baker)

for the Elite) which made him the youngest driver ever to win that award.

Nathan recalled his Elite days very fondly and mentioned that he used to drive 8 MPG on the road to race meetings. He calculated his fuel mileage occasionally and reckoned that the car got 40 mpg at a sustained 100 mph! 'The Elite was a very good car. At Brands Hatch, for example, one could approach the hairpin at great speed and simply throw the car sideways and catch it on the steering and throttle to take it around. Other drivers would pull alongside in horror thinking the Elite was going to go straight on.

'The first time I saw an Elite cornered this way I was up against Warner and Leston. They shot by me at Snetterton and went into Riches, which is the right-hand bend after the pits, with the cars just sideways on! One of them managed to wave at me! The manoeuvre absolutely stunned me, but within a year I was doing the same thing.'

Nathan sold 8 MPG in 1963 after a year chasing the new Lotus Elans. He felt the Elite's competitive edge was lost when the Elan became fully sorted, and although it was never a match for the Elite in cornering power, the Elan's horsepower was far superior.

In 1989 the car was part of Bill Friend's collection and had been retired after several seasons of historic racing. Roger Nathan was invited to drive his old mount at a Lotus test day at Goodwood when he paid Friend the highest compliment by stating that the car was just as he remembered, and once behind the wheel the many happy memories came flooding back.

Racing modifications

That the Elite was in reality a racing car for the road was evidenced by the relatively few modifications which were required to put a car on the race-track; that and the significant percentage (some experts put this as high as one out of four cars) that competed in some form of motor sport. The Elite could be raced 'right out of the box' and still perform commuting duties from Monday to Friday. Numbers on the doors were all that was necessary.

Of all the Elites, the Series I was probably the ideal racer. It was lighter, lower and more stiffly suspended than the Series II cars and with a Stage I head and single SU it was no mean performer, although at the time there were numerous manufacturers who built high-performance parts for the Climax engine to satisfy the need to go faster. Derrington, Cosworth and others supplied heads, camshafts, intake manifolds, exhaust systems and the like.

A Stage II or Stage III engine increased the performance considerably, which usually went hand in hand with the installation of alloy front brakes. As might be expected, the 'hotter' engines did, in fact, produce more heat, so a light alloy shield for the starter motor and the engine bay, adjacent to the four-branch exhaust manifold, was highly recommended. Close ratio gears in the MG box and double-laced wheels (60 spokes as opposed to the standard 48 on the single-laced rim) completed the full race specification on most of the early Elite competition cars.

A word here on wheel size and tyre specifications. Colin Chapman designed the Elite to run on 4-inch wide rims, which meant that the car slid during hard cornering. When front and rear alignment was correct and there was no movement due to worn bearings or Metalastiks, and the tyre pressures were set properly, the Elite's cornering was absolutely neutral. It could be balanced on the throttle or steering wheel and beautiful four-wheel drifts were precisely what the car was designed to accomplish. If there was a fault, it was an over-abundance of roll stiffness up front which encouraged the inside front wheel to lift when the Elite was pushed hard through a corner.

The state of the art in racing tyres in the early 'sixties in England was the 'L' section Dunlop R5. In America, it was the Goodyear Bluestreak. But even at 5 inches wide (about the maximum the Elite could wear at the rear) both the Dunlop and the Goodyear still allowed the car to slide. In later years, as tyres got stickier and smaller wheels were fitted in order to use lower profile and thus even wider rubber, the Elite stopped slipping in a corner. This abundant adhesion encouraged a different driving style, that of flying into a corner, cranking the wheel and simply driving around the apex. Unfortunately, the Elite was not designed for this kind of technique and proved it by a willingness to get up on two wheels with potentially disastrous results.

The Elite was also sensitive to tyre pressures and was usually happiest with a couple of pounds difference, front to rear, with the higher pressure at the back. Experimentation netted absolutely neutral cornering. A little oversteer or understeer could be negated by adding a few pounds of air to the tyres at the end of the car that was doing the most sliding.

The NACA duct

As discussed in Chapter 1, the Elite was designed with a fully ducted radiator. This meant that after the air passed through, it was directed (in part) down the transmission tunnel to cool the rear brakes and differential. In road use the system worked quite well, but under racing conditions it was found that the carburettor intakes were getting nothing but hot air which resulted in a loss of horsepower.

The first person to effectively deal with this problem was Peter Lumsden, although Chapman experimented with several kinds of vents in the prototypes, including one on the left flank of the engine bay in Lumsden's own car! Lumsden fashioned an air scoop out of aluminium sheet and placed it on the bonnet directly over the carbs. This solved the problem but the men at Hornsey thought Lumsden's scoop (David Buxton used a similar device on his first racer, 500 KRA) looked too unsightly to use on the works cars. Chapman thought at once of Frank Costin and called him for advice. Costin studied the situation for a moment and announced that Lumsden's 'raised duct' was the best kind of inlet for the slope of the Elite's bonnet, but there was another type available, slightly less efficient, but fortunately much more elegant. This was a submerged opening called the NACA duct.

Costin explained that after the Second World War the National Advisory Committee for Aeronautics (NACA) in America embarked on a number of studies of air flow in relation to jet aircraft. One of the subjects was air induction systems and numerous designs were considered, including one of their own which was a triangular-shaped submerged inlet. This type of air intake was nicknamed the NACA duct and eventually found use in many kinds of aircraft.

The NACA duct, with its characteristic curved sides and ramp floor,

The NACA duct was positioned to dump air over the intake of the forward carburettor. It was angled toward the car's centreline to pick up the air flow as it veered off to the back of the wing. (Author)

A NACA duct incorrectly positioned. (Foster Cooperstein)

Flow-through ventilation was facilitated by an exhaust placed in a low pressure site; here is one type done in a Perspex rear windscreen on Mike Ostrov/Hank Mauel's No 95 racing Elite. (Author)

Forced air ventilation was accomplished on racing Elites by tapping into the heater plenum which was fed by the intake at the base of the windscreen. A hose fitting was placed over the hole to the plenum and a length of air hose was clamped to it and then aimed at the driver. (Author)

contributed negligible aerodynamic drag because it was not stuck up in the airstream, yet at the same time provided a significant ram effect at its exhaust end, just the thing for the Elite, and besides, Chapman thought it looked great. As it happened, Costin had used the NACA duct before, on the Vanwall Formula 1 car, but its use on the Elite marked the first time that it was fitted to a road car. Interestingly, the later Team Elite cars abandoned the NACA duct in favour of a length of flexible tubing which extended from the radiator opening to the forward carburettor.

Most Elites meant for serious competition work ran with stripped interiors for reasons of both weight savings and ease of maintenance and cleaning. Additional weight was saved by replacing both the rear window and the side window framing and quarter-lights with Perspex screens.

In warmer climates ventilation needs were handled with vent holes in one or more side windows and, for a flow-through effect, similar openings in the back window. An oil cooler was also required to combat elevated ambient temperatures, as was the cutting of vent holes in the fibreglass panel forward of the steering rack. This exhausted the lower half of the radiator into the engine bay as well as the front wheel wells.

Many racing Elites were fitted with Lotus 18 seats which were extremely lightweight fibreglass buckets supported by an equally delicate tubular steel framework. A long-range fuel tank of 10-gallon capacity was available from the works. This tank featured a 3½-inch diameter filler tube which required the large Aston-style aluminium flip-up cap.

When the Series II Elite was introduced, with its softer spring rates and raised ride height, the touring customer noticed little difference other than, perhaps, a slightly more compliant ride, but the racers experienced a dramatic increase in body roll and less precise handling. At first the change to a 'hard ride' specification meant swapping the front wishbones and trunnions for Series I units and fitting Series I rear springs with a longer spacer tube to make up for the loss in spring length.

The racers finally got around to having custom springs wound to a shorter length (to lower the ride height) and a stiffer rate than standard Series II or, for that matter, SI items. Some, like Les Leston, used Lotus 15 springs in their Elites. Whatever the case, care had to be taken in the selection of shock absorbers because the Series II type had longer rods which bottomed on full bump when springs in SI length were fitted. Even Konis bent (or broke!) under these conditions.

The rear ride height could also be adjusted by changing the length of the tube which supported the lower spring perch. A few racers split this tube in half (lengthwise) and then segmented the halves like bearing shells. Hose clamps kept each segment in place but they could be removed to lower the car or added to raise it.

Besides the S4-12 gearbox, ZF also made a limited slip differential for the Elite, but these units were extremely rare and very costly and only a few cars were known to have used them. Apparently, these limited slips were also larger than standard which required some modification of the chassis. The Series II rear wishbones were easily modified to accept spherical rod end bearings, and a few racers made the change to

Comparison of the standard petrol tank and the long-range (10 gallon) alloy tank. Notice that the filler neck on the long-range tank is larger in diameter (3½ inches). (Author)

The adjustable ride height on Mike Ostrov's Elite shows how low an Elite can go. (Author)

eliminate the possibility of rubber ball failure and to provide a precise means of adjusting toe-in. Others preferred to simply replace the rubber with a bronze ball (split in half to fit) to eliminate any unwanted movement.

The Costin nose

When the Frenchman Jean François Malle secured an entry for his Elite in the 1961 Le Mans 24 Hours, he set his sights on the Index of Thermal Efficiency. He also enlisted the aid of 'Jabby' Crombac to look after the car's preparation. Crombac was still smarting from the previous year's fiasco (see the Chapter on Le Mans) and wanted every possible advantage when going into this race. Since aerodynamics were so important to the Index, he contacted Frank Costin to see if there might be a way to give the Malle Elite an edge over the others.

Frank accompanied the Elite to Le Mans (it had been at Willie Griffiths's shop in England for engine preparation) for the April test days. Using strips of plasticine he altered the Elite's frontal contours and then 'wool-tufted' the trailing surfaces. He then sent the drivers out to make high-speed runs while he observed, from a chase car, how the tufts behaved. Frank recalled using the roads around the circuit for this purpose (besides the race-track) and on one occasion it was pouring with rain yet Malle had to hit 100 mph in traffic to get the data Costin required.

Armed with mountains of figures and photographs of wool tuft flutter, Costin set to work to modify the front of the Elite in order to improve its penetration in the airstream and to lower its aerodynamic drag. He did this by removing the front bumpers, parking lights and indicators and then building up the leading edge until it was completely parabolic in curvature. Perspex covers were moulded for the headlights to fair them into the wings which were raised $\frac{3}{16}$ inch immediately behind the lights. Two holes were drilled into the covers to prevent misting.

The air intake was reduced in size by about 30 per cent which approximated to the shape of the opening Costin had designed for the

The Costin nose on the restored DAD 10. (Fred Scatley)

Lotus Eleven. An oil cooler was fitted in front of the radiator, but it protruded through a slot in the bottom of the nose so Costin faired it in as well. The rain gutters were removed, a NACA duct was installed in the bonnet, and the windscreen was installed flush with the bodywork by means of a flat, light alloy surround which was fastened in place with countersunk bolts.

Lotus also installed a specially moulded wing tank, but more on this in a moment. During the race, Malle's co-driver, Robin Carnegie (the Earl of Northesk), reported having better acceleration and an additional 500 revs as a result of the front end mods. Top speed down Mulsanne was 142 mph which, interestingly enough, was the same as Jim Clark's Elite in 1959. Unfortunately, the race ended for the Malle/Carnegie Elite in the ninth hour when the fuel tank split.

Costin oversaw his modifications to two other Elites, Les Leston's DAD 10 and David Hobbs' Mecha-Matic equipped racer. Frank recalled that he had several sets of headlight covers left in his workshops which were sold off, presumably to owners who wished to copy the 'Costin nose'. Some conversions were close while others missed the mark by a wide margin.

A final observation on the Elite's aerodynamics is that, arguably, the car may have been one of the most efficient designs of all time. Despite its extraordinarily light weight, it hugged the road at high speed and never lost its composure in cross-winds or while cornering. Some cars were criticized for getting light at the front or at the back when driven flat out, while others suffered from aerodynamically induced over- or understeer. By the mid-'sixties cars were sprouting spoilers and other appendages just to keep them on the ground. The Elite needed none of it, thanks to Frank Costin's reverse camber line and the all-important negative angle of incidence.

Chapter 8

Long-distance racing: Le Mans, the 'Ring and Sebring

Le Mans

In the 1950s the greatest sports car race in the world was the Le Mans 24 Hours of Endurance held at the Sarthe Circuit in France. A quarter of a million spectators saw the annual event in person, while millions more listened to the commentary over the radio or watched it on TV and newsreels. Magazines featured lengthy articles on the cars and drivers and added to the excitement by analysing teams and their potential for winning months before the race was run.

Even the most jaded car enthusiast was awestruck by 'Le Vingt-Quatre Heures du Mans' because of the magnitude of racing flat out for 24 hours. The drivers had to contend with poor visibility, rain, morning mists, ground fog and a three-mile long straight called Mulsanne where the fastest cars nudged 200 miles per hour before braking hard and gearing down for an acute right-angle corner. The overall winner covered over 2,500 miles during the race which began at 4pm on Saturday and ended at 4pm on Sunday. To win, place or show in any of the several classifications was a fantastic achievement which was praised by the press and public alike. To merely survive was remarkable because, on the average, 75 per cent did not. In the 1950s, if a manufacturer of sports cars wanted to be taken seriously, the cars had to compete at Le Mans; their sporting image, not to mention the reputation of their product, was at stake.

Of course, in those days Le Mans racing cars were easily recognizable, and similar, if not identical, models could be purchased from works or dealer showrooms. To be able to drive the same kind of car that raced (or was placed) at Le Mans was an exciting possibility both to the average enthusiast and the car builder's advertising department.

Fortunately, the Le Mans organizers sought to accommodate as great a variety of racing cars as they could and in 1959 there were four ways to win at Le Mans. The foremost was an overall placing in the Grand Prix of Endurance—the winner was the car that covered the greatest distance in 24 hours of racing. Within the GP of Endurance were up to six classes based on engine size. The largest was 5 litres and the smallest was 501 to 750cc. A class win in the GP of Endurance was worth untold publicity, not to mention a handsome cash award as well.

The next category was the Index of Performance. This was a handicap based on engine size and a distance, which the Le Mans organizers calculated, that should be achieved in the 24 hours. Because the winner was the car that exceeded this theoretical mileage by the greatest percentage, a driver could not ease off, no matter what his position was in class, for fear of falling below the car's potential. The Index of Performance was hotly contested because the cash prize was almost as large as a win in the Grand Prix of Endurance. Generally, cars with the very largest or the smallest displacements held the advantage.

The last way to win at Le Mans was the Index of Thermal Efficiency. This category was initiated in 1959 and consisted of a complex formula which included average speed, the weight of the car with a full fuel load and the car's rate of fuel consumption. A high top speed and low fuel consumption were essential but, oddly enough, light weight was not. Le Mans observers reckoned the Index of Thermal Efficiency had been designed to favour French cars, specifically the 750cc DB Panhards. Interestingly, such a car won this class in 1959, but as we will see later in this chapter, the Elite spoiled what otherwise would have been a string of French victories.

Lotus at Le Mans

Colin Chapman's fascination with Le Mans was no less intense than that of the most zealous of enthusiasts. The difference was that Chapman had set a personal goal of a Class win at Le Mans and he meant to accomplish this feat in a car of his own design. The success of his first aerodynamic racer, the Mark 8, convinced Chapman that he was progressing in the right direction. The Mark 8 was the first of the Lotus all-out racers and was strong, light in weight, terrifically 'slippery' and unbelievably fast considering its MG powerplant and 85 brake horsepower.

By the time his next design, the Mark 9, was beginning its shakedown runs, Chapman felt that he was ready to have a go at the big time and submitted the first Lotus entry to the Automobile-Club de l'Ouest for consideration for the 1955 edition of the 24-hour endurance race. 'Consideration' was the operative word because initial entries had to be sent in six months before the race and the French exercised considerable latitude in the acceptance of some car-makers. Fortunately, Chapman had a man in France, 'Jabby' Crombac, to make sure all the paperwork was in order. When the acceptance arrived there was much to celebrate—Chapman's dream was on the verge of coming true.

A Mark 9 went to Le Mans with Chapman and Ron Flockhart doing the driving, and was well up in class when it was disqualified for reversing out of a sand-bank after a spin. The marshals were terrified of another accident because a few hours earlier a Mercedes Benz had crashed into a stand of spectators, killing more than 80.

Chapman was undaunted and not only vowed to return, but predicted a Lotus victory. The following year saw three Lotus Elevens entered, and by the time the chequered flag fell one of them had won the 1100cc Class, taken a 7th overall and been placed 4th in the Index of Performance. Chapman was delighted, not only by the win but by the publicity and the resulting interest in Lotus cars. Le Mans introduced Chapman's designs to a whole new audience and quite a number of them beat a path to his door with cash in hand.

By the time entries were submitted for the 1957 event, business was booming at Hornsey. There were constant enquiries from the press for test cars, there were the Motor Show exhibits and a regular flow of cars overseas to international markets. Lotus had arrived, and to celebrate they prepared five Elevens for Le Mans. These were the so-called high back and curved cockpit designs which ended up being probably the

Group portrait of the Elite entry at Le mans in 1959. Far left is the Videlles/Malle entry, centre Lumsden/Riley and right, Clark/ Whitmore. Jim Clark (in neck-tie) and John Whitmore stand behind their car as do Peter Lumsden (in hat) and Peter Riley (blond hair and glasses). The apparent presence of a no 58 is something of a mystery, as no car with that number took part. (Henri Beroul)

fastest front-engined 1100cc sports racers of all time. When the race ended at 4pm on the Sunday afternoon, Lotus Elevens had taken a 1st and 2nd in the 1100 class, 1st in the 750 class (with a short-stroke 1100), 1st and 2nd in the Index of Performance and 1st in the Biennial Cup which was awarded to cars entered for two consecutive years. The men from Hornsey took home half-a-dozen trophies, a million francs in prize money and an untold fortune in publicity value.

The press hailed the event as Britain's finest achievement ever at Le Mans because besides Lotus's heady victories, a team of D-type Jaguars not only won the race overall, but took 2nd, 3rd, 4th and 6th as well! To say that Chapman was the most successful and confident 29-year-old car-maker in the world was probably pretty accurate, because following Le Mans he began preparations for the début of the Elite and the Seven and, several months after that, the Fifteen!

Elites at Le Mans in 1959

Chapman tried to duplicate the Eleven's dominance of the '57 Le Mans by entering four cars the following year. Unfortunately, the team went down to dismal failure when two of the cars crashed, one stopped when its distributor drive sheared and the last soldiered home to an 8th in Class and 20th overall following an off-course excursion in the sand-bank at the end of Mulsanne.

As explained in Chapter 6, Colin Chapman came to the realization in 1959 that he was trying to juggle too many projects in too little space with too few personnel. It was all he could do to prepare three Fifteens for the 24 Hours; the Elite had to be left to privateers.

Peter Lumsden and Peter Riley teamed up in Lumsden's own Elite which was registered WUU 2 (this car was chassis 1003 that saw considerable development work at Hornsey). Both men were relatively new to international racing but had been quite successful at the club level, Lumsden in a Lotus 9. He believed the Elite was ideally suited to long-distance racing and planned to use his annual vacation in the summer of 1959 to contest both Le Mans and the 1.000-kilometre race at the Nürburgring in Germany!

The Clark/Whitmore Border Reivers Elite during the Le Mans scrutineering. (Henri Beroul)

The Videlles/Malle entry during scrutineering. Notice the works registration number loaned to Jabby Crombac for the occasion. Considerable interest is shown by spectators behind. (Henri Beroul)

Lumsden converted his Elite to Stage III tune (albeit with twin SUs as opposed to Webers), and fitted an oil cooler and an auxiliary oil tank which was controlled by a petcock in the cockpit. This tank, incidentally, was topped up by means of a filter tube and cap in the centre of the panel at the base of the windscreen. Lumsden ran the car at several club meetings prior to Le Mans and besides the differential coming adrift at Silverstone he discovered that underbonnet temperatures climbed quite high during the course of a race—to the detriment of power output, because SUs (or Webers, for that matter) did not like pre-heated air. He solved the problem by fitting a raised air scoop above the carb intakes.

In June 1960, *Sports Cars Illustrated* magazine published a road test of Lumsden's Elite (written by David Phipps) which indicated that the car weighed 1,375 pounds with a full fuel tank (presumably oil in the auxiliary too). The magazine accomplished a 16-second quarter-mile time with a speed of 95 mph. Top speed was an observed 123.

The second Elite was entered by Ian Scott-Watson of the Scottish

Border Reivers Racing Team. This organization was the patron of Jim Clark and he and John Whitmore were paired for the 24 Hours. Both Clark and Whitmore had shown great skill with a wide variety of cars and both would go on to take championships behind the wheel of Elites.

The Border Reivers' Elite was their second for Clark, the first having been one of the pre-production prototypes. The third Elite entered in the 1959 Le Mans race was arranged by 'Jabby' Crombac for two French drivers, Jean Claude Videlles and Jean François Malle. Interestingly, of all the drivers Videlles had the most experience at Le Mans, having raced DB Renaults and Panhards since 1954.

The new 1300cc GT Class had not yet been approved by the Automobile-Club de l'Ouest so the Elites raced with the 1500s. At flagfall, the Clark/Whitmore car shot away in sprint fashion while Lumsden and Riley stuck to a pre-race strategy of fixed lap times. Clark and Whitmore were circulating at 105 mph, about 5 mph more than the other British entry, but were troubled with lengthy pit stops because of a fried starter motor.

The French entry had problems with heat as well when their Elite burned completely to the ground. Apparently the engine timing was advanced by a slipping distributor which superheated the exhaust pipe. The fibreglass caught fire and engulfed the entire car while Videlles waited in vain for it to extinguish itself. He had been told that fibreglass didn't burn!

Meantime, Lumsden and Riley motored on to the chequered flag and a 1st in Class, an incredible 8th overall and a 2nd in the Index of Thermal Efficiency. Their car averaged 94 mph for the 24 hours (and 2,259 miles) of racing and recorded an amazing 18.97 mpg. The Clark/Whitmore Elite finished 2nd in Class, 10th overall and 5th in the Index. Who could have been bold enough to predict that this magnificent first effort was the first of a string of victories that would continue for five more years?

Elites at Le Mans in 1960

Fired with enthusiasm, Elite owners took to Le Mans seemingly in droves, and six were entered in the 1960 event. Two were Team Elite

The Team Elite entry for Buxton/Allen in 1960. Notice the Team logo on the door. Bill Allen stands by. (Henri Beroul)

entries, one came from France (again sponsored by Crombac) and three were private cars from Great Britain, although, as will be seen in a moment, one of these had heavy works involvement.

As detailed in Chapter 6, the Team Elite entries were for David Buxton with Bill Allen and John Wagstaff with Tony Marsh. The French team consisted of Roger Masson and Claude Laurent while the three remaining British entries were for Michael Parkes with Sir Gawaine Baillie, Jonathan Sieff (heir to the Marks and Spencer chain), who had not yet named a co driver, and lastly car owner Michael Taylor, who had named Innes Ireland and Alan Stacey as his drivers.

The 2-litre Elite

Michael Taylor's Elite was very special because it began life as a notion Colin Chapman had for an overall win at Le Mans. Chapman was delighted with the 130 mph speeds (on 100 bhp) which his Elites were turning in on Mulsanne and wondered how the car would go with another 80 or so horses. The powerplant he had in mind was the Climax FPF twin cam, in 1960cc capacity.

Chassis number 1255 was set aside for the project. This was a Series II Maximar body/chassis and was chosen for its strength and light weight. (Elite restorer Anthony Bates examined this car and found, interestingly enough, that it had polyester doors.) Of course, numerous changes had to be made to the car to compensate for the greater weight and power of the engine.

The first task was to beef up the front suspension by fitting the double wishbones, anti-roll bar and $10\frac{1}{2}$-inch disc brakes from the Lotus 18 Formula car. The 18 also contributed its steering rack which was mounted ahead of the wheel centre. Tyres were 500 × 15 in front and 600 × 15 at the rear, which required some wheel well modifications to obtain clearance. Because the Le Mans regs required GT cars to carry a spare tyre, and those of the 2-litre were so wide, the entire back of the spare tyre well was cut out so that the wheel could be loaded from the boot. Stiffer springs and externally adjustable shock absorbers completed the suspension modifications.

A wing tank was fitted to the left side (as opposed to the usual position in the right wing) and an exhaust cut-out was made in the right-hand side of the engine bay. The wing tank, incidentally, was made of light alloy and was fitted inside the torsion box aft of the wheel well.

Len Street recalled building quite a few special fuel tanks for the Le Mans cars. On one occasion, 'We got in a special aluminium 20-gallon tank for the boot and had to test it for leaks. We painted the seams with washing-up liquid, plugged up all the openings and hooked it up to the works air line set to 3 psi. While we were out to lunch someone used the air line to blow up a tyre but he put it back without resetting it. When I got back the tank looked like an oil drum in aluminium. I sat down with another chap and together we beat the thing square and it didn't leak!'

In order to install the FPF, several cuts had to be made to the engine bay but once in place, it was mated to a ZF transmission and a ZF limited slip differential with a 3.2:1 ring and pinion. Formula Junior seats, a single Lucas windscreen wiper and dual master cylinders for the braking system completed the specifications.

Unfortunately, the first drive down Tottenham Lane showed something was seriously amiss. Apparently the weight distribution was too far forward or the steering geometry was not right because at speed the car understeered mightily. It also seemed to be a little short on brakes. Rather than sort out the car, which required time and staff he simply could not afford, Chapman decided to sell it but with a full report on its problems and the offer of works technical advice on how to put them right.

Unfortunately, the car never got a chance. Taylor, who planned originally to co-drive with Innes Ireland, was badly injured practising for the Belgian Grand Prix, the very race in which Lotus driver Alan Stacey was killed. When Jonathan Sieff was asked if he wanted to drive the 2-litre instead of his own car, he agreed.

As if some kind of cloud hung over the project, young Sieff's luck suddenly turned bad as well. He preferred to put a few miles in in his own Elite but one of the mechanics had assembled a rear tyre with a normal inner tube instead of the racing type which had a lock nut to secure the stem to the rim. 'Jabby' Crombac described what happened in his book, *Colin Chapman, The Man and his Cars*. 'While accelerating out of the Tetre Rouge corner at the beginning of the long Mulsanne straight, a bout of wheel spin caused the tyre and the tube to slip on the rim, so that the valve itself was torn out of the tube. A mile further down the straight, when the car had virtually reached top speed, the tyre deflated completely and Sieff had a monumental crash. He was found lying badly injured in the garden of a house, having been thrown clear over a wall.'

Years later, Innes Ireland recorded in his memoirs that he followed Sieff to the hospital with Roy Salvadori and was ushered up to the operating room. Sieff's life hung by a thread and Ireland plunged into 'the depths of appalling depression'. Stacey was dead, Michael Taylor was badly injured and his own experience with the 2-litre was that it had no brakes to speak of and flat out it handled like a ship at sea. Later that night in a hotel room at Le Mans, the team manager, Stan Chapman, told Ireland that if he wanted to race the 2-litre John Whitmore was standing at the ready. Ireland wisely declined and the car was packed up and sent home.

Shortly after Le Mans, David Buxton acquired the car (under the Team Elite banner) and gave it to Bill Allen for a minor club event at

The Masson/Laurent entry being pushed to the victory area after their class win. A check of the records indicated that they had actually won the Index as well and were awarded a duplicate prize to Wagstaff and Marsh. Note the jubilant supporters including Jabby Crombac, whose hand appears to be in the quarter window. (Henri Beroul)

Rufforth Airfield in Yorkshire. Allen recalled that the race began in light rain and because the acceleration was so good he had managed to put the car into first place by the first corner. When he turned the steering wheel for the right-hander, the car did not respond at all and understeered straight off the circuit. He pulled in after a few slow laps and pronounced the car unfit to race.

Back at Buxton's, the FPF was removed and sold and the car placed on stands in the back of the workshops. When Buxton's company went into receivership it was still there and was finally sold by Lloyds and Scottish Finance Ltd in 1962 to pay off creditors. In 1989 the car was owned by Jim Castle in England, and apart from being powered by an FWE it was the same as it had been 30 years before at Le Mans, even down to the scars on the bonnet for the leather securing straps.

Returning to 1960, that year saw the inauguration of the 1300cc Class, and the Elite's lone competitor that year was an Alfa Romeo SZ that blew its transmission in the ninth hour. The same malady befell the Parkes/Baillie Elite in the sixteenth hour while clutch problems stopped the Team Elite car of Buxton and Allen, hardly 60 minutes later. It was up to the Elites of Wagstaff/Marsh and Masson/Laurent to carry on. The French Elite was the fastest of the pair and averaged 90.9 mph for the 24 hours. They were placed 1st in Class, 13th overall and 2nd in the Index of Thermal Efficiency, or so the Le Mans organizers thought when the car was forced to pit in the last hour to repair an electrical problem. The Wagstaff/Marsh Team Elite car came in 14th overall and was credited with 1st in the Index which provided them with a cheque for 30,000 francs. They had averaged 89.4 mph for 2,146 miles and had obtained 21.87 mpg.

Crombac, Masson and Laurent, on the other hand, reckoned that their race average was 90.95 and their fuel consumption of 22.57 mpg should have given them the Index win. When they were allowed to examine the official records some seven days later, they were proved right. An error had been made in the official calculations which showed their fuel consumption at 21.25 mpg. The Automobile-Club de l'Ouest was forced to award the French Elite a second first prize and an equal amount of cash!

Elites at Le Mans in 1961

Five cars were entered for the 1961 Le Mans classic, two from France, two Team Elite cars and one from the UDT/Laystall Racing Team. As we will see in a moment, the UDT car was another very special Elite.

The Team Elite cars, in their new livery of green racing stripes over white, were for Clive Hunt with the American 'Doc' Wyllie, and Trevor Taylor with Bill Allen. The Hunt/Wyllie Elite ran like a train, picking off place after place, until the nineteenth hour when it retired due to a split fuel tank. The Allen/Taylor car fared much better, taking a 1st in the 1300 Class with a new record of 93.12 mph and 12th overall.

The only other Elite to finish the race was that driven by Kosellek and Massenez. This car was entered by the French Lotus importer and besides finishing right behind the Team Elite car for a 13th overall and a 2nd in Class, it also scored a 2nd in the Index of Thermal Efficiency.

The other French Elite, owned and co-driven by Jean François Malle, the brother of the well-known film director (paired with the English driver, Robin Carnegie), was the first Elite to sport the so-called

The Bill Allen/Trevor Taylor Elite during scrutineering for the 1961 event. (Henri Beroul)

The French Lotus importer entered this Elite in 1961 for Kosellek and Massenez. They finished the race 2nd in Class and Index and 13th overall. (Henri Beroul)

This is the Malle/Carnegie Elite during scrutineering and before the Costin nose was fitted. A split wing tank spoiled a superb effort during the race. (Henri Beroul)

'Costin nose' described in detail in the previous chapter. This was done for a specific attempt at the Index of Thermal Efficiency. The modifications worked to the tune of 142 mph down Mulsanne, but their race was brought to an abrupt end in the ninth hour when a wing tank split.

The 750 Elite

The UDT (United Dominions Trust)/Laystall Team, which had been campaigning Lotus 18s in Formula 1 and 19s in sports car events, decided to contest the Index of Performance (by then exclusively DB Panhard territory) with a new type of Climax engine installed in a special Elite. Unfortunately, little is known about the modifications to the body/chassis except that it was rumoured to be extremely light in weight, with single panel bonnet and boot lids and minimum thickness lay-ups for the floor and sides of the body.

Much was known about the engine, on the other hand; it was a twin cam, four-cylinder unit displacing 742cc and named the FWMC (featherweight marine competition). Interestingly, the engine was almost precisely half of the new 1500cc V–8 being developed by Coventry Cimax for the new Formula 1. The engine was rated at 81 bhp at 8,000 rpm and when installed in the Elite it was fitted with a specially tuned exhaust system that terminated in megaphones. The resulting exhaust note was shattering, and track-side observers reckoned it was easily the noisiest car in the race.

In 1957 an Eleven, fitted with a 750cc short-stroke FWA, won the Index, so it was expected that an Elite with similar displacement but 30 per cent more power would positively run away from the opposition. Cliff Allison and Mike McKee shared the driving assignment for this Elite, which was entered in the Sports as opposed to GT, and they jumped to an early and commanding lead in the Index. By the tenth hour it appeared the Panhards would be vanquished, but an oil pump drive broke and the car was withdrawn. Despite its promise, there is no evidence that the 750 Elite was ever raced again.

Elites at Le Mans in 1962

By 1962, the Lotus Elite had raced and won at Le Mans for three consecutive years which, by any standard, was a long time to remain competitive. Most observers thought that this would be the car's last appearance at Le Mans, especially after Colin Chapman announced that he would never again enter one of his cars in the 24 Hours.

It seems that a two-car team of new Lotus 23s had been rejected at scrutineering because of over-sized fuel tanks, too large a turning circle, insufficient ground clearance and the fact that the front wheels were held on by four studs and the rears by six. Despite works mechanics and machinists working all night to put the cars into compliance, including building new four-stud hubs for the rear wheels, the cars were still turned down. The stewards were concerned that a four-stud rear hub might be too weak if the original design called for six.

No amount of reasoning or slide rule demonstrations would convince the inspectors. Mike Costin explained that the cars were running 1-litre engines even though the power train had been designed to handle up to 2 litres. Of course, the 1-litre Lotus 23 was tailor-made to win the Index of Performance, a fact not lost on the French organizers.

The Hobbs/Gardner Team Elite entry in 1962. Notice the full plexiglass side windows and the partial radiator blind. (Henri Beroul)

Even the presence of Colin Chapman failed to persuade them and in the end he swore an oath never to return.

Interestingly, Chapman agreed to sell the Ford-powered 23 (one used a short-stroke Ford 1600 twin-cam and the other a Climax FWMC) to a French driver named Bernard Consten, under the proviso that he enter only endurance races and use the four-stud hubs. Consten went on to win his class in the Clermont-Ferrand 6-Hour race and in the 1,000 Kilometres at Montlhery. Chapman felt he was vindicated but, nonetheless, he never did return to Le Mans.

It was left to Team Elite to continue the Elite tradition, and this they did by entering two cars, one for David Hobbs and Frank Gardner and the other for Clive Hunt and Doc Wyllie. Two manufacturers sought to spoil the fun, Alfa Romeo with two of their 1290cc SZ coupés, and Abart with no fewer than four Simca/Abarth 1300 coupés.

Instead of contending with their competition, the Team Elite cars took off after a pair of new Porsche-Abarth 1600cc coupés. By the twenty-second hour the Hobbs/Gardner Elite was in 8th place overall and led not only the Alfas and Simca/Abarths but both the Porsches as well. The Team Elite cars were motoring absolutely flat out and were timed at nearly 140 down the Mulsanne straight.

A problem, which was later found to be a burned exhaust valve, caused the Hobbs/Gardner car to slow a little which allowed one Porsche to squeeze by at the chequered flag. Both Elites had additional troubles with generators vibrating themselves to pieces. Apparently the Team chose not to use the old Buxton ruse to solve the problem. It seemed that Lucas electrics, especially starters and generators, were put to the test in the Elite and under racing conditions suffered failures from heat and vibration. Because the Le Mans regs allowed repair but not replacement, Buxton's mechanics used to

The Frank Gardner/ John Coundley Team Elite Le Mans entry in 1963 which burst its engine in the sixteenth hour. (Henri Beroul)

The Wagstaff/Ferguson Team Elite car during scrutineering. This car finished 10th overall and 1st in Class. (Henri Beroul)

The last Elite to race at Le Mans, the Team Elite car of Clive Hunt and John Wagstaff. The effort resulted in another class win. This car is currently owned by John Wagstaff. (Henri Beroul)

keep two deep buckets of water handy in the pits. 'Fire extinguishers,' they said, but at the bottom of one was a new starter and the other a new generator. So when a Team car pulled in with a burned-out unit, the mechanics would remove it and bounce it up and down in their hands, exclaiming to the official pit observers, 'Hot, hot!' They would then toss it into the right bucket under the pretext of cooling off the part, and minutes later would pull out a new one which, of course, was identical with the old. No one ever caught on, even the drivers.

Happily, the generator difficulties did not significantly hinder the two Elites' progress and the Hobbs/Gardner car took not only a 1st in Class but also a 1st in the Index of Thermal Efficiency, while coming in 8th overall. The Hunt/Wyllie Elite finished 3rd in Class (beaten by an Alfa), 2nd in the Index and 11th overall. Both cars broke the previous year's class record, Hobbs/Gardner averaging a terrific 99.6 mph and Hunt/Wyllie 96.7, an outstanding achievement which gave rise to much celebration in Team Elite headquarters in Derbyshire and at the works in Cheshunt.

Elites at Le Mans in 1963

When Team Elite arrived at the Sarthe in 1963 with a pair of cars, they already knew that production of the Elite was about to end in only a few months' time. The new Elan was 'on stream' and already showing more profit than its predecessor. Still, enthusiasm was high, and the Team wondered aloud, 'Wouldn't it be something to pull off the fifth Elite win?'

As already highlighted in Chapter 6, the entry consisted of Pat Ferguson with John Wagstaff, and Frank Gardner with John Coundley. The latter car burst its engine in the sixteenth hour while lying 13th, but Ferguson and Wagstaff kept their car together and finished 10th overall and 1st in Class. They took 3rd in the Index of Thermal Efficiency and averaged 94.0 mph.

1964, the end of the dynasty

As the deadline approached for the 1964 Le Mans, Clive Hunt announced that the Team would be retired at the end of the year. As mentioned earlier, one Elite had been kept by the Team primarily for John Wagstaff to use in long-distance races. It was really because of tradition that Hunt decided to go for one last victory in France.

Wagstaff and Hunt drove the Elite in their typical flawless fashion and despite constant generator troubles averaged 92.6 mph and covered 2,222 miles in the 24 hours. They ended up 22nd overall in a field of 25 finishers which was, incidentally, the largest number of cars to go the distance since 1953! Wagstaff and Hunt walked away with another class win, the sixth for the Elite and a record not broken since, not even by the Porsche 911.

A production Lotus would never again race at Le Mans. The 1300cc Class record set by Hobbs and Gardner in 1962 was finally broken in 1966 by an Alpine Renault and the class itself was retired in 1968.

Years later, David Buxton reminisced, 'Although we didn't know it at the time, we were also participating in the twilight of the private, entrepreneurial racing car owner/driver, works sponsored or recognized or not. Due to economic factors I feel those days are gone for ever and the major part of the sport seems to have lost much of what, for me, was its real value.'

The Elite Record at Le Mans, 1959–1964

Year	Car no	Drivers	Position in Class/overall	Index of Therm Eff	Index of Perf	Miles	Mph	Mpg	Weight in pounds
1959	41	Lumsden Riley	1st/8th	2nd	5th	2,259.3	94.1	18.9	1,377.8
	42	Whitmore Clark	2nd/10th	5th	11th	2,150.6	89.6	19.0	1,433.0
	38	Videlles Malle	Fire in ninth hour						
1960	44	Masson Laurent	1st/13th	2nd*	19th	2,182.8	90.0	21.2	1,428.6
	41	Wagstaff Marsh	2nd/14th	1st	12th	2,146.7	89.4	21.9	1,466.1
	42	Buxton Allen	Clutch failure during seventeenth hour						
	43	Baillie Parkes	Transmission failure during sixteenth hour						
	Unknown	Taylor Ireland	2–litre car that did not start						
	Unknown	Sieff (no co-driver)	Crashed in practice						
1961	38	Allen Taylor	1st/12th	—	13th	2,234.9	93.1	Unknown	Unknown
	40	Kosselek Massenez	2nd/13th	2nd	14th	2,231.1	92.9	19.9	1,477.1
	32	Wyllie Hunt	Split fuel tank during nineteenth hour						
	51	Allison McKee	750cc car failed in tenth hour with broken oil pump drive						
	41	Malle** Carnegie	Split fuel tank during ninth hour						
1962	44	Hobbs Gardner	1st/8th	1st	3rd	2,390.5	99.6	19.6	1,388.9
	45	Hunt Wyllie	3rd	2nd	6th	2,319.9	96.7	19.8	1,388.9
1963	39	Wagstaff Ferguson	1st/10th	3rd	9th	2,256.9	94.0	20.7	1,477.1
	38	Gardner Coundley	Engine failure during sixth hour						
1964	43	Wagstaff Hunt	1st	—	18th	2,222.7	92.6	Unknown	Unknown

* Awarded duplicate 1st in Index ** This car fitted with 'Costin nose'

The Nürburgring

The fact that the Elite compiled its string of victories at Le Mans with deceiving ease belied how difficult such an accomplishment really was. Endurance racing required a special type of driver—one who could maintain concentration for very long periods of time despite the hypnotic effects of a race course lined with trees and fence-posts. Luckily, the Elite required a very light touch and its balance and stability at high speeds made few demands on its drivers.

Peter Lumsden emphasized that the ''Ring' and Le Mans were onl two weeks apart and his drives in 1959 marked the Elite's first appearance on the Continent. Still, the early wins were met with scepticism and the feeling that, somehow, Lotus had been very lucky.

It will be recalled that Peter Lumsden planned on spending his summer vacation in 1959 racing his Elite at Le Mans and the Nürburgring in Germany. The annual endurance race at the ''Ring' covered a distance of 1,000 kilometres and was run on the tortuous circuit high in the Eifel Mountains, one lap of which consisted of over 170 corners!

Lumsden and Riley teamed up for the race and at flag-fall set out in pursuit of no fewer than 16 Alfa Romeos! Much of the race was run in the rain, yet under these difficult conditions the lone Elite pulled away from the Italian contingent by some 30 seconds per lap! Lumsden and Riley won the 1300cc Class going away.

A view from atop the Team Elite transporter unloading a car at the Nürburgring in 1962. (Wagstaff collection)

Mechanics conducting a final check before the start of the 1000 Kilometres at the 'Ring. (Wagstaff collection)

WUU 2 returned to the ''Ring' in 1960, but this time the win went to the Elite of John Wagstaff and Alan Stacey. Their race was not without incident; in the closing stages the steering rack came adrift and allowed the entire steering column to move up and down in its mounts.

In 1961 three Elites were entered, WUU 2 for Lumsden and Riley, a car for the German drivers, Degner and Braun, and the 'automatic' of David Hobbs which was to be co-driven by Bill Pinckney. This interesting Elite will be discussed in detail in Chapter 12, but Hobbs was so fast in practice and the car was fitted with such a non-standard gearbox that the organizers moved his car from the GT category to the 1600cc Sports Class. No matter, Hobbs and Pinckney finished 1st anyway, ahead of several Porsches. The GT class, 1300cc, was again won by Lumsden and Riley with the German Elite taking 3rd.

Special recognition is given here to Peter Lumsden and Peter Riley, whose success in long-distance racing was second only to that of Team Elite. Both men were members of the BRDC, nominated, incidentally, because of their skill behind the wheel of the Lotus 14, and their exploits served as the exemplars for the host of Elite racers that followed.

Sebring

The 12 Hours of Sebring was the American equivalent of Le Mans, the 'Ring and other European long-distance events. At least that was the theory, but more on that in a moment. The town of Sebring is in the state of Florida and was noted for its United States Air Force bomber base, where road racing promoter Alec Ulmann staged an annual 12-hour endurance race. The event had full FIA sanction for the World Sports Car Championship and, as a result of this, attracted the top teams from Britain and Europe as well as the US. In addition to points standings, the prize money was also pretty good.

Although Ulmann did his best to mimic the great European long-distance races, Sebring never seemed to take itself all that seriously. Scoring and time-keeping were notoriously inaccurate and several events had the dubious distinction of having corrected versions of the official results published days after the race was run and everyone had gone home. No one seemed to be immune from the bungling, not even the course marshals. For example, in 1962 Stirling Moss and Innes Ireland's NART Ferrari was disqualified for an illegal refuelling. The trouble was, the black flag was not given to the drivers until three hours after the incident!

The reason for this casual attitude was probably Sebring's party atmosphere. Southern Florida was a welcome change for the Europeans with its bright sunshine and warm climate. There were also the sponsors' hospitality suites and the parties which continued essentially non-stop during race week. The festivities attracted many entertainment personalities, not to mention Hollywood starlets. It was said of Sebring that a good time could be had by all no matter where one finished (or thought they ended up) in the race.

The circuit was 5.2 miles in length and consisted of a combination of billiard table runways and poorly surfaced access roads. It featured 15 corners and was extremely difficult to 'read' because of the lack of prominent features. The straights were long and thus very fast, even though the surface was quite bumpy, especially across transition roads. The 12-Hours was also somewhat unique among long-distance races because it started in daylight and concluded in darkness.

1959

The Elite's first appearance at Sebring was in 1959 when Colin Chapman brought chassis numbers 1013 and 1015 for himself and Jay Chamberlain, the American importer. Car number 45 was driven by Chapman and Pete Lovely and they covered 160 laps (the winning Ferrari did 188) at an average speed of 70 mph (the Ferrari managed 80 mph) for a 21st position overall and 2nd in Class. Chamberlain and Sam Weiss drove car number 46 to a DNF due to a blown engine.

The American enthusiasts' press hailed the Elite as lovely to look at but not fast enough for the Sebring course. The cars, incidentally, received a great deal of attention and there was always a crowd of people in the pits trying to get a closer look. Recall that both of the Sebring cars were prototypes with the early type of shock absorber towers and wing fuel tanks.

1960

Chamberlain returned to Sebring in earnest in 1960 with a team of three Elites, entered under the Lotus Cars of America banner. They were painted in American racing colours, dark blue with a white racing stripe, and looked quite smart despite headlight covers fashioned from aluminium pie-plates!

Car number 55 was driven by Chamberlain and Charles Evans and finished the race 25th overall and 3rd in class behind two Alfa Romeos. The fastest Elite was number 57 driven by Phil Forno and Frank Bott. They were leading the class by miles when Bott was forced off course by a backmarker and rolled his Elite on the 57th lap. Luckily, Bott walked away unhurt but enormously shaken because he had witnessed another Elite's accident early in the race.

On lap 5, car number 56 (driven by Sam Weiss and Jim Hughes) had also rolled but with tragic consequences. Hughes was behind the wheel when he entered Sebring's 120 degree corner and realized that he was going much too fast to make the turn. He shot down the escape road

Jay Chamberlain in car 55 during Sebring scrutineering. Just behind is the Elite of Phil Forno and Frank Bott which rolled during the race. Notice the pie-plate headlight covers. (Photographer unknown)

and straight for a photographer who had illegally set up his tripod in the centre of the roadway.

Hughes desperately flung the steering wheel to swerve out of the way but the car caught a rut and rolled, spilling its driver into its path and killing him instantly. The wildly careening Elite struck the photographer, who never looked up from his camera, and killed him as well.

Following the race a pall hung over the Lotus pits, and after Chamberlain had taken care of the grim arrangements, he sped away from the course only to be arrested for reckless driving. Because he was from out-of-state, he was taken to the local police station and booked, despite his explanation of the day's tragic events.

1961–2

As will become clear in the next chapters, Lotus Cars of America and the works at Cheshunt were in deep turmoil in 1961, so there was no participation at Sebring. The following year saw two Elites entered, from two Lotus importers at opposite ends of the country.

Car number 68 was entered by Dutchess Auto in New York for Peter Pulver and Newton Davis. Elite number 69 was entered by Ecurie Shirlee in California for Don Hulette and Burk Wiedner. The California Elite caught fire and did not finish while the car of Davis and Pulver motored steadily to 29th place overall and well back in Class.

1963

Another pair of Elites was entered in 1963 for John Bentley/John Gordon and Lee Lilley/Edward Graham. Both cars ran without drama and finished in 38th (Bentley/Gordon) and 39th place (Lilley/Graham) overall and 6th and 7th in Class behind a gaggle of Simca Abarths and an Alfa SZ.

1964

The entry list for the 1964 Sebring 12 Hours showed two Lotus Elans and a Lotus Cortina for Jim Clark, Colin Chapman and Ray Parsons. A lone Elite was listed as a reserve but, as luck would have it, was allowed on the grid at the last minute. The Elans disappeared early, the Clark/Chapman/Parsons Cortina finished 21st overall and 6th in Class, while the Elite, entered by Dutchess Auto and again driven by Davis and Pulver, finished 36th overall and 4th in Class, beaten by a lone Réné Bonnet and a pair of Simca Abarths.

With that, the Elite's long-distance racing career in America ended. While not as auspicious as in England and Europe the car, nonetheless, demonstrated the stoutness to go the distance which was a fact not lost on American enthusiasts. The paradox, as will be discussed in Chapter 10, was how could the Elite be so strong on a race-track but so fragile on the street?

Chapter 9

Marketing the Elite

As we have seen, the Elite presented all manner of challenges to the young Colin Chapman and his small company, but, as it happened, these were nothing compared to what lay ahead when the time came to market the car. Until that time Lotus was an engineering shop and racing car builder and selling its products was relatively easy—just win races and drivers would line up at the door with cheque books in hand. Of course, the Elite was proving to be quite a racer in its own right, but Chapman wanted a much bigger slice of the pie. To succeed financially, the Elite had to be sold as a road car to customers all over the country and, eventually, the world.

A works advertisement from Sports Car & Lotus Owner *magazine.*

Works Elite sales brochures, one for each year of production. (Author's collection)

The philosophy

From their earliest conversations, both Chapman and Kirwan-Taylor agreed that the Elite, in accordance with its name, would be a grand touring car by the strictest definition—nothing more or less than an elegant means of high speed transport for two. Unfortunately, the very first Elites were more racers than touring cars and they demanded the attentive hands of skilled mechanics. This was nothing that a dedicated dealer network could not provide, of course, but in 1957 Lotus cars were sold direct from the factory. There was no network. There were no dealers.

Initially, this presented few problems. Elites were not yet sold overseas and the early cars were serviced at Tottenham Lane. Advertising consisted of race reports in the enthusiasts' press and continued exhibition at the major motoring and racing car shows. The car magazines were spreading news of the Elite far and wide but one still had to travel to north London to lay hands on one.

At first, Chapman loaned cars to journalists for driving impressions only. He did not want the Elite to be put through an actual road test with stopwatches and Tapley meters until the development phase was completed and all of the pre-production problems had been worked out. As it turned out, the first factory-authorized road test did not appear until 1960, but more of that in Chapter 11.

Despite the subjectivity of these early 'driving impressions', enthusiasts lined up at Hornsey in earnest; they wanted cars to test drive and, having done that, they wanted cars to buy. Of course, most of

An aerial photograph of the Lotus works at Cheshunt. Row after row of Elites are visible in the field next to the main assembly buildings. (A.N.E. Bates)

these potential customers were racing drivers, but in order to relieve the pressure (and interruptions) at 7 Tottenham Lane, Chapman arranged a deal with Alexander Engineering Ltd to distribute cars to one dealer, an associated company by the name of Michael Christie Motors Ltd in Haddenham, Buckinghamshire. This arrangement would serve as a pilot programme for the larger scheme to come.

Elite colours

No one was more aware of the visual (and thus sales) impact of paint colour than Peter Kirwan-Taylor. His early expeditions to the European motor shows introduced him to the importance of colour and how visual excitement could be created by certain paint jobs. He also appreciated how light played on colour and how the designers in the late 1950s were beginning to utilize different hues to promote highlights and emphasize contours. In the Elite's case, the right choice could enhance the feeling of lightness and accentuate the body's curvature, while the wrong ones could make some features seem to disappear entirely. The preferred colours tended to be the lighter ones which also photographed better under the lights of the auto shows.

As part of his research, Peter Kirwan-Taylor discussed form and texture with a friend, Robert Erskine, who operated a successful art gallery in London. Although Erskine's favourite engineered object of the twentieth century was the jet engine, he entertained Peter's idea that the automobile had potential as well, even if Peter did dislike the use of metallics on plastic.

Kirwan-Taylor had come to the conclusion that the Elite was shown to the best advantage in certain pastels. In fact, he purchased an expensive box of French chalks (which he still has) to study the possibilities. When it came time to list the colour options for the Elite, Kirwan-Taylor chose three of them from his box of chalks, deep (sunburst) yellow, cobalt (light) blue, and permanent (lime) green. In deference to international racing colours he also listed red (Italy), dark blue (USA),

It is easy to see why white became a popular colour. Here a fine English oak creates interesting patterns on the paintwork. (Derek Duncan)

British racing green (UK), moonstone grey—to mimic silver, which was Germany's racing colour—and white, which was an industry standard.

To complement, and in some cases to intensify, certain of the Elites' paint finishes, Kirwan-Taylor also convinced Chapman to offer a variety of upholstery colours. These included black, red, yellow and natural tan. An Elite in light blue with a red interior (although lime green with yellow comes close) remained one of the most visually startling yet, to some observers, the most pleasing combination available.

Unfortunately, several of the early colours proved to be unstable due to their solvents being incompatible with the early polyester resins and primers. As we will see in later chapters, this problem was never completely solved and a number of owners of the first Elites found that their cars changed colours like a chameleon. Inexplicably, not all cars were affected, but a few of the early reds went to orange, some of the dark blues changed to greyish blue or lilac and moonstone grey often became a kind of lavender pink. While some of these changes were not unattractive, they were not what the customer ordered and they became a painter's nightmare when the time came to match panels after a collision repair. In time, the situation improved, but over half of Kirwan-Taylor's colours were eliminated in the process.

More dealers and the irrepressible David Buxton

By the time production of Maximar-bodied Elites reached full capacity, it was apparent that the lion's share would be going to the USA, so great were their initial orders. That the American market played an enormous role in the success of the Elite, and Lotus itself, will be discussed later in this chapter, but it occurred to Chapman in 1959 that, for the time being, he could sell his cars direct from the factory and through a few specialized dealers sprinkled throughout the United Kingdom. He really did not need to develop anything more sophisticated than that.

In time, Chapman would name several hand-picked 'Lotus Centres' that, by their enthusiasm and the skill of their service departments, were deemed qualified to sell the Elite. One of the first was David Buxton Ltd in Derbyshire. His understanding for, and no doubt his love of, the car did much to promote Lotus's fortunes in the early Elite days.

David Buxton was a successful club racer who campaigned an Elite, 500 KRA, with considerable verve. His company, David Buxton Ltd, was the distributor for Maserati, TVR and Piper Aircraft and, as we have seen in an earlier chapter, it was also the first patron of Team Elite. He advertised heavily and the pen and ink artwork of his ads attracted considerable interest. Oddly, Buxton emphasized the Elite's racing attributes much more than its touring capabilities, and his ads often touted the most recent race victory.

Buxton also got on well with Colin Chapman and after he lost his dealership and gave up Team Elite, he went to work for Lotus as Sales Manager at Cheshunt. Years later, he was involved with a boat-building company, Moonraker Boats, which Chapman himself eventually purchased. It seems Buxton's automobile troubles were caused by the use of some highly imaginative financing schemes which the Government frowned on, and by representing pre-owned automobiles as slightly newer than they really were. Buxton was also quite flamboyant and as a result of this he was highly visible and any foible was likely to

As leading Lotus Distributors we are now able to supply the Lotus Elite Series Two to latest production specification, in component form for £1299.

This latest facility, bringing the finest compact grand touring car built today within the range of a far greater section of the sports car market, also gives the purchaser a wider choice of equipment combinations than would be available with a normal production line car.

The Component Elite, which is supplied cellulosed, wired and trimmed, requires only the use of hand tools and 25 man-hours to completion, and a fully comprehensive workshop manual is available.

David Buxton Limited, who for the past two years have been entrusted with the racing and preparation of the Works Team Elite cars, and having gained Class and Thermal Efficiency Index wins at Le Mans, can now also offer the Component Elite with stage II and Stage III modifications to Team Elite Specification, at a competitive cost. For further details, please contact our Head Offices and Showrooms at 59-61 London Road, Derby; telephone Derby 40526 (5 lines).

Componently Elite!

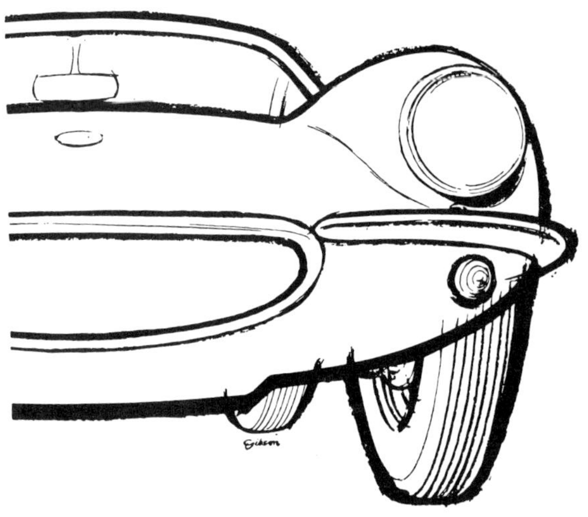

David Buxton Limited

Dealers in High Grade Automobiles, Executive and Private Aircraft

Advertisement for David Buxton Ltd. (Autosport Magazine)

get picked up by the newspapers and publicized. There was no question—he 'stepped over the line' on occasion, but whatever sales success the Elite enjoyed in the early days was because of the wit and considerable charm of David Buxton.

The Chequered Flag and others

After the Hornsey works were closed there was no place in London to buy a Lotus until Graham Warner's Chequered Flag Ltd sports car specialists in Chiswick became a distributor, and eventually a second showroom was opened in the Midlands. Their recognition was instant, at least among racegoers, because they sponsored Graham Warner's LOV 1. Warner's exploits were covered in an earlier chapter, but the magazine adverts almost always featured LOV 1 in a lovely four-wheel drift. In time, the Moto Baldet Group in Northamptonshire and the Waltham Cross Service Station in Cheshunt also came aboard as Lotus Centres to sell the Elite and the new Elan.

High cost and big problems

The Series I Elite cost £1,300 plus the mandatory British Purchase Tax which raised the total to £1,951 ($5,450.00). Therein was the main reason why grand touring customers were slow to respond to the Elite. Two thousand pounds was Jag and AC Bristol territory, not to mention Porsche and Alfa Romeo, and enthusiasts were not quick to warm to the idea of high-priced, small-capacity sports cars, regardless of the high level of performance.

Then too, there was much about the Elite that the average enthusiast simply did not understand. Peter Kirwan-Taylor recalled the buyer resistance to the early wing fuel tanks. Never mind the negligible change in weight distribution, full versus empty, the touring customer worried about stories of leaks and the possibility of fire in the event of a collision.

He was also unsure about the monocoque, especially with each new tale of a diff breaking loose, and there was that problem of changing colours. *Sports Car and Lotus Owner* magazine published a few random comments overheard at the Motor Show in October, 1959:

'Oh look, it hasn't got any back brakes.'

'Why have you changed the method of construction? I know for a fact you have gone over from glass fibre to plastic.'

'Those brake drums look awfully thin.'

Slowly, sales withered away to a trickle. Chapman had extended his credit to the limit and every penny was committed to the new factory at Cheshunt. Then, his accountants broke the news that his company had lost £29,062 (nearly $80,000.00) by the end of 1959. As if that were not enough, news came from America that Jay Chamberlain, the US distributor, was in trouble and the docks in Long Beach, California, were lined with half a million dollars worth of Lotus Elites. By mid-1960 the situation had worsened. Bristol was 'on line' and anxious to complete its contract. New body/chassis spilled on to the fields next to the Cheshunt factory by the score.

If it were not for the sales of sports racers and formula cars (spurred by Lotus's first F1 victory in May 1960 by Stirling Moss at Monaco), and the soon to be legendary Seven, there would have been no cash flow at all and Lotus, very likely, would have gone bankrupt. Then Bristol Aircraft handed Chapman a bill for £100,000 and informed him that it was due and payable!

Enter Peter Kirwan-Taylor, who at the time was representing the in-

THE CHEQUERED FLAG

LOTUS ELITE

SAFETY, SPEED, ELEGANCE, COMFORT, ECONOMY

LEADING DISTRIBUTORS IN LONDON AND THE MIDLANDS

In every showroom a faultless array of hand picked sporting machinery, every marque, in every colour at your price. All facilities are immediately available, insurance, hire-purchase, and the best part-exchange allowance. Visit us first for really excellent sports cars at our very competitive out-of-season prices.

THE CHEQUERED FLAG
(London) LTD.
Tel. : CHI 7871/2/3
High Road, Chiswick, W.4

THE CHEQUERED FLAG
(Midlands) LTD.
Tel. : 89282/3
Arkwright St., Nottingham

THE CHEQUERED FLAG
(Competition Cars) LTD.
Tel. : EDG 6171/2
Gemini House, High St., Edgware, Middx.

Advertisement for The Chequered Flag. (*Autosport* Magazine)

Cash flow all but stopped as Elite production spilled on to the fields next to the works. (Lotus)

terests of his bank (Hill, Samuel & Co Ltd) in high-level meetings on the British aircraft industry. One of the principals was George White, a member of the main Board of Directors of Bristol Cars who also had director's responsibility for Bristol Plastics. Peter had met White many years earlier and he knew him to be keen on high-performance cars. After one of these meetings White enquired if Peter was still a Director of Lotus and if so they needed to talk! During the course of a lunch the two men worked out a plan by which Lotus could reduce its debt in quarterly payments. Kirwan-Taylor had bought some time. Now what?

The Elite kit

Chapman knew that the only way out was to lower the price of the Elite and convert his tremendous inventory into cash. Fortunately,

The Elite kit is displayed in an unusual exhibit at the London Motor Show. Note the disbelieving looks of the journalists. (Photographer unknown)

there was a way he could do it without losing money! The trouble was that to do so would break a promise Chapman had made to himself, that nothing would be allowed to diminish the image of the world's most advanced small GT.

Charles Fox, Lotus Public Relations Officer, called a press conference and handed out the following release:

PRESS EMBARGO DATE: OCTOBER 1st, 1961

'Firstly gentlemen, we would like to thank you for coming to this press conference and we would like to give you a brief resumé of Lotus Elite marketing policy for the next twelve months.

'Lotus Components Limited are pleased to announce that they have now concluded arrangements whereby they can offer the Lotus Elite Grand Touring car to an improved specification in component form for assembly by the home builder.

'These components are presented in a form which can easily be assembled by the inexperienced amateur and the total cost of the car by this method is £1,299 and, of course, cars built in this way are not subject to Purchase Tax.

'Lotus Cars Limited will continue to build complete cars for home and export as hitherto to both standard and Special Equipment specifications.

'Over the last decade, Lotus have established an enviable reputation as the world's leading manufacturer of cars in component form, during which some 1,500 cars have been supplied, and all this experience has been put to good use in ensuring that the major sub-assemblies, as offered for home assembly, of the Elite have been designed in such a way that they can be assembled by the average person in 25 man-hours. They have also been prepared so that no further parts or specialized assembly operations whatsoever are required. A more detailed specification of the chassis body unit, as it will be supplied to the customer, is in the appendix.

'A fully comprehensive Service Manual is available to would-be car builders and, with the aid of this, assembly becomes simplicity itself.

'In order to allay any possible remaining worries that may exist, the Factory offers free technical inspection of the car if returned to the Factory after registration and also a free 500-mile service.

'One hardly need reiterate to members of the Press the advanced technical specification and completely unmatched overall performance of the Elite in respect of speed, road-holding and fuel economy. The basic specification of the car has been further substantially improved by the adoption of a twin SU carburettor, 80 bhp Coventry Climax 1216cc power unit and interior trim of the more luxurious type previously supplied on the export market only. Incorporated with this is a further improvement in sound dampening and consequent interior noise level.'

The Elite kit was delivered by truck and consisted of a fully trimmed, wired and plumbed automobile with the engine and gearbox, front and rear suspension systems and differential requiring installation. The works' estimate of 25 hours for assembly was probably pretty accurate if the owner had several people to assist in fitting the larger assemblies and was at least partly familiar with automotive mechanics. An added benefit of self-assembly was gaining an intimate knowledge of the Elite's underpinnings and what it would take to service them.

A works press photo showing the Elite kit in knocked down form. (Edward Sear)

An aside to the announcement of the Elite kit was a new price structure for complete cars which reflected the financial squeeze. The standard Series II cost £1,375 plus £631 Purchase Tax (£2,006 or $5,600.00 total). The Special Equipment Elite was priced at £1,495 plus £686 PT for a total of £2,181 or $6,400.00. By the end of production the standard car in kit form had risen to £1,375 and the SE to £1,495. Oddly enough, the rate of Purchase Tax dropped slightly because a built-up Elite went for £1,891 and the SE for £2,056.

The Press Release made mention of a comprehensive service manual. This was actually a workshop manual which was written for the Series II Elite—there had been nothing available at the works or dealers for the Series I! The shop manual was written by Mike Costin and illustrated by artist James Allington with the latter given an Elite for his efforts. Another point made in the Press Release was about the more luxurious interior trim, which was the new Royalite panelling. By then, only four body colours were available, the so-called cirrus white, light blue, tartan red and sunburst yellow. Interior trim colours were pared down as well and included black, red and tan.

The Elite kit was a complete success and in a matter of months eliminated the inventory at Cheshunt while providing much-needed capital. There were even stories around the works that completed cars were disassembled to satisfy demand. As we will see in the next chapter, the situation in America also began to improve and Chapman must have breathed a sigh of relief, although it took his personal attention in the States to revitalize the Lotus name. On returning home he began the design of the Elan.

The Super series

When David Buxton joined Lotus as Sales Manager in about 1961 he came up with the idea of a Super series of Elites to mimic the Porsche Super 90. These cars could be taken directly to the race track and entered in competition, although when fully trimmed they could also be driven on the road for even more performance than could be had with the Special Equipment version. Unfortunately, only sketchy information has survived on production numbers and prices for the series. The following equipment and accessories list was published by the factory in January 1962, and although the Super 100 is identified, the specifications were probably identical for the 95 and 105 also:

Optional equipment and accessories Lotus Elite range

Item		Price ex-Factory £	
Respray to customer's own single colour		45.0.0.	
Respray to customer's own two-tone colours		55.0.0.	
Irving seatbelts	each	8.10.0.	+
Large capacity screen washers		3.0.0.	
Pirelli Cinturato tyres, extra per set of 5		4.7.6.	*
2 Dunlop 450 × 15 R5 tyres and tubes (front) 2 Dunlop 500 × 15 R5 tyres and tubes (rear) plus 1 spare Dunlop 500 × 15 R5 tyre and tube	extra	46.6.0.	+
Alternative final drive ratios (4.9:1, 3.7:1, 4.5:1)	each extra	2.0.0.	
Chromium Monza fuel filler cap (for standard fuel tank)		4.10.0.	=
Le Mans fuel filler cap with $3\frac{1}{2}$ in (89mm) diameter neck, for long-range fuel tank		10.7.6.	+
SU electric fuel pump, piping, etc		6.5.0.	+
Racing suspension front and rear		40.2.10.	+
Light alloy front brake calipers		32.7.0.	+
Five Red Spot wire wheels	extra	6.2.6.	+
Stage II, 90 bhp engine conversion, SU carburettors,	Standard Elite	35.0.0.	*
	Special Equipment	25.0.0.	*
Stage III, 100 bhp engine conversion, SU carburettors	(racing only)	260.0.0.	+
Alternative pair Weber 40DC0E2 carburettors, manifolds and linkage		17.11.0.	
Competition clutch		17.10.0.	+
Close ratio gears fitted (MG gearbox)		27.10.0.	=
ZF four-speed all-synchromesh gearbox		96.0.0.	=
Cold air NACA duct in bonnet		12.10.0.	+
Heat shield over starter motor		2.0.0.	+
Oil cooler, air duct and piping		15.11.6.	+
Chromium plated wire wheels	each extra	12.10.0.	
Crating of assembled Lotus Elite, if required		22.0.0.	

= Available for regular model only
* Available for regular and Special Equipment models only
+ Standard equipment on Super 100

LOTUS CARS LIMITED, DELAMERE ROAD, HERTS, ENGLAND
Telephone: Waltham Cross 26181 Cables: Lotuscars London. Jan.62.

The Japanese connection

With the US absorbing the lion's share of Elite production outside the British Isles, only a few cars managed to trickle to the more remote corners of the world. And once there, they tended to disappear into obscurity, their owners delighting in them until the need arose for major service or repair. Once stung with exorbitant or shoddy work or hit with impossible delays in obtaining even the most ordinary parts, the

The dashboard and steering wheel of the Honda S600 sports car were strongly influenced by the Elite. (Honda)

love affairs tended to end rather quickly.

But not in Japan. Although only three were imported in 1960, three more in 1962 and one in 1963, their effect on the Japanese enthusiast and the enthusiasts' car-makers was completely out of proportion to their number. Six of the original seven survive to this day, incidentally.

Koichi Sugita, one of the original owners of an Elite in Tokyo, recalled, 'The shock that an Elite gave car manufacturers in Japan seems to be the same as it did to me. That is evidenced by the fact that, among the seven imported, three were bought by car manufacturers for their testing. Running performance with conventional cars is usually designed so as to absorb the shock from the ground with twisted ladder type frames and strong springs. With the Elite, it is designed to allow enough wheel stroke by using soft springs and to check pitching by strong shock absorbers. This idea was a shock to both car manufacturers and enthusiasts.'

Honda, Toyota and Suzuki were the three manufacturers that bought Elites for study, and apparently pleasure as well, for when the Honda Company opened its Suzuka racing circuit in 1963 the official course car was Mr Soichiro Honda's Lotus Elite. He used his car for his daily commute until the mid-'sixties when he handed the keys over to his son who owned the car for several more years.

Honda built its first sports car in 1964, the S600. Besides extremely compact dimensions, a low carriage and generous suspension travel, the car also featured a dashboard, gear lever and steering wheel that were quite familiar to Elite owners.

While Suzuki never did venture into the sports car market, Toyota built a pair of cars in the late 1960s, the Sports 800 and the 2000GT. The aerodynamics of the 800 and the Chapman strut rear suspension of the 2000, complete with towers that intruded into the cabin, had obvious origins. The Elite continued to exert influence, especially on suspension design, for years to come. The number of owners increased as well and in 1989 there were almost 30 cars in Japan.

Elites in Japan, 1989

No	Chassis no	Engine no	Registration	Colour
Series I				
1	1006	7548	400 FKX	Silver/green
2	1026		1205EV (Germany)	Blue
3	1120	7591	657 OAR	Green
4	1195	7683	USA	Blue
5	1221	8210	4394 MP	Red
6	1239	10187 (8214)	567 WKP	Red
Series II				
7	1333	8907		
8	1352	10504	VBW 808	Silver/brown
9	1441	8941	Milano	Pale yellow
10	1446	9381 (9012)	8188 MP	White
11	1476			
12	1531	9125		
13	1690	10848	490 YNN	Copper brown
14	1781	9558	OO 5608	White
15	1811	10585	5 BWR	
16	1834	8165	2078 UR	Red
17	1837	9135	Fuyo Trading	
18	1850	10177	8550 PF	Grey
19	1853	9128	Fuyo Trading	Red
20	1861	9364	Fuyo Trading	
21	1878	9711	9871 AT	Blue
22	1885	9238 (10381)	BRC 439B (USA)	
23	1946		3004 AT	Brown duo-tone
24	1951	10826	Fuyo Trading	
25	1965	10763	Fuyo Trading	White
26	1974	10785	Fuyo Trading	
27	1992	10771	Tokyo Shoji	
28	2025	10183	DJA 855C	Orange
29	2032		EUX 708C	Yellow

Chapter 10

The Elite in the USA

Jay Chamberlain

Jay Chamberlain first made the acquaintance of Lotus in 1954 in his foreign car repair shop (called Jay Chamberlain Automotive) which was located in Burbank, California. His small garage catered for British cars owned by employees of the numerous motion picture and television studios that dotted the area, and their affluence was reflected in the surprising variety of marques Chamberlain maintained both for road use and for the race-track.

Chamberlain was a racer himself, and although his origins were with the Southern Californian oval dirt tracks, he came to prefer road racing in a Jag-engined 'special' he designed and built himself. One day a customer called at the garage with photographs of a new racing car he had ordered from England. It was called a Lotus Nine, but the name, Chamberlain recalled, 'went right over my head'. It was not until the car had arrived and was uncrated in his shop that he took notice. He was awe-stricken by the aerodynamic concept and the advanced engine and suspension design, and was so taken with the car that he decided to order one for himself.

Chamberlain's Mark 9 arrived in early 1955 and he spent the season enjoying himself immensely while picking up club wins at Palm Springs, Torrey Pines and San Francisco. Meanwhile, his business prospered which enabled him to build a new and more spacious shop on a larger piece of land just down the street next to the Warner Brothers' Studios. There was a showroom, upstairs offices and a multi-car service bay underneath. A nice coincidence at the Grand Opening was the arrival of a letter from Colin Chapman congratulating Chamberlain on his success with the Nine. Chapman also took the opportunity to describe the new Eleven which Chamberlain thought sounded good enough to place an order for. He took his second Lotus to 17 wins in 21 starts at every circuit on the Pacific Coast from the Canadian to the Mexican border.

Jay Chamberlain at Pomona in 1958. (Joe Smith)

Chamberlain and Chapman met at Sebring, Florida, in 1956 during the 12 Hour enduro and they hit it off at once. In fact, Chapman invited Jay to England to discuss the possibility of his becoming the US distributor for Lotus cars. In June, the announcement was made in *Road & Track* magazine that Jay Chamberlain Automotive (new car sales were actually handled by a company called Lotus Cars of America, formed by Chamberlain and backed by several wealthy investors) had become America's sole Lotus dealer. During the next two years Jay proved his dedication by selling 64 Elevens.

In 1957 Chamberlain was invited by Chapman to drive an Eleven at Le Mans. He and Mackay Fraser took 1st in Class and 2nd in the Index of Performance, a stunning victory for a pair of Americans in a British car at a French long-distance road race. As a way of saying 'Thanks', Chamberlain bought Lotus a dynamometer and then trained the mechanics how to use it. A strong friendship grew between Chapman and Chamberlain, and on subsequent trips to the UK Jay often stayed at the boss's house. On one of these visits Chamberlain was told about the new Elite. He predicted great success, especially at a list price projected at $4,100.00 (the dealers' net cost was $3,555.00). At the time, the top-of-the-line Eleven sold for £1,953 ($5,467.00) so the Elite, he thought, being a true dual-purpose car, ought to do well.

LOTUS CARS OF AMERICA
OVERSEAS DELIVERY

	Dealer Cost	*Factory Retail*
Lotus Elite	$3,555.00	$4,159.50
OPTIONAL EQUIPMENT		
Heater	58.00	65.00
Radio	92.75	106.00

Delivery charges to the following cities in Great Britain:

Cheshunt (factory)	$25.00	Southampton	$65.00
London	38.00	Glasgow	73.00
Liverpool	53.00		

International Touring Documents should be arranged as follows:

1. Carnet de Passage en Douanes (Passport for car)..................$25.00
2. International car license plates.. 7.00
3. Associated membership in the Royal Automobile Club......... 12.00
4. English registration....................... for 12 months............ 35.00
   for 3 months.............. 10.00

Continental deliveries (drive away) can be arranged for in most principal cities in Europe. Listed below are a few delivery charges:

Paris	163.00	Geneva	140.00	Madrid	338.00
Cannes	150.00	Frankfurt	125.00	Barcelona	300.00
Nice	150.00	Dusseldorf	203.00	Lisbon	320.00
Marseilles	150.00	Rome	335.00	Brussels	135.00
Amsterdam	173.00	Naples	355.00	Vienna	250.00
Rotterdam	173.00	Copenhagen	265.00	Cherbourg	180.00
LeHavre	180.00	Stockholm	320.00	Hamburg	205.00
Zurich	140.00	Gibraltar	338.00		

PAYMENT

A deposit of $500.00 is required at the time of order for the car to be placed. The balance for the full payment including cost of the car, accessories, registration, etc, must be paid at least 30 days prior to the departure of the customer from the United States.

The first US Elites

In March 1959, chassis numbers 1013 and 1015 were shipped to Sebring for the 12 Hour race. As we have seen, one car was driven by Chapman and the other by Chamberlain, and while Jay's faltered and

Jay Chamberlain's showroom and service facility on Lankershim Boulevard in North Hollywood. (Bud Lewis and Associates)

Below *A Lotus Cars of America (Jay Chamberlain) advertisement.* (*Sports Car Graphic* magazine)

Below right *Jay Chamberlain in a publicity photo tries out a new Lotus Fifteen.* (Bud Lewis and Associates)

did not finish, Chapman took a 2nd in Class. After the race the cars were trailered to Burbank, cleaned up and installed in Chamberlain's showroom. In July, the first of the Maximar production arrived with chassis numbers 1047, 1052, 1053 and 1054.

Chamberlain advertised heavily in the enthusiasts' magazines and campaigned an Elite in West Coast club racing. His car was easily recognizable because of its red colour with silver accenting on the nose. He also set up a small showroom and service garage expressly for

Jay Chamberlain in his Sebring Elite at Pomona in 1959. Notice the wing tank and the damaged front end. (Photographer unknown)

the Elite on Ventura Boulevard in Studio City, an area heavily populated by well-heeled entertainment personalities. He also hired the public relations firm of Bud Lewis & Associates in Hollywood to promote the car. This they did by publishing press releases, handling exhibits at the local auto shows and other public events. They also scored heavily by getting the Elite into several episodes of the popular television series '77 Sunset Strip' as the personal transport of one of the programme's detectives, Jeff Spencer (actor Roger Smith).

Initial sales were very good. The car was doing well at the races despite, as we will see later in this chapter, a confusing situation over its classification. And the enthusiasts' response was as hoped for— instant appeal and recognition as an exotic and sophisticated GT car.

A little sleight of hand

When Chapman began to feel the big financial squeeze described in the previous chapter, he started shipping Elites to California in ever increasing numbers. His accountants had worked out a deal with the bank to employ letters of credit against which Lotus purchased materials and paid their creditors, like Coventry Climax and Bristol. Of course, word of Lotus's problems spread quickly in the industry and Tony Caldersmith, then Service Manager at Cheshunt, recalled having to wait at Coventry Climax while a Lotus cheque was cleared before he could take delivery of a batch of engines.

The letters of credit were based on factory invoices for Elites which had been sold, or, in the case of cars going to Chamberlain, bills of lading for cars shipped. It was thus vitally important for Chapman to load cars bound for America even if Chamberlain had not paid for them. Chamberlain was not upset about this at first, because sales were going well and there was no reason to believe he could not move even a backlog of Elites. As it happened, his backers bought some of the surplus just to keep a continuous stream of cash heading back to England.

The factory chassis list showed how much Chapman depended on the American market because 200 of the first 364 Elites went to

This picture was part of a magazine lay-out on Chamberlain's Sebring Elite. Posed in front of Griffith Observatory in Los Angeles, the car was red with a silver accent on the nose. (Photographer unknown)

Chamberlain. In all he was invoiced for 269 Elites, or over half of the production to that time. At first, this extremely risky financial tightrope worked satisfactorily. Chamberlain sold cars out of his showroom and consigned them to dealers in other parts of the country; demand seemed steady enough and response from the first owners was positive.

Price, paint, parts and politics

Then Chapman raised the price which forced a corresponding increase in the States to $5,244.00. Unfortunately, as in England, this placed the Elite against the likes of Jaguar, AC Bristol and Porsche, to name but a few, and enthusiasts baulked at paying that much money for so small a GT, especially one with paint problems.

At first, the colour changes were subtle. Red lost its depth and the light blue turned to lavender in only a few months, but longer exposure to the California sunshine resulted in some doors, bonnets, boots and bodies that were entirely different shades. Even the lime green and pale yellow were affected. Then, the doors on random cars developed a curious texture not unlike cobblestones and a line of Elite owners with complaints became a daily occurrence at Jay Chamberlain Automotive.

Both Chapman and Chamberlain were at a loss to explain what was happening and fibreglass experts offered only guesses. Chapman finally sent Robin Read (Sales Manager before David Buxton) and Ron Hickman to California for a look. Their analysis of the problem laid the blame (critical word 'blame', because if fault was found in the manufacturing process then Lotus would have to honour, and therefore pay, the warranty claims) with the sun, or more precisely the ultraviolet rays which they theorized were stronger in California than in England.

They believed that ultraviolet was penetrating the paint layers and reacting with the epoxy resin and hardener, causing a migration of one or more of these chemicals to the surface. In other words, it was definitely a manufacturing problem and Lotus agreed to pay for new paint jobs which were arranged by Chamberlain with local shops. One of these was Bruno's Corvette Repair (more of Bruno's in the chapter on restoration) in North Hollywood. The proprietor, Felix Brunelle, had his own ideas about the Elite's colour changes.

Brunelle discounted the ultraviolet theory (UV will not pass through plain window glass, let alone layers of paint) and reasoned that the problems resulted from using primers incompatible with polyester resins, exposure to heat causing the solvents and the resin to interact. Brunelle also theorized that Maximar occasionally painted Elite bodies at a different time of day (and with a different paint mix) than the doors and lids, which explained why not all cars suffered from differential fading.

The cobblestone texture which took months (years in the case of the author's Elite) to appear on doors was due to an imprecise combination of resin and catalyst. Epoxy required exact proportions to effect a complete cure and if either was measured incorrectly, or inexactly, the mix would 'work' for years to come, especially if exposed to heat—like California sunshine!

As more Elites took to American roads (and race-tracks), maintenance and repair became virtually impossible. This was because there was an insufficient parts inventory to service a few cars, let alone hundreds. Chapman could not afford to set up an adequate spares store in England for his own customers, so Chamberlain had to order, often on an individual basis, even the most ordinary supplies, like bearings bushes, valves and gasket sets. Some Elites were laid up for weeks despite Chamberlain's reliance on the telephone to advise Chapman of the situation.

As might be imagined, the once congenial conversations turned cold and antagonistic. Both men were under enormous pressure and feared the loss of their businesses, not to mention their hard-earned reputations; and both had to routinely invest their own money just to keep the Elite alive despite their common acknowledgement that it had the potential for stellar success and would, no doubt, set standards which the rest of the industry would mimic for years to come. Consider, then, their monumental frustration.

Then came news of the long-awaited Series II with its improved and more reliable rear suspension. But shortly after the cars started to arrive in California came the final blow. Chamberlain received a box of angle-iron from Cheshunt with a letter informing him how to install differential reinforcing straps.

Jay felt he could do nothing more and watched helplessly as row after row of Elites stacked up on the docks at Long Beach. The situation reached crisis proportions when Chamberlain refused to sell any more cars. In desperation, Chapman sent his confidant, Fred Bushell, to negotiate with Chamberlain. At these meetings, incidentally, Chamberlain always had one of his employees sitting in to witness the proceedings in case of any future legal action, a practice which seemed to make his guest uncomfortable. Interestingly, he had for some time taped all of the transatlantic telephone conversations on a Dictaphone for the same reason. Chamberlain and Chapman, incidentally, had never possessed a written contract—they became business associates over a smile and a handshake!

When Chamberlain refused to negotiate the issue of warranty claims and Chapman's emissary left in stalemate, Jay's financial business part-

Above *Jay Chamberlain leads a pack of historic racers at Riverside in 1988.* (Author)

Above right *Jay Chamberlain leans against his car between races at Riverside. He used number 152 in the 'sixties as well.* (Author)

ners got panicky, especially after Bushell urged them to replace Jay with someone more cooperative. They saw their profits tied to Lotus and not Jay Chamberlain and decided to lever him out. Gaining proxy of a few shares held by a long-time Chamberlain employee was all that was needed to gain control, and Jay was summarily dismissed. Lotus Cars of America went into voluntary bankruptcy, and as a result of this action all assets and records were locked up, disposition to be decided by the court. A sheriff was posted at the door to bar Chamberlain (or anyone else for that matter) from interfering with the seizure of the company's assets. He could not even clean out his desk.

Epilogue: Jay Chamberlain

Of course, Jay Chamberlain was devastated by the dismissal but he knew nothing could be done until the hearing some months away. Alas, the inevitable suits against Lotus Cars of America would eliminate whatever assets he could salvage. Chamberlain decided to go to Europe and try his hand at professional driving. British Petroleum assisted in the purchase of two Lotus 18s, one a Formula Junior and the other a Formula 1. After a year of campaigning with little success and no income, he returned to California only to find criminal charges waiting for him. It seems that Lotus had alleged excise tax fraud and the forgery of certain warranty claims. The trial took place in Los Angeles and Chamberlain was found not guilty on all counts.

Chamberlain may have been exonerated but he found himself not at all clear of the stigma, so he left California and went to work at a Porsche agency in Florida owned by an old friend. In time, he moved to Arizona and bought into a VW dealership and regained his reputation, if not his love affair with Lotus cars. In fact, neither Chapman nor Chamberlain ever forgave each other or exchanged another word.

Then, out of the blue, in 1985 Chamberlain accepted a ride in an Eleven at the inaugural Palm Springs historic races which marked the first time he had sat in a Lotus for over 20 years. In no time he was up with the leaders but what delighted those who knew him was that Jay was obviously enjoying himself immensely. Chamberlain had finally come full circle and made peace. Today, he and his son, Jaime, are familiar sights in California and Arizona vintage racing, both taking turns behind the wheel of his ex-Sebring (1960) Elite!

Western Distributors

Before the dust had settled on Lotus Cars of America, Chamberlain's primary financial backer, Dr Jack Briggs, formed Western Distributors

Western Distributors advertisement. (Sports Car Graphic magazine)

and hired Peter Hessler to sell Lotus cars again. Bushell and Read made another trip to California and pronounced the Elite alive and well.

However, in little more than a year, Western Distributors succeeded in taking a faltering Lotus reputation and ruining it completely, not only in Southern California but in other parts of the country as well. Their plan was to get rid of the cars by any means available (they even tried a lease arrangement, $135.00 a month with no money down) with minimal or no regard to preparation, repair or normal servicing. Elites that required major work, like paint jobs, were simply sold off, considerably below market value, and the headaches passed on to someone else.

For example, a foreign car dealer in Encino, California, operated by Frank Millard (and owned by Roy Rogers of motion picture fame), bought a dozen Elites from Western Distributors and sold them for $2,995.00 each! At this rate the cars sold very quickly, but they went without warranty or the promise of service! And therein was the cruellest blow to unsuspecting buyers. Dealers sold Elites but refused to service them (in most cases they simply could not). Western Distributors sold Elites at wholesale prices to foreign car dealers all over the country as window dressing for their showrooms, but woe betide the buyer who eventually needed his car fixed. There were neither parts nor trained mechanics.

The Elite buyer found himself completely on his own in a sophisticated car that demanded knowledgeable attention. Eventually, of course, the chickens came home to roost and the more persistent owners learned that their cars originated from Western Distributors. As the number of irate callers increased, it became difficult to move more Elites and sales began to drop off. This necessitated a return trip by Lotus's Financial Director, Fred Bushell, who immediately identified the problem as being Peter Hessler's failure as a business manager. Alas, before poor Hessler could be removed he was killed in a Lotus Formula Junior at Riverside and with that, Dr Briggs announced that he had had enough and dissolved the distributorship.

Bob Challman and Ecurie Shirlee

One of the dealers who bought Elites from Western Distributors was Bob Challman who operated a showroom and repair garage in Manhattan Beach, California. His company was called the Ecurie Shirlee Corporation (named after his wife) and was significantly different from the rest because of the proprietor's belief in the car and its potential. Challman also planned to be around for a while and set up a comprehensive service department, headed by master mechanic Jim Nieland, complete with a paint booth and a fibreglass repair area. He also accumulated a parts store and attempted to give the Lotus buyer (Challman also sold the Seven and Formula Junior 18) a degree of dealer stability unknown since the days of Chamberlain Automotive.

When Western Distributors folded, Challman contacted Cheshunt and proposed that he take over Lotus sales in the United States. Colin Chapman thought enough of the offer to come to the United States himself and negotiate the deal. As it happened, there were other inquiries to distribute Lotus cars, so Chapman wisely assigned only certain territories to specific dealers. The most prominent became Challman, who supplied cars to Southern California, Arizona and Utah, and Dutchess Auto in New York, who covered the eastern seaboard.

Bob Challman license plate frame. (Foster Cooperstein)

Chapman returned to England with a semblance of a dealer network and $850,000 worth of orders for Elites, Sevens and Formula Juniors!

A bonus to prospective buyers was that Chapman lowered the dealer price of the standard Elite to $4,138.00 ($4, 780.00 retail), the Special Equipment to $4,435.00 ($5,310.00 retail) and the Super 100 to $5,725.00 ($6,780.00 retail). Not inexpensive by any means, but at least the new Elite owner did not have to hire a detective to locate his dealer or rush out to find a paint shop experienced in fibreglass.

YOU are Cordually Invited
to THE LITTLE Opening OF
A NEW Sports CAR AGENCY?
it will take place on Monday
Zvening THE 12th OF February
between 7&11 p.m. The Sheriff & bank Willing.
THE BATH ROOMS ARE CLEAN & INSIDE THE BUILDING.
DANCING! a 1/4 TON oF CofFeE aNd
DoNuTS, RACE filmS aNd MAYBEE
FEW DANCE GIRLS..

COLIN CHAPMAN vehicles will be on Display
for YOUR APPROVAL

THANK YOU

2301 SEPULVEDA BLVD.
FRontier 6-8833

BOB CHALLMAN
ECURIE SHIRLEE CORPORATION

Below *Invitation to Bob Challman's grand opening.* (Bob Challman collection)

Below right *Bob Challman in front of his sign on the day of his grand opening celebration.* (Photographer unknown)

A jazz band in the showroom on the left entertains guests at Challman's grand opening. Note the white Elite inside. (Bill Norcross)

THE ELITE IS NOT DELIVERED RACE-READY

CONTRARY TO SOME DELIGHTFULLY FLATTERING FOLK TALES, THE ELITE IS NOT DELIVERED RACE-READY. THIS MYTH ARISES, NO DOUBT, FROM THE FACTORY PRACTICE OF ROAD DRIVING EACH NEW CAR. BY THE SAME TOKEN, THESE FACTORY JAUNTS DO HAVE VIRTUES AND ONE SHOULD NOT BE DECEIVED BY THE FRESH, VIRGINAL APPEARANCE OF A NEW ELITE. COLIN CHAPMAN'S CREWS HAVE A BIT OF A GO WITH EACH NEW ONE. IT'S RATHER AN OLD WORLD TRADITION. NOTHING BEATS AN ENGLISH COUNTRY ROAD FOR RELIEVING ANY MAIDENLY TENSIONS THAT MIGHT INHIBIT A NEW MACHINE, AND WILLFUL TENDENCIES CAN BE DISCOVERED AND CORRECTED BEFORE THEY BECOME EVIL HABITS. THE CHAPMAN SUSPENSION HAS BEEN THOROUGHLY SCRUNCHED AND WIGGLED TILL IT CARRIES THROUGH FAST CORNERS ON ALL FOURS WITH THE TENACIOUS GRACE ONE EXPECTS FROM A LOTUS. THE OVERHEAD CAM COVENTRY CLIMAX GETS A THOROUGHGOING PHYSICAL ON THE TEST BENCH EVEN BEFORE IT GOES INTO THE CAR, AND ON THE ROAD THE GIRLING DISCS GET A BRISK EXERCISING ALONG WITH THE CLUTCH GEARBOX COMBO TO ASSURE A PROPER ASSORTMENT OF CHANGES. IN SHORT, A NEW ELITE HAS HAD AT LEAST A TASTE OF THE FAST HEEL AND TOE WORK THAT LIES AHEAD IN HIGH SPEED TOURING OR PRIZE COMPETITION. TO THE OWNER WE LEAVE THE DETAILS OF FINAL BREAK-IN AND THE SELECTION OF VARIOUS RACING ACCESSORIES, PLUS PAINTING ON THE NUMBER, A DANDY JOB FOR A DECORATIVE CREW MEMBER. AND IF YOU DO COME OFF A WINNER, THERE IS A COMFORTABLE INSIDE PASSENGER SEAT TO CARRY HOME YOUR TROPHY.

If you live in the Pacific Southwest we will be pleased to arrange for you to examine and drive the Elite. For those in more remote areas we can supply information through correspondence and put you in touch with owners in your area.

Exclusive agents for Lotus cars in Southern California, Arizona and Utah.

BOB CHALLMAN Ecurie Shirlee Corporation
SHOWROOMS AND SERVICE FACILITIES
2301 SEPULVEDA BOULEVARD
MANHATTAN BEACH, CALIFORNIA
FRONTIER 6-8833

SPECIFICATIONS

Dimensions: *Wheelbase, 88"; Length, 130' Width, 58"; Height, 46"; Weight, 1,376 lb*

Engine: *Four-cylinder, overhead-ca Coventry Climax; 1216cc, 79 bhp @ 630 rpm, Twin S.U. carburettors.*

Fuel consumption: *Range, 30-40 mpg.*

Transmission: *Four speed, synchromes on top three. ZF Four speed synchromes optionally available. Top speed: 120 m.p.*

Suspension: *Front, independent by com bined coil-spring-damper units and tran verse wishbones incorporating anti-ro bar. Rear, independent by Chapman stru system with long coil spring damper unit double articulated drive shafts and trailin links.*

Steering: *Rack & pinion, (2.5 lock to lock, your choice right or left side.*

Brakes: *Girling hydraulic, 9½" discs, ou board front and inboard rear. Handbrake on rear.*

Price: *$4,780 P.O.E.*

LOTUS ELITE

A Bob Challman advertisement from Road & Track *magazine.* (Road & Track)

Bob Challman's Super 100 in action at Pomona in 1963. The fox tail was the driver's trade mark. (Charles Ferron)

Challman, in fact, made himself very easy to find and advertised heavily in *Road & Track* magazine. His series of ads featured clever pen and ink artwork by Jon Dahlstrom and, if a little condescending in presentation, they nonetheless helped to regain a large measure of Lotus's pride.

Challman took himself seriously (perhaps, on occasion, too much so because he once turned the author out of his showroom for being barefoot!) and made known his expectation that his Elites be returned for service on the dot. One little item Challman insisted on was a valve job at 20,000 miles and while this operation certainly benefited performance (20 thou came off the head along with the carbon) the day or so lay-up in the shop gave his mechanics ample time to give each car a thorough inspection. They checked suspension bushes, tightened rear brake disc bolts (see Chapter 13) and tended to the myriad details which went into keeping an Elite sound.

Challman's system obviously worked because an Elite maintained in his shops usually commanded a premium on the resale market. He was also successful at selling new Elites and quickly disposed of the last of the Chamberlain/Western Distributors inventory. As an example of how long some cars languished on the docks or in some other storage, the author's Elite (chassis 1461) was invoiced to Jay Chamberlain in October 1960, but was not sold by Bob Challman until September 1962!

Challman raced a Lotus Nine in Cal Club (California Sports Car Club, a region of the SCCA) and, on occasion, his personal Elite. When he was named a distributor, he ordered a white Super 100 and when it arrived he campaigned in earnest. His best season was 1963 when he finished 2nd in the West Coast Championship.

Then Chapman announced the Elite kit, for sale in the United States, direct from the factory! The standard Elite went for $3,995.00, the SE for $4,295.00 and the Super 100 for $5,495.00, and these prices included crating, shipping and insurance and import duty! The factory had, in one stroke, undercut its entire American dealer network!

The other blow came in 1963 when Chapman announced the signing of an agreement with the British Motor Corporation for the BMC dealers to carry Lotus. Challman, Dutchess Auto and the rest became

1962 LOTUS ELITE GRAND TOURING COUPE SERIES TWO

	P.O.E. (no extras)
Regular Model (SCCA E Production)	$3,995.00
Special Equipment Model (SCCA E Production)	4,295.00
Super 100 Model (full-race SCCA C Production)	5,495.00

Above prices include crating, cost of shipment and insurance, Import Duty.

Lotus announce the introduction of a revolutionary United states marketing scheme for the Lotus Gran Touring range:

1. The 1962 Lotus Elite range in 24-hour assembly kit-form, may now be ordered direct from the Factory for early shipment to you at any United States Port of Entry.
2. Direct marketing enables the car to be offered at a substantial saving (no distributor/dealer mark-up; no Excise Tax).
3. Easy, safe payment by Letter of Credit arranged by your Neighbourhood Bank (full details supplied).
4. Kit may be assembled with hand tools, from clear directions contained in the comprehensive Shop Manual supplied with each car (in under 24 manhours); no previous experience required. Kit is ready-painted, trimmed, wired and piped; power unit installed. Just bolt up suspensi assemblies and connect wiring and brake systems. Ad gas and water—then GO!
5. 24-hour Factory low-cost parts service to any region U.S.A.
6. The Lotus Elite is the *only* Grand Touring car availabl which may be used both for family motoring and SCC Production racing without special "one-purpose" prepar tion.
7. Write or cable today to the Factory for full particula of this outstanding car—by airmail return.

LOTUS, DELAMERE ROAD, CHESHUNT, HERTFORDSHIRE, ENGLAND
TEL.: WALTHAM CROSS 26181 CABLES: LOTUSCARS LONDON

14 SPORTS CA

Above *This advertisement devastated American dealers because they had agreed not to sell kits and their prices for complete cars were substantially greater.* (*Sports Car* magazine)

Above right *Bob Challman in 1982 at Laguna Seca looks over the author's Elite.* (Author)

ordinary neighbourhood car dealers with no territorial rights whatsoever.

Challman immediately filed suit for a rumoured one million dollars, but it was ultimately withdrawn in frustration. The Elite days were over. It was time for the new Elan and Lotus Cortina, cars that could be purchased and serviced at any BMC outlet in America. Or so it said on paper.

Club racing—the SCCA

The SCCA (Sports Car Club of America) was the organizing body for amateur sports car racing in America in the 'sixties, and besides setting safety standards and driver licensing programmes it also determined car classification. This was quite a different process from that in Great Britain or Europe, where cars were classed by engine displacement, because in the States production cars were grouped by speed potential regardless of engine size. The theory, of course, was that racing would end up being closer with cars of equal potential competing together, and, all in all, the system worked pretty well even if, at times, politics and vested interests saw to it that some cars ended up with a slight edge.

By the time the SCCA was faced with the Elite, the car had already established its dominance of the 1300cc class overseas. At the time, however, there were some dramatic differences between American and European race-tracks. Many US circuits were still airport courses which were flat and tended to have mostly acute corners, the type of courses which favoured coal cart suspensions and high torque/horsepower engines. European tracks, on the other hand, consisted of elevation and camber changes with as many sweeping corners as tight ones. On this type of track the Elite excelled with its supple suspension, powerful brakes and high-revving engine.

Nonetheless, the SCCA feared a similar 'runaway' in the US, so they placed the Elite in a class with much larger-engined cars. This was 'E Production' which included Austin Healey 100-4s and 6s, Alfa Veloces, TR-3s, Elva Couriers, Sunbeam Alpines, Porsche 1500s and 1600s, Morgan Plus 4s and MGA twin cams. The standard Elite with its single SU and cast iron exhaust manifold did pretty well in this company, but the SE and the Supers simply blew them all away.

The SCCA did not want to do battle with Colin Chapman over the Elite as it had with the Seven. It seems that the American club had painted itself into a corner over the options list on the Lotus Super Seven and in the end had to declare the full race version (the so-called SCCA 109E, built expressly for American racing) essentially too fast to race! Chapman was furious and cited numerous examples of the SCCA's favouritism, for example the Ferrari 250GT with up to six Weber carbs, or cars being allowed to run in production classes without the required number having been built, like the first Cobras, the Simca Abarth and Abarth Porsches.

Rather than get into a technical inspector's nightmare by listing acceptable options, the SCCA decided to classify the Elite based on stage of engine tune. The Stage I Climax kept the car in E Production, Stage II in D (Alfa Romeo Supers and Giulias, Arnolt Bristols, Healey 3000s, MGB 1600s, Porsche S-90s, TR-4s and TVR 1600s). The Stage III or Super Elites went into class C which included cars like the AC Bristol, Alfa Sprint Zagato, Daimler SP250, Jag 120 to 150S, Morgan Super Sports and the TVR 1800. During its competitive life span in the US,

Mike O'Neil racing with an early SCCA roll bar at Santa Barbara in 1967. (Photographer unknown)

Norman Hart rolls his Elite at Santa Barbara in 1960 and escapes without injury. Notice that he has nearly fallen completely out of his car. (Barry Taylor)

the Elite did well although it never approached the all-conquering reputation it enjoyed in Europe.

Roll bars

Interestingly, the SCCA pioneered the use of roll bars in club racing and made them mandatory long before their value was appreciated in Europe. Initially, the Elite was considered strong enough, because of the windscreen hoop, to race without one although experience with the back of the roof caving in during a roll-over proved the wisdom of their installation.

Although Elites tended to look bad after a shunt because fibreglass splintered and disintegrated so dramatically, the safety of the material was readily apparent in that damage was almost always localized at the point of impact. Tremendous amounts of energy could be dissipated in the Elite's collapsible structure before harm came to the driver. If the Elite had a weakness in a roll-over or a bad crash, it was the ease with which the doors parted company with their attachment points. Other than that, the car had an admirable record of allowing its drivers to walk away from the most fearsome of crashes, and even then the cars could be put right again, as we will see in Chapter 13.

Chapter 11

On the road

When the Lotus Elite was introduced to an amazed public in October 1957, there was absolutely no equivalent in all of motordom. The fibreglass monocoque aside, there was no other grand touring car in the world that featured four-wheel independent suspension, a light alloy overhead cam engine, four-wheel disc brakes and an aerodynamic shape that was universally acclaimed as being not only beautiful but also extremely low drag as well. That the Elite was built to 'an advanced specification' was evidenced by press reaction, using words like 'sensation', 'landmark' and 'milestone' to describe the car. When the Elite appeared at the race-tracks, at the hands of Ian Walker and John Lawry, the public's interest grew ever more intense, as did that of the motoring press.

Unfortunately, as we saw in Chapter 2, the Elite's début was somewhat premature because of the lengthy development period which was necessary to get the car ready for production. As a result, the prototypes differed in significant details from later cars, so Chapman was understandably reluctant to offer them for magazine road tests. As the months passed after Earls Court, requests for cars became more persistent until, finally, several enquiries were tinged with scepticism that the Elite might not even be a serious effort. Chapman had to do something to appease the media.

Technical explanations

For some of the questions put by press and public alike, it became apparent that the Elite may have been exciting at first acquaintance but it was also somewhat misunderstood. To correct this, Chapman provided the magazines with press packages which included photographs of the monocoque (the Earls Court show prototype) under construction, and background information of its design and construction.

Principal to this discussion, of course, was a short dissertation on GRP and its use in the construction of the Elite's body/chassis. There was also a description of the car's engine, suspension and drive train. One of the interesting bits of information released through Hornsey was that the bare body/chassis weighed 200 lb, or 10 lb more than the Lotus Eleven spaceframe complete with its alloy bodywork.

Sports Car and Lotus Owner published this kind of technical article in November 1957, and *MotorSport* did the same in February 1958. *The Motor* did a complete appraisal of the Elite in its June 22 1960 issue, but this article was a little different in that it consisted of an analysis based on their own observations and testing. Among other items they explained the geometry of the Series II suspension. They also announced that wind tunnel tests had placed the Elite's drag coefficient at 0.29 which was extraordinary considering that most other cars of the period could achieve no better than 0.4, and the really good ones were between that and 0.3.

Driving impressions

Unfortunately, the technical articles appeased no one, and the clamour for road test cars persisted. Chapman partly gave in by announcing that a few cars would be loaned for 'driving impressions'. No road tests,

Above *A publicity photo of one of the three works cars used extensively for magazine road tests.* (Michael Boys)

with stopwatches and Tapley meters for performance tests, just 'scat of the pants' subjective impressions.

Sports Car and Lotus Owner was the first to publish a driving impression and the article was written by none other than Ian Walker, and his comments were about EL 5. 'It is the most exciting car I have

ever driven, let alone owned, and I must confess I find myself looking into shop windows to see the reflection as I pass by!'

Walker was very careful not to give much away because his response to 'What'll she do?' was a simple statement that he did not know. 'Up to this point I have restricted revs to 6,500, which represents a speed of 108 mph with the rear axle ratio fitted (4.55 to 1). Assuming one used 7,000 rpm and a touring axle of 3.9 to 1, the theoretical top speed would be 136 mph. From the way the car pulls and accelerates right through the speed range I would imagine that this theoretical top speed would be quite possible.'

Walker went on to say that hills did not slow the car at all and the high average motorway speeds into which the car settled only became apparent when coming up behind other vehicles. The rate of closure was very fast indeed.

Walker praised the Elite's road-holding which he said inspired more confidence than any car he had ever driven. Corners could be taken under full power and a slide or drift could be easily adjusted by either steering wheel or throttle. The brakes were impressive and stopped the car in a straight line with no sign of fade.

Walker said that he liked the driving position and found it extremely comfortable, although the seats were not of the 'armchair variety'. All of the controls came readily to hand and were situated in exactly the right places. The instruments were easy to read and the only thing he found wanting was with regard to the accelerator pedal, which he felt was not long enough.

The next driving impression to be published in the enthusiasts' press was by David Phipps in the November 1958 issue of *Sports Car and*

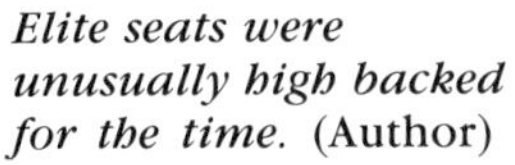

Elite seats were unusually high backed for the time. (Author)

Lotus Owner. Phipps went on to become the most prolific writer on the Elite in the 'sixties because he also contributed articles in *Motor Racing* and *Autosport* besides authoring the *Profile Publication* on the Lotus 14. He was so enthusiastic about the car that he bought one for himself and used it extensively in the UK and on the Continent.

In the first couple of paragraphs of Phipps's *Motor Racing* article (May 1958) he clarified Chapman's dilemma. 'The Elite received so much publicity on its (premature) announcement in the autumn of 1957, followed by adverse criticism as time went by and production models failed to materialize, that it would perhaps be timely to give an idea of the amount of development work which has taken place in recent months. No one who saw the Elites raced last year can doubt the car's performance potential, although not until one has driven an Elite can the manner in which it performs be appreciated.'

After explaining development problems such as body trimming, sound damping and 'making the doors fit', Phipps went on to say that the car had to be made into a 'touring car, acceptable to all and not just to rabid enthusiasts who will put up with a certain amount of inconvenience to obtain a vehicle in which road worthiness and performance are virtually unsurpassed.'

Phipps, apparently, felt that the Elite was so different from the normal sports car that a description of the driving position was in order. He described the seating position as so low that the feet and seat were nearly on the same level, and that the angle and size of the steering wheel might appear a little unusual at first.

To demonstrate his objectivity, he complained that the handbrake pressed hard on the driver's left knee during a long journey, but to even matters out, the vertical door handle did the same to the driver's right knee. Other than that, his impressions were very similar to those of Walker, even down to the ease with which the Elite could be steered on the throttle. Phipps described certain geography, which readers undoubtedly recognized at once, to explain how the Elite handled: 'The limited wheel lock required on the relatively mild hairpins of the Col de la Faucille, in the Juras, made it much less tiring to drive than a car with conventionally geared steering, and the attractive wood-rimmed wheel provided a good grip at all times.'

The gearbox on Phipps's car proved to be a little stiff above 5,500 rpm, but was actuated by 'a ladies' clutch—smooth and progressive'. He did mention that the noise level was considerable, but all of the faults were quickly forgotten by comparison with the Elite's performance, road-holding and reliability. He ended the article by stating that the Elite in Stage I tune was ideal for Continental cruising at around 105 mph, although its maximum was over 115. And all this while averaging over 35 miles per gallon.

And so it went for a while—motoring journalists expressed their delight at how the Elite looked and how it felt to drive. They also liked how the car handled and stopped, but they noted their displeasure at the noise it generated, the ease with which the Firestone tyres lost their treads and the sparseness of the interior. All but band leader Chris Barber, that is. In the February 1960 issue of *Sports Car and Lotus Owner*, he explained how he removed the headliner from his Elite when it began to droop during a trip to Monaco in the summer. He later had the roof flocked like current production Elites because he felt it was a more attractive and practical finish. This flocking, incidentally, was not a paint but a kind of felt that was sprayed on to the fibreglass. Tony Caldersmith remembered that only one or two cars had this type of head liner.

Ready for the road

The publication of driving impressions bought Chapman a little more time to refine his GT. By the time he was ready to offer cars for road tests, the Elite's appointments, while not exactly plush, were a far cry from a 'closed sports/racer'. For example, the exposed tops of the shock absorbers were covered with neat fibreglass housings which were included in the interior mould. An upholstered fibreglass cover concealed the spare tyre and provided a rigid shelf to stow items while travelling, including small pieces of luggage. When the cover was removed, the recess was deep enough to carry two spare tyres, a feature some designers, including Morgan, thought necessary for grand touring and one which Lotus frequently mentioned in their sales literature. There was even a simple tool roll stowed in the boot which consisted of an adjustable spanner, pliers, a plug wrench and a screwdriver.

Sound-deadening material was glued to the floor and transmission tunnel and these surfaces were finished with a carpeting (grey in colour) which had zippers over the door hinge mounts to allow easy access for adjustment. The seats and door panels were covered in leathercloth, a type of vinyl, which was available in red, black, yellow or natural tan, although yellow was eventually eliminated in Series II production.

As we have seen, the initial range of paint colours was surprisingly extensive and included lime green, BRG, light blue, dark blue, yellow, white, red and grey, although for a nominal fee the works would spray a car to suit a customer's preference. As production of the Maximar cars stabilized, the colour choice was pared down to light blue, yellow, white and red. Silver-painted wire wheels were standard, but accor-

Derek Duncan wanted to see for himself if the Elite really was a Gran Turismo so in 1963 he took his car for a drive around Switzerland. The peak in the background is the Lauterbrunnen Breithorn at 12,399 feet. (Derek Duncan)

The Elite dashboard featured a full compliment of instruments. Notice that the shape of the panel somewhat resembled the profile of the car. (Author)

6 SME was not one car but rather a works registration number transferred to any car that needed to be put on the road for photography, testing or transportation. (Spillman and Ramsey Ltd)

ding to the options list chrome-plated rims were available on special order. Also optional were a Smith's radio and a Smith's heater/demister unit.

No one wanted to drill a hole in the bodywork to fit a normal radio antenna (although some Elites had aerials mounted on the leading edge of the roof), so an effort was made to utilize the rear bumper. Unfortunately, the stainless steel by itself proved marginal at noise suppression. It was discovered, however, that the bumper could be made to work by filling its cavity with silver foil and then running a copper wire down the centre and soldering an end to the antenna wire which led to the radio. Only a few cars used this rather exotic solution especially after someone fitted a normal antenna in the boot and found it worked perfectly. Although FM signals could be received without significant engine shielding, AM stations were lost to ignition-induced static.

Standard fittings to the interior included a courtesy light, windscreen washers, parcel trays for both the driver and passenger (later in production only the passenger was treated to this shelf), map pockets in the doors, two-speed windscreen wipers and instrument lights on a rheostat. As mentioned earlier, the side windows on SI cars were stored in fabric envelopes while the SII Elites had pockets in the seat backs for this purpose.

The instrument panel featured a large (4 inch diameter) tach and speedo flanked by smaller fuel, ammeter and combined water temperature and oil pressure gauges. A novel and highly useful fitting was a stalk which protruded from the corner of the dash panel, near the steering wheel rim. A downward movement of the stalk sounded two powerful horns while an upward flick flashed the lights for overtaking.

6 SME

Chapman employed a clever licensing ruse when the time came to put a works car on the road for development, publicity or magazine work. He simply took some numbers off a hook on the wall and stuck them on the car. The registration he used for the Elite was 6 SME but he had used 9 EHX on the Lotus Nine and XAR 11 (also DEC 494) on the Eleven. The practice was of course, frowned on, by the authorities and over the years they had given Chapman several warnings.

When it came time to loan cars to magazines for road tests, which usually took several days to conbuct, he had no choice but to properly register the cars. From 1960 onwards he used three Elites for road tests and publicity photos and they wore consecutive registration numbers, 6573 AR, 6574 AR and 6575 AR.

Road tests

Road & Track magazine in America had the distinction of publishing the first road test of a Lotus Elite in their January 1960 issue, but they did so by obtaining a privately owned car. The chassis number was 1047 and it was the first Elite invoiced for export to Jay Chamberlain.

The first thing *R&T* noted was how tiny the car appeared, but also how easily it accommodated drivers (and passengers) over six feet in height. They thought the seats were 'among the very best we've ever tried, for comfort' and the steering wheel was angled for straight arm driving. In short, their impressions echoed those published in earlier accounts. By May 1960, *The Motor*, *Autosport* and *Autocar* had published their own tests. As can be seen from the accompanying table, the objective data was strikingly similar. It is interesting to note here that all UK road tests were conducted on Bristol-bodied Series II Elites. Chapman believed that they were a better road car than the Maximar versions.

Contemporary road test data (all cars tested were Stage I)

Magazine	Price	Weight (lb)	$\frac{1}{4}$ mile time (sec)	$\frac{1}{4}$ mile speed (mph)	Top speed (mph)	Mpg
Road & Track	$5,244.00*	1,420	18.0	73	111	30/35
The Motor	£1,949 (inc PT)	1,456	18.4	—	111	34.1
Autosport	£1,949	—	17.4	80	108	30/40
The Autocar	£1,949	1,456	18.8	75	112	34.4

* The exchange rate in 1960 was $2.80 to the pound ($2.80 × 1,949 = $5,457.00)

All testers found the pedals spaced just right for the 'heel and toe' technique and the other controls were an equal delight. The gearbox, on the other hand, was too stiff and the brakes required very high pedal pressures at low speeds. For example, *Autocar* recorded 100 lb effort to stop the car from 30 mph at 0.70g. The distance this manoeuvre took, incidentally, was 43 feet. Despite small overall dimensions, the testers praised the amount of elbow room inside and the fact that, with the side windows removed, no rain entered the cockpit and a cigarette could be lit without shielding the match!

The testers found the noise level too high, the side windows a little fiddly, the absence of a boot or bonnet stay inconvenient, and the engine vibration around 4,500 rpm in top gear a little annoying.

When the slide rules and stopwatches were set aside, however, the comments on how the Elite behaved on the road were universally

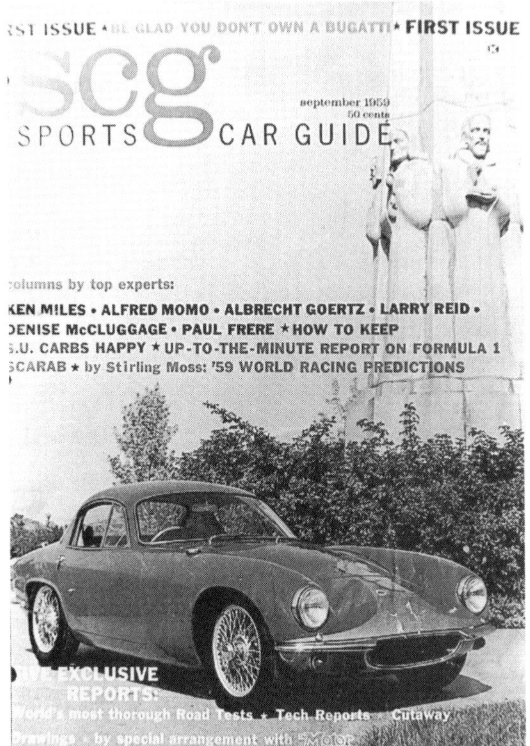

superlative. *The Motor* said, 'An immensely desirable property for anyone who wants to enjoy covering big daily mileages.' John Bolster, writing for *Autosport*, remarked, 'In Greek mythology there were gentlemen called centaurs who were half man and half horse and I am sure that I became half Bolster and half Lotus as I flicked the Elite through the corners.' And finally, *The Autocar* summed it all up by stating, 'An outstanding performance is obtained from a relatively small engine, and the controllability and safety in handling are as high as in any car tested by this journal.'

Of course, that much motor car had a price and the magazines said so. 'Expensive in relation to its size and weight.' 'The Elite is not a cheap car.' '. . for the well-heeled enthusiast.'

The Elite kit

When the Elite kit was introduced in October 1961, the criticism from the press that the car was too costly evaporated at once. Of course, in order to take advantage of the savings one had to be mechanically minded and have a fair knowledge of hand tools. The works quoted the average assembly time was a matter of 25 hours, but this depended to a large degree on the number of helpers available because some assemblies were both heavy and awkward to install, never mind how few bolts were required in their attachment.

Detailed assembly instructions were supplied by Lotus as well as an offer for a complete check-over at Cheshunt, just to make sure everything was in order. For a year or so, most Elites sold in the United Kingdom were in kit form which prompted the American magazine *Car and Driver* to do an article on home assembly. In the July 1962 issue it printed a story entitled 'The Lotus that Came in a Crate' which detailed how a British physician, Dr Kenneth MacDonald, put his car together.

Interestingly, *Car and Driver* thought 'partly knocked down' was a better description than CKD (completely knocked down) because the body/chassis arrived completely painted, glazed, trimmed and wired. The doors were in place and adjusted, the steering gear was on, the brake piping was attached and all the lights and instruments were installed.

The hardware that required installation included the engine and gearbox, differential and rear brakes, drive shaft, fuel tank, the exhaust system, wheels, seats and the boot and bonnet lids. Dr MacDonald encountered few snags and was particularly surprised to find the only adjustment to the fibreglass was the need to enlarge the gear lever opening.

With three helpers, one of whom was his daughter who kept the assembly instructions at the ready, Dr MacDonald built his Elite in 36 hours. 'About the only thing that marred the first rapture of owning and driving a self-assembled Elite was a high level of resonant noise within the body.' The story had a happy ending, however, because the Doctor was able to cut the din by about half with little expense by adding a layer of thick felt under the carpets on the transmission tunnel and the spare tyre platform.

Testing the Special Equipment Elite

As detailed earlier, the Special Equipment (SE) Elite was identified by a silver roof and (the advertisements promised, due to twin carbs and a four-branch exhaust) more spirited performance than the standard car. In 1963 both *Road & Track* and *The Motor* tested the SE version and found only top speed (117.5 for *The Motor* and 115 for *R&T*) to be improved. Oddly enough, quarter-mile acceleration was the same. The reasons for this included the fact that the Elite had gained weight and was up to about 1,500 lb. The SE was fitted with the ZF and a 4.2 diff and as a result was slightly slower off the line than the standard car with the MG box and 4.5 final drive. As it happened, fuel economy suffered as well, and *Road & Track* averaged 32 mpg while *The Motor* got only 27.5.

Of course, the Elite never was much of a drag racer, so the acceleration curve was a lot less important than what happened when the engine was up on revs. Both of the testers agreed that the car had lost none of its ability and had the added bonus of the ZF gearbox which was a sheer delight to use. The Royalite interior scored high marks as well for its functional good looks. Alas, the criticisms were the same as they had always been. The car was too noisy, the boot and bonnet lids had to be held up by hand because there was no provision for support rods or counter-balancing springs, and the hand brake was marginal in holding power. Most owners fashioned their own bonnet stay, incidentally, by shaping a block of wood to fit under the right-hand hinge. A length of dowelling served the same purpose for the boot.

The Elite clubs

In 1969, Michael and Sue Taverner formed Club Elite for the purpose of keeping alive a car the factory seemed to want to forget. Parts sources were drying up, fewer garages were interested in servicing the car and owners were getting desperate for help. The Taverners published a simple newsletter every month for five years which grew into a world-wide registry of cars and owners. The enthusiasm of this group was evident not only in the gathering of the normal historical information but also in the development of a technical library for service and repair.

The Taverners turned the club over to Michael Frazer in 1974 who guided the organization for two years before a proper committee was formed with Miles Wilkins (see Chapter 13) elected as Chairman. Miles held this post for nine years when the club went through another reorganization. Miles, who also operated Fibreglass Services (an Elite restoration business), was able, through his purchasing power, to convince some of the old suppliers to tool and reproduce Elite parts. He also discovered all of the Elite's idiosyncrasies and passed this information to members so they could do their own service and repair. For the first time in years, Elite enthusiasts had not only a place to get Elite parts, but also an expert to tell them how they were to be installed. Miles also used the newsletter to detail preventive maintenance as well. He went on to expand the scope of the club by promoting social events and an annual test day at the Goodwood circuit where owners could exercise their Elites at racing speeds.

In 1987 a new committee was elected with John Chatwin as Chairman. The new organization reaffirmed the Club's purpose as a link between owners to keep the cars on the road, but with a new emphasis on social events which included an annual general meeting and exhibitions at major historic car shows. Club Elite also promised to keep members posted on the efforts of members who were involved in

Right *Club Elite (Great Britain) insignia.* (Club Elite)

Far right *Club Elite of North America insignia.* (Club Elite NA)

historic racing and to involve themselves in a cooperative project with Club Elite of North America to locate and identify every Elite that still existed.

Club Elite of North America

After several hesitant attempts to follow the lead of the club in England, Bill Hutton (see Chapter 13) came to the aid of American and Canadian Elite owners by forming Club Elite of North America in 1971. Because of the tremendous size of the geography of the United States, Bill's organization was based strictly on correspondence by means of a bi-monthly newsletter. His emphasis was also on the historical and technical aspects of the Elite, and his newsletters featured articles on Elite history, maintenance and repair.

As it happened, Bill also entered the Elite parts business and was able to assist club members in securing much-needed hardware, either from his own stores or overseas. Bill (and his wife Barbara, who did the typing) ran Club Elite of North America for half a dozen years and developed the newsletter from a simple typewritten sheet to a pictorial leaflet.

After Bill Hutton gave up the reins of the club, the organization saw a succession of secretaries (in reality, President, Secretary and Treasurer!), including the author, Barry Swackhamer and Alex Bollinger. In 1989 the head of the Club was Mike Ostrov whose goal was to complete the task of registering every Lotus Elite known to man. The results of his efforts are given in Appendix II—the Elite chassis list with the names of current owners and their country of residence!

Dennis Ortenburger and 1461

I have owned 1461 since 1966 and my experience with the car is probably the same as most owners, except perhaps that I have owned my car a little longer than the average. My Elite has had a distinctive paint job for over 20 years (originally it was cobalt blue which had been polished through to the primer on the roof and wing tops) which I have long maintained was good for another 10 mph top speed. Others, however, have likened the yellow racing stripes (over BRG) to a kind of Christmas wrap where the ribbon goes completely underneath the package, rather than a real racing car with its stripe draped properly on top.

The Elite is a superb road car and long-distance tourer as long as it is absolutely right. Unfortunately, mine on purchase was not. There was

The author's Elite at a concours in 1971. (Author)

The author buckling up for a ten lapper at Laguna Seca. (Marlene Ortenburger)

a horrible clutch imbalance that threatened to vibrate the car to bits and the ratios in the MG box seemed all wrong for American roads. A ZF gearbox, meticulous balancing and spot welding the pressure plate springs in their seats solved the initial problems. That and the addition of more sound-damping material quietened the car to the point where Marlene (my faithful sidekick since 1965) would fall asleep in the passenger seat after a 20-minute ride. Of course, I could still hear the clutch-driven disc making contact with the flywheel on pulling away from rest, and at 100 mph normal conversation was quite impossible, but the sounds were not all that unpleasant. In fact, if a little fantasy was indulged, like pretending I was chasing John Wagstaff through the Mulsanne kink, the noise was oddly pleasurable.

The Elite has always reminded me of a front-engined Formula Junior in the way it dives into corners, although certainly a more comfortable one, due to the great seats and the surprising amount of room there is in which to work—even for the author's six-foot frame. All of the controls (save the brakes) respond to the lightest touch and the smallest of inputs, although even the brakes (1461 has alloy calipers front and rear) can be made to work better on the street with significantly less pedal effort by having the friction material replaced with a modern metallic compound.

My first decade with 1461 ran the gamut from commuting, to touring, to light *concours* duty with a slalom thrown in now and again for diversion. The *concours* scene was a peculiar one where the competitors always seemed ready to die twice, one on seeing a fly land on their paintwork and again on observing the speck it left. Unfortunately, for those really interested in detailing their Elites, concours judges are not much impressed with the car. There is not a lot of chrome or light alloy to polish and fibreglass never quite approaches the perfection of surface of steel, and these are among the things deemed vital to the normal *concours d'élégance*.

The next ten years were spent in historic racing which proved to be satisfying and, at the same time, a little frustrating. It was exciting to be able to lap (eventually) places like Riverside and Laguna Seca as fast as the boys did in the 'sixties, but it was also a little annoying to see cars like bug-eye Sprites pulling away on the straights and then having their drivers tell you later that it's hard to cheat in a Lotus Elite. Still, the exhilaration of driving a car as well mannered and above all as safe as the Elite was loads of fun. That, and to find the early driving impressions were absolutely correct, that the Elite really could be set up for a high-speed corner and without moving the steering wheel, the direction of the nose could be altered by simply pushing or lifting off the accelerator.

My Elite's career came full circle when, in 1983, I retired the car from racing and returned it to the street and a gentler pace of life. A little battle-scarred and stone-chipped and a mite loose in the joints was the extent of the wear and tear of the exercise. Oh, and the steel timing gear still makes a terrible metallic whirring noise and the Webers have an awful bark when they are punched open, but the pleasure I derive from slipping behind that outrageously large diameter steering wheel has not diminished in 23 years!

The author in close company at the Monterey Historic in 1983. (Ron Brown)

Chapter 12

Miniatures, replicas, special Elites and the copycat

Elite miniatures

The hobby of collecting model cars is a delightfully infectious pastime that has experienced extraordinary growth since the days of the Elite. What began as simple toy cars have progressed to precision miniatures which feature, in some cases, amazingly accurate detail. The size of the cars can range, for example, from over 10 inches in length ($\frac{1}{18}$ scale) to a couple of inches ($\frac{1}{43}$) with the latter, in recent years, having become the collectors' standard. Prices of new examples and the value of older models can run from a few pounds to hundreds, and manufacturers can be found worldwide. Interestingly, the Elite is represented in both the toy category and the precision miniature, as well as a few other types that fall somewhere in between.

SMTS (Scale Model Technical Services) was a die-cast metal miniature, made in England in $\frac{1}{43}$rd scale. The manufacturer supplied four Elites (all were available in 1989) which were superbly detailed renditions of DAD 10, LOV 1, the Lumsden/Riley Le Mans-winning WUU 2, which is pictured here, and a road version in the SE colour scheme.

Bandai was a Japanese-made tinplate model in $\frac{1}{18}$th scale, and was a toy that came equipped with a friction motor. It was produced in the 1970s and was exported to toy stores in the UK, America and Europe. Although lacking in many details, the model has a certain charm despite the words 'Lotus Elan' stamped on the undercarriage and on the box! This Elite came in either red or blue.

Super Shells were plastic kits, made in England in about $\frac{1}{43}$rd scale. The Elite was offered in the 1970s as a slot-car body, devoid of a chassis and wheels. A later version included these items so that a display model could be assembled. Made of surprisingly hefty plastic, the Super Shells Elite was slightly bloated in appearance and lacked many details but was significant because it was one of the first attempts to model Chapman's monocoque GT.

Lancer was a vacuum-formed, transparent shell made in the USA in $\frac{1}{24}$th scale. During the slot-car rage in the 1970s, numerous manufacturers built body shells for proprietary slot-car chassis. These shells were very flimsy, vacuum-formed pieces that lacked detail and substance. They nonetheless apparently took paint well and looked good enough to enable slot-car racers to field a wide variety of cars on their grids.

Superbly detailed SMTS 1/43rd white metal Elites could be obtained as kits or ready built. (Author)

This 1/18th scale Elite was a tin-plate Japanese toy made by Bandai. (Barry Swackhamer)

This plastic Super Shell Elite kit was manufactured in England in the 'seventies and is now quite rare. (Author)

This curious shell was a slot car body built in 1/24th scale and made in the USA by Lancer. (Author)

Scuderia Scale was a vacuum-formed shell made in the USA in about $\frac{1}{25}$th scale, and was another type of slot-car shell that consisted of a thin, vacuum-formed body, undercarriage and dash panel. Apparently, the instruction sheet explained that a display model could be built up using bits scavenged from other kits, such as Revell's Austin Healey 3000.

Grand Prix Models were die-cast, white metal kits made in England in $\frac{1}{43}$rd scale. Before SMTS came on to the modelling scene, the Grand Prix Models' Lotus Elites (one version was a road car and the other was the Hobbs/Gardner 1962 Le Mans winner) were state-of-the-art miniatures. Typical of white metal kits of the '70s, they required much finishing and fiddling to end up with a nice display piece, but the detailing was quite good as was the proportion and feel.

Roadace Models were solid resin miniatures made in England in $\frac{1}{100}$th and $\frac{1}{200}$th scales. Roadace was the name of a road racing parlour game

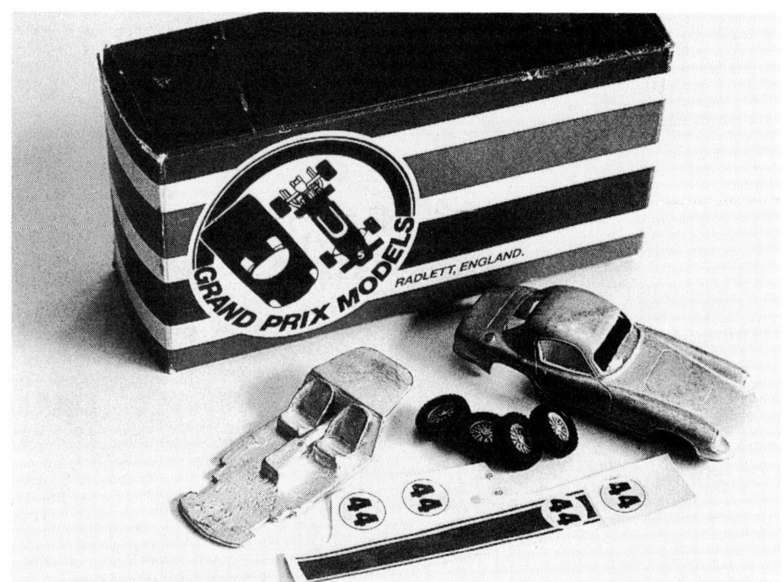

Grand Prix models 1/43rd scale white metal kit. (Author)

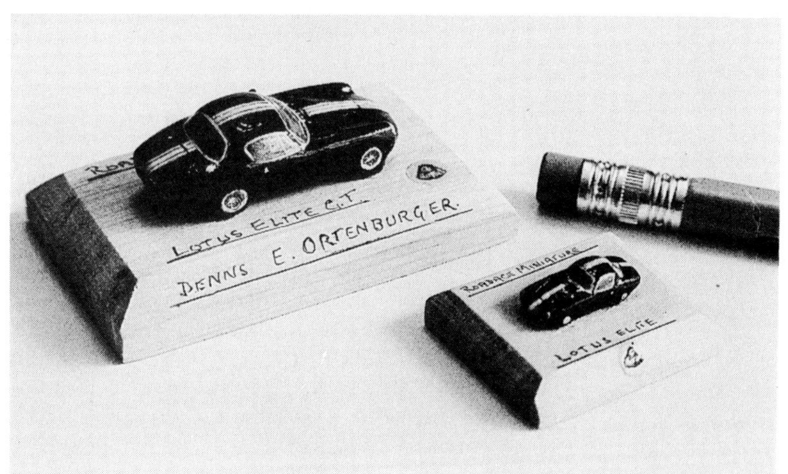

Roadace miniatures came in 1/100th and 1/200th scale and were made of resin. (Author)

Kogure of Japan manufactured this highly detailed plastic kit in the mid-'seventies. The instruction sheet resembled real car assembly. (Author)

game and a series of sports car miniatures manufactured in the mid-1960s. The game pieces were $\frac{1}{200}$ scale and were superb (considering their tiny size) renditions of the real thing. Roadace models were larger, at $\frac{1}{100}$th scale, and were hand-painted to an almost unbelievably high standard of detail by the man responsible for Roadace, Ken Dolton.

Kogure's plastic kit model of the Lotus Elite was a superb $\frac{1}{20}$ scale miniature of Japanese manufacture. The extremely detailed kit was moulded in red plastic and was powered by a small electric motor. Interestingly, the engine was mounted in front and drive was taken to the rear wheels by a shaft! Two batteries were held in the boot. The Kogure was available in the mid-'seventies but was a rare item even in established model outlets. Today it is as rare as the Roadace models.

The Kellison replica

The fibreglass car body industry in the United States took off a little slower than it did in the UK, but by the early 1960s there were several well-established companies supplying a variety of shells for proprietary chassis. One, by the name of Kellison Inc, in Lincoln, California, manufactured a delightful array of sports car bodies including, among others, a Sting Ray coupé, D Jag, 1932 Austin and Lotus Elite!

The Elite was, according to Kellison sales literature, an exact duplicate of a 1962 Lotus Elite coupé outside body shell with all flanges, openings and lids! 'Includes inner and outer hood, doors and deck lid sections. Body shell fits all Triumph TR2, 3 or 4 chassis or build your own custom chassis. Wheel base 88 inches. 130 inches long by 58 inches wide by 46 inches high. Per kit $595.00.'

In 1989 Jim Kellison was still in business building fibreglass Cobra replicas. In a conversation with Barry Swackhamer, past Secretary of Club Elite USA, Kellison recalled the Elite with mixed emotions. The

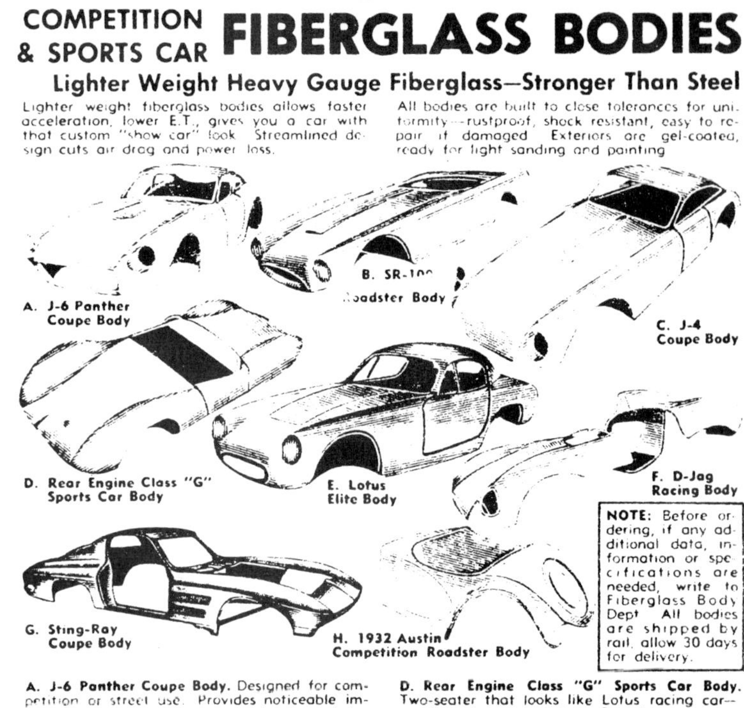

COMPETITION & SPORTS CAR **FIBERGLASS BODIES**

Lighter Weight Heavy Gauge Fiberglass—Stronger Than Steel

Lighter weight fiberglass bodies allows faster acceleration, lower E.T., gives you a car with that custom "show car" look. Streamlined design cuts air drag and power loss.

All bodies are built to close tolerances for uniformity—rustproof, shock resistant, easy to repair if damaged. Exteriors are gel-coated, ready for light sanding and painting.

NOTE: Before ordering, if any additional data, information or specifications are needed, write to Fiberglass Body Dept. All bodies are shipped by rail, allow 30 days for delivery.

A. J-6 Panther Coupe Body. Designed for competition or street use. Provides noticeable improvement in handling, roadability and increased speed. Complete with all paneling, including inner fender panels, floor pan, dash panel. Includes inner and outer doors, deck and trunk lids. Body shell is of 1-pc. construction (doors, hood, deck lid are separate). Reinforced doors and hood come in two sections. Other features: lipped and flanged hood openings; scooped hood to clear air cleaners, door jambs installed and drilled for hinges; door jamb rubber sealing mounts installed, doors are assembled, ready to bolt in position; door striker plate box installed, grille openings cut and flanged, driveshaft tunnel and transmission cover installed, deck lid cut out and reinforced. Overall body size; 66" wide, 49" high, 6" ground clearance.
No. 79-5377F—Per Kit **$550.00**

B. SR-100 Roadster Body. Fits Chev or Ford shortened chassis. Corvette and T-bird available as outside shell only. Ideal for competition or show car use, gives you performance and handling characteristics similar to European sports cars. No inner paneling — deck, trunk, and doors molded in, can be cut for functional use. Complete with hood, deck and door stiffeners—provisions for easy installation of hinges and locks. Ready for light sanding and painting. Overall body size: 165" long, 68" wide. Wheel base: 99 to 101" (100" optimum), front tread: 54" to 56", rear tread 55" to 58". Height to cowl: 35½", weight of shell: 125 lbs.
No. 79-5626F—Per Kit **$295.00**

C. J-4 Coupe Body. For competition use only—available as outside shell only. No inner paneling but doors are included (not assembled). Hinge boxes are already installed in body for mounting doors. Does not include seat buckets, firewall, dash, or inner fender panels. Ideal low priced fiberglass body for the buff who wants to construct a car to his own individual taste. 98" wheelbase, tread width 56" to 60".
No. 79-5627F—Per Kit **$329.95**

D. Rear Engine Class "G" Sports Car Body. Two-seater that looks like Lotus racing car—excellent for competition. Complete with nose section, tail section, and two doors (doors not assembled). Also includes dash panel, two bucket seats. No inner paneling included. Wheelbase: 86" to 90", tread width: 48" to 52". Weight: 60 lbs.
No. 79-5628F—Per Kit **$195.00**

E. Lotus Elite Body. Exact duplicate of 1962 Lotus Elite Coupe outside body shell, with all flanges, openings, and lips. Includes inner and outer hood, doors, and deck lid sections. Body shell fits all Triumph TR 2, 3, 4 chassis, or build your own custom chassis. Wheelbase: 88"; 130" long x 58" wide x 46" high.
No. 79-5629F
Per Kit **$595.00**

F. D-Jag Racing Body. Replica of D-Jag racing car body includes tail section and nose section only plus two bucket seats. (Doors and lower body panels can be easily made of flat stock aluminum or body metal). Wheelbase can be made to any length (determined by width of doors). Wheelbase: 90" to 92", tread width: 46" to 51"; 160" long x 60" wide x 29" high. Weight 90 lbs.
No. 79-5630F—Per Kit **$249.50**

G. Sting-Ray Coupe Body. Complete outer shell only—no inner paneling. Includes doors (not assembled) and deck lid. Does not include dash panel, upholstery, floor pans, or inner fender panels. Excellent body shell for building up a sports car gosser.
No. 79-5631F—Per Kit **$595.00**

H. 1932 Austin Competition Roadster Body. "Must" for the roadster enthusiast! Design of this body permits exceptional weight transfer to rear axle—provides superior front end stability. Body is well reinforced and includes firewall with integrated flange.
No. 79-5348F—Per Kit **$129.50**

All fiberglass bodies are shipped from our California warehouse. Payment in full is required to facilitate handling. Our usual 100% satisfaction or money back guarantee applies.

NOTE: Before ordering, if any additional data, information or specifications are needed write "Fiberglass Body Department."

NOTE: Allow 30 days delivery on all bodies. All bodies will be shipped by rail.

The ubiquitous J.C. Whitney catalogue in America listed the Kellison line of plastic car bodies. The Lotus Elite was 'an exact duplicate of a 1962 Elite'. (J.C. Whitney)

moulds were originally intended to provide replacement panels for damaged Elites, but Kellison saw a way to construct a relatively inexpensive replica by mounting his shell on a Triumph chassis. Alas, he sold only two complete bodies for this purpose and in 1969 he broke up the moulds and hauled them off to the dump.

The GPJ replica

Another attempt at an Elite replica apparently only got to the prototype stage before the project was abandoned. This one was conjured up in the replicar phenomenon that began in earnest in the 1970s and showed no sign of abating at the end of the '80s. These cars, usually sold as kits, were a significant advance over the fibreglass body shells of the 1950s and '60s because of more highly developed assembly methods that almost guaranteed satisfactory results. A few replicars in recent times were so well done and finely detailed that it was difficult on first acquaintance to distinguish them from the genuine article.

The GPJ Company of Toronto, Canada, was a kit car assembler, one of several such businesses in North America whose sole purpose was to build up and detail DIY automobiles. GPJ displayed a plastic Porsche Speedster at the 1985 Toronto Kit Car Show that defied detection. They also displayed a partially finished Lotus Elite body shell which had been moulded by their shops.

GPJ apparently intended to manufacture the car in kit form around a proprietary engine and suspension system. Unfortunately, the project fizzled out while still in the prototype stage. Pity—it looked interesting.

The fastback special

An often-photographed customized Elite of the 1960s was the handiwork of one of the contributors to this book, Anthony Bates. As will be detailed in the next chapter, Tony operates one of the world's premier Elite restoration shops, but in 1963 he was a pilot with the RAF who had just acquired the 1962 Motor Show Elite, finished in 'Amazon metallic green' and chrome wire wheels, no less.

The car was in extremely poor condition, despite its youth, so the first order of business was a complete restoration. On stripping the finish off the back end, Tony found 'about 90 per cent filler' but the real drama was that Lotus could not supply a new rear section for at least four months. Tony decided to build his own mould (while in the service he had spent some free time taking courses on the use of fibreglass), but since his first child was getting too big to travel in her mother's arms, he thought he might alter the cabin to take a third seat in what was originally the spare tyre recess.

Rear view of A.N.E. Bates' superb fastback Elite. (A.N.E. Bates)

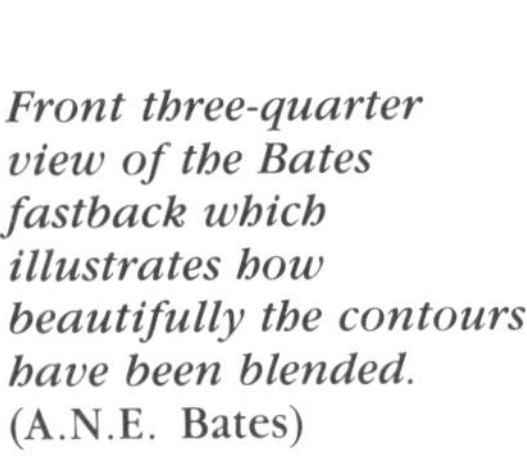

Front three-quarter view of the Bates fastback which illustrates how beautifully the contours have been blended. (A.N.E. Bates)

To Tony's eye the only visually pleasing solution to a revised roof line was a fastback. This design also allowed sufficient headroom for the third passenger and greater luggage capacity than the original. Work began with the construction of a wooden pattern from which the mould would be taken. Interestingly, Tony was able to do this without cutting or dismantling the car, other than removing the boot lid.

The wooden pattern was lathered with polyester filler and laboriously shaped and sanded, a process, Tony recalled, that took weeks to complete. After the roof, which included a new tail section, was pulled from the mould and grafted on to the body, the pattern was altered to make a mould for the opening rear hatch, as on the Jag XKE coupé. Yet another mould was made for the interior skin so as to keep the finished look of the original. The job was completed by fabricating a special fuel tank that incorporated a recess for the spare tyre.

The results were superb, both aesthetically and in the quality of workmanship. The Bates family enjoyed the fastback for several years and then sold it to a fellow RAF pilot. In 1989 Tony assumed that it still resided in England, although exactly where was not known because its registration had been allowed to lapse and the owner had not responded to the registry.

The Modsport special

An American serviceman by the name of Phil Cannon was completing a two-year tour of duty in Europe in 1976 when he spied an advertisement in *Motor Sport* magazine. The car was described as an Elite with Elan 26R components, including a full race twin-cam engine. On viewing the Lotus, Phil was told that the car had been successful on the racetrack before being retired in 1972 and trimmed for street use.

Close inspection revealed some clever engineering that incorporated the rear section of an Elan backbone chassis into the Elite's structure. A roll bar was welded to the Elan chassis member as were two parallel bars that extended forward on the Elite's underside to the engine bay. Most of this reinforcement was neatly covered with fibreglass.

The suspension was Elan 26R in the rear and fabricated upper and lower wishbones in front. Koni double adjustable shock absorbers were used at both ends of the car with adjustable spring perches in front. Spring rates were 128 psi in front and 100 in the rear. Adjustable anti-roll bars were used, 1 inch in diameter in front and a half an inch in diameter at the rear. The brakes were Elite discs in front and Elan discs in the rear but separate master cylinders were fitted along with a balance bar to adjust fore and aft bias.

A 3.77 limited slip differential with sliding spline half shafts was used as was an oil cooler with an electric pump to circulate the lubricant. The wheels fitted to the Modsport Elite were $8\frac{1}{2} \times 13$ inch, Kong-Heath centrelock magnesium items.

The engine was a dry sumped Ford twin-cam equipped with the big valve option and Chris Steel rally cams. Cooling was handled by what Phil Cannon called a monster radiator canted over 30 degrees and topped with a Kenlow electric fan. An engine oil cooler was installed just ahead of the radiator. The horsepower rating was 145 bhp and the car went like blazes. Cannon lost no time in writing his cheque and arranging for transport to the States.

The Modsport Elite on display at a club gathering. (Phil Cannon)

The powerplant for the Modsport Elite is an Elan twin cam. (Phil Cannon)

Back home in Pennsylvania he began competing in autocross and achieved several FTDs and a series championship. In 1988 the Modsport Elite was treated to a complete strip down and re-paint, and Cannon's plan was to continue competing in this most unusual Elite.

The convertible special

As mentioned in an earlier chapter, one of the reasons why Chapman wanted to end production of the Elite was to build an open sports car, something the Elite could never have been short of a major re-design of its structure. In Chapman's original specification, the Elite's roof played a critical role in 'tying' the monocoque together. That this section was very highly stressed was evident on some early attempts at fitting fabric sun roofs and the resulting stress cracks that immediately appeared at the corners of the opening.

Still, the idea of an open Elite intrigued many enthusiasts and when a damaged car was brought to the '60s Lotus specialists Terry Eglington and Len Street in Enfield, they decided to have a go. The wrecked Elite had lost its top so the windscreen surround and its steel hoop were the first to be repaired.

A pair of $1\frac{1}{2}$ inch square tubes were welded to the door hinge posts. These tubes extended back to the rear wheel arches inside the door sills. A second pair of tubes, curved this time, were mounted inside the wheel wells and picked up both of the sill tubes and a transverse member that lay adjacent to the diff box in the boot. All of the aft reinforcement was covered in fibreglass to aid rigidity.

According to Len Street, the car looked good and behaved well. Sadly, no one thought to take a picture and the current whereabouts of this convertible Elite are unknown.

The automatic Elites

In 1961 a certain red and blue Elite, registered 5649 UE, began to win every British club event in sight and a few long-distance events on the Continent as well. The car also created a degree of controversy at many of these meetings because it was fitted with an automatic transmission. Not that automatics were particularly frowned on, but the car was definitely a 'one-off' Elite and, therefore, not homologated with the FIA.

The car belonged to David Hobbs and the gearbox was designed and built by his father for installation in small-displacement saloons. The box was called the Hobbs Mecha-Matic Transmission, model number 1015. Howard Hobbs was an Australian who emigrated to England in 1929. His life's work was the design of engine transmissions and he spent 12 years working on the Mecha-Matic.

The design utilized disc-type clutches to change a planetary gear train rather than conventional contracting bands. As a result of this there was minimal power loss which had been the major liability of contemporary automatics. The Mecha-Matic was a four-speed and featured a positive selection of intermediate gears besides a slot in which the transmission shifted completely for itself. The Mecha-Matic allowed for full engine braking yet was safety valved to prevent over-revving in case of a careless manual down shift. It was comparable in size and weight to normal gearboxes. Unfortunately, it was also very costly, so despite initial interest from Ford (GB), Volvo and others, the Mecha-Matic never caught on and the senior Hobbs was left to make hi fortune on transmissions for trains and buses!

Young David had raced a Morris Oxford in 1959 and a Jag XK 140 in 1960, both with Mecha-Matics, but unfortunately with little success. Then, in November 1960, he bought an Elite from The Chequered Flag sports car garage in Chiswick, and decided to go racing, again with one of his father's transmissions (albeit with the down change safety valves and the two start device removed). The rest, as they say, is history.

Hobbs's Elite, incidentally, was a very highly developed car. The engine had been brought up to Stage III specs by Cosworth and numerous racing modifications had been done to the body/chassis by his mechanics, Ken Taylor and ex-Lotus 'wrench' Henry Lee. Included in these modifications were the installation of full plexiglass screens in the doors and rear window, the removal of all trim and several of the lightly stressed interior panels. The boot was treated to a 15 gallon fuel tank and twin SU pumps and the battery was moved to the passenger footwell to reduce current loss in starting. The car was also fitted with a 'Costin nose' later in its career.

Seats were Lotus Formula Junior and the transmission tunnel 'radio' panel received oil temperature gauges for both engine and transmission. In an early outing Hobbs's Elite suffered a front wishbone failure when the subframe broke, so Taylor welded in a bar connecting the wishbone mounts on both sides of the car. Diff straps were installed by him as well.

Hobbs's first half-dozen races showed great speed, but niggling problems prevented a good finishing position except at the Silverstone Club meeting in mid-1961 where he was placed second in several races. The first big win came at the Lord's Taverners meeting at Brands Hatch where he took 1st, beating no less than Les Leston in DAD 10. Interestingly, Hobbs's and Pinckney's win at the Nürburgring came despite seven pit stops for engine oil; a clue, perhaps, to Hobbs's only serious trouble which was a rod that ventilated both sides of the block at the very next outing at Pescara during a three-hour enduro.

From then on Hobbs never looked back and ran up a string of 14 consecutive wins! His speed and consistency did not go unnoticed and in 1962 he joined the Peter Berry Racing Team to campaign a 3.8 and an E type Jaguar. He took the Elite out occasionally but crashed it heavily at the Clermont-Ferrand three-hour race. Lotus provided another body/chassis, which reportedly had been damaged in a road accident. In any case, all of the undamaged, original hardware, including the Mecha-Matic, was installed in the 'new' body/chassis. Hobbs evidently retired the car shortly thereafter but not without first offering it to various car magazines to test.

In December 1962, for example, *Motor Sport* magazine drove the car and reported achieving 0 to 80 mph in 16.2 seconds and 100 mph in under half a minute. Speed in gears were 44, 62, 82 and 106 mph, and the only disadvantage of driving in 'automatic' was valving that would not engage 4th gear until 5,000 rpm! Otherwise, changes were relatively smooth which allowed relaxed motoring.

Interestingly, both Stirling Moss and Jim Clark took keen notice of David Hobbs and his Mecha-Matic and they ordered their personal Elites so equipped. Tony Bates, who owns an Elite with the Jim Clark paperwork (an owner after Clark wrecked the car which required a new body/chassis and a ZF gearbox), noted that both Clark's and Moss's Elites were Special Equipment versions with yellow bodies and silver roofs. In a conversation with Len Street, Bates learned there were some problems with the Mecha-Matic.

Colin Chapman told Street to give the car (chassis 1659, registered HSH 200) a good run before handing it over to Jim Clark. He and an engineer took it to Birmingham and back via the M1 motorway. On the way back they slowed for the first exit; the box, sensing a change of speed, decided to change down, but was confused enough to try it at 80 plus miles per hour. The result was two twisted half shafts (no diff box damage), a bent steering wheel and the windscreen popping out after being hit by the engineer's head. Fortunately, he had the presence of mind to grab it before it completely left the car! This incident highlighted a problem with the Hobbs box which concerned the oil and the sensing of the pressure at which gear changes had to be made.

The Rochdale Olympic copycat

While the Elite was widely recognized as the world's first fibreglass monocoque, many enthusiasts also believed it to be the only example of an all-plastic body/chassis. This was not the case, however, because the Elite had a contemporary which was an almost exact copy of Chapman's original concept. The automobile was called the Rochdale Olympic, and although it existed in the shadow of its progenitor it was, nonetheless, quite an interesting car.

It all began in 1952 when Rochdale Motor Panels of Lancashire introduced its fibreglass automobile body shell. Until then the founders, Harry Smith and Frank Butterworth, had built aluminium bodies for special builders in the 750 Motor Club. They saw fibreglass as the material of the future and began experimenting with shapes and moulds.

Their first shell sold for £47 and was adaptable to a number of proprietary chassis. By 1955 Rochdale Motor Panels had produced a line of bodies which ranged from touring applications to racing, with a Ferrari lookalike. The quality of the Rochdale product was good and the prices were low, an unbeatable combination which ensured a steady stream of customers.

In 1956 the company took a significant leap forward by introducing a 2 + 2 GT coupé body shell for the venerable Ford 10 chassis. This was quite different from previous designs because it included inner wheel well panels, the engine bulkhead, a battery box, dashboard and part of the floor section in the primary mould! Windows and doors were supplied as well, all for a very reasonable £140. Over a thousand of these bodies were sold in a five-year production run, but by 1959 the company had made enough money to consider another advance in its product line.

The introduction of the Elite had not gone unnoticed, and Smith and Butterworth reckoned a similar car should not be beyond their capabilities. A friend of the company and an owner of a Rochdale GT coupé by the name of Richard Parker was asked to help in the design of the Rochdale monocoque. Parker was an engineer who worked at Bristol Aircraft (most suspicious, this!) and had a good knowledge of aerodynamics and plastic technology.

In mid-1959 the prototype Rochdale Olympic (named after the forthcoming 1960 Olympic games in Rome) hit the road, and after 18 months and 30,000 miles of testing was pronounced fit for production. Its monocoque required only two master moulds; the one for the

Rear three-quarter view of the Rochdale Olympic. Notice the tail-light lenses and the sun roof. (Paul Narramore)

Frontal aspect of the world's second GRP monocoque. Construction details were remarkably similar to the Elite. (Paul Narramore)

undertray was fully enclosed save for openings for the radiator, sump, trans and diff drains. All of the inner panels, engine bulkhead, dash panel, wheel wells and the like were laid-up as the upper body cured in the second master mould.

Like the Elite, the Olympic featured a built-in steel hoop over the windscreen and a front subframe, also fabricated out of steel, which supported the radiator and front suspension. Other metal reinforcements were bonded in various parts of the body/chassis to support the engine, gearbox and rear suspension. Interestingly, the body colour was incorporated in the gel coat with good, if not quite perfect, results. The works offered a paint job as an option!

Initially, the Olympic was offered only as a completely outfitted and trimmed body/chassis which required installation of Riley front suspension, a Riley engine (1.5–litre) and gearbox and a BMC rear axle. The works supplied all of the above for the unbelievably reasonable price of £670! If a buyer had a scrapped 'donor car' from which to remove the parts, the fully equipped body/chassis could be purchased for only £250.

In 1963 the Olympic was sufficiently revised in specification to call it a Phase II model. The bodywork, however, remained unchanged except for a slightly larger bonnet opening and an opening rear windscreen which, in the interests of weight-saving, was formed in Perspex. The front suspension was changed to Triumph Spitfire (including its disc brakes and rack and pinion steering) and the engine and gearbox options became the trusty Riley 1.5, the BMC 1-litre, or either the Ford 105E or 116E 1500cc pushrods.

In Phase II form, the Olympic could be purchased as a 'quick-build' kit (according to the works about 50 hours of assembly time) for £735, or as a complete car, taxed and tested, for £930. Extras included a fresh air heater and demister, laminated windscreen, rear seats, polished aluminium bumper caps, jack and spare wheel (!) and safety belts.

On the road the Rochdale Olympic proved to be a spirited performer. The 116E Ford engine took the car to a top speed of 114 mph and 0 to 60 in 11.5 seconds. The car weighed about 1,600 lb and road testers reported excellent handling, especially over rough surfaces, and good brakes. The Olympic was an inch shorter than the Elite, about 3 inches higher, 5 inches wider and shared the same tail-light lenses. It also had roll-up windows and *Motor Sport* magazine stated that 'anyone who takes a good deal of trouble in assembling his car can claim to have a "British Porsche" for the ridiculously cheap price of £735.'

Although Rochdale Olympic owners admitted that their cars lacked the Elite's pedigree, they also felt that they were not only more robust but more reliable as well. For example, Derek Bentley, of the Rochdale Register, reported in 1988 that he had covered 210,000 miles in his Phase I with minimal attention and service.

By the early 1970s Rochdale Motor Panels had turned its attention to non-automotive projects which were proving to be more profitable than cars. The Olympic had been in production for nearly ten years and total output numbered about 400 cars. Not bad for the world's second fibreglass monocoque.

Chapter 13

Restoration and maintenance

Because of its racing record, milestone automobile status and the fact that the Elite is capable of delivering all of its original performance and driving pleasure on today's roads, the car is a perfect candidate for restoration or preservation in good working condition. That, and the fact that in 1989 several cars were sold for over $25,000.00 (£13,900) in the USA and £25,000 ($45,000.00) in England, means that it makes excellent sense to take care of these cars in their old age. Fortunately, even the most neglected example can be brought back to its original, if not better than new, condition. As we will see later in this chapter, today's restorer is well taken care of by the existence of clubs and businesses that specialize in the Elite.

Fibreglass

Of benefit to 'do it yourselfers', fibreglass has lost much of its mystique over the years and many repairs are well within the capability of the amateur. The quality of both polyester and epoxy resins and their hardeners has improved as well so that new work tends to be stronger than the original material. The only drawbacks to home fibreglass work are the amount of physical hand work involved and the mess this process generates. There is also the potential health hazard in that fibreglass dust is easily inhaled unless some form of respirator or filter mask is used.

While a complete discussion of fibreglass repair is beyond the scope of this book (most retailers provide free advice), a few points will be highlighted to explain some kinds of typical Elite damage. For a better understanding of fibreglass, the reader is referred to any number of good texts on the subject including the excellent *How To Restore Fibreglass Bodywork* by Miles Wilkins (Osprey, 1984). Miles, incidentally, played a vital role in the later history of the Elite, but more on his contribution later in this chapter under 'Fibreglass Services'.

The keys to good fibreglass work are twofold—structural integrity and finishing. Structural integrity simply means making a strong repair, and this comes from using cloth saturated in properly mixed and catalysed resin to build up a damaged area. There are numerous plastic fillers on the market which sand and shape easily, but they are brittle and have no strength and should be used for nothing more than filling minor imperfections like sanding scratches or forming the gel coat. Random mat should be used in places open to view because this type of cloth does not 'telegraph' its pattern to the surface as does the woven type. The latter has superior strength, however, and can be used to good advantage in making repairs to interior load-bearing panels.

As discussed in an earlier chapter, the Elite's body/chassis was made of fibreglass cloth made rigid by the addition of a catalysed polyester resin, or in the case of most of the doors, and many boot and bonnet lids, by an epoxy resin. In both instances, although particularly with epoxy, exact proportions of catalyst (hardener) and its resin must be used to effect a thorough cure. If done carelessly, and if too much

The finish on 'double dimple' Elites, including the rear suspension recesses, was extremely well done. Notice that the Series I pick-up point was left in the mould. (Author)

hardener is used, the repair ends up unnecessarily brittle, while too little results in a soft or sticky area that may never set up and become completely rigid.

In finishing off a fibreglass repair, a great deal of hand sanding is required to smooth the new surface and to match the level of the original panel. Progressively finer grades of paper are necessary to feather the edges of the newly glassed surface so that it blends into the original without a 'scar' line. Because finish sanding is so time-consuming and laborious, it is usually the step that the amateur or cut-rate repair shop minimizes, resulting in a faint outline (or worse) to identify the site of the repair.

Tiny air bubbles result in any hand lay-up, and when sanded these appear as pin holes in the surface. These holes must be finished separately with a special kind of filler lest shrinkage, and thus surface irregularities, occurs after paint is applied. A truism is that the quality of a paint job is only as good as the surface it is sprayed on, so hours spent in finishing fibreglass pays off when the colour goes on.

Patience, stamina and a tolerance for discomfort (fibreglass dust is extremely irritating to the skin) are necessary to do a fibreglass job satisfactorily. The reward, of course, is a repair as strong as the original and completely undetectable. Waves, patches and outlines on the Elite are evidence of hasty or careless work.

The body/chassis and stress cracks

Fortunately, the Elite's fibreglass monocoque is both strong and reliable and has successfully withstood years of hard use and exposure to all kinds of elements. Inspection, except for the diff box, is relatively easy and damage is quick to spot.

The most common damage, other than from impact, is stress cracking or hair-line breaks in the top layer of the surface. Most of this kind of damage is superficial and occurs when a panel has been flexed excessively, impacted slightly or subjected to both high and long-term loads. The cracks appear in various configurations, including 'spider webs', concentric circles, parallel lines and checking in star-like or ran-

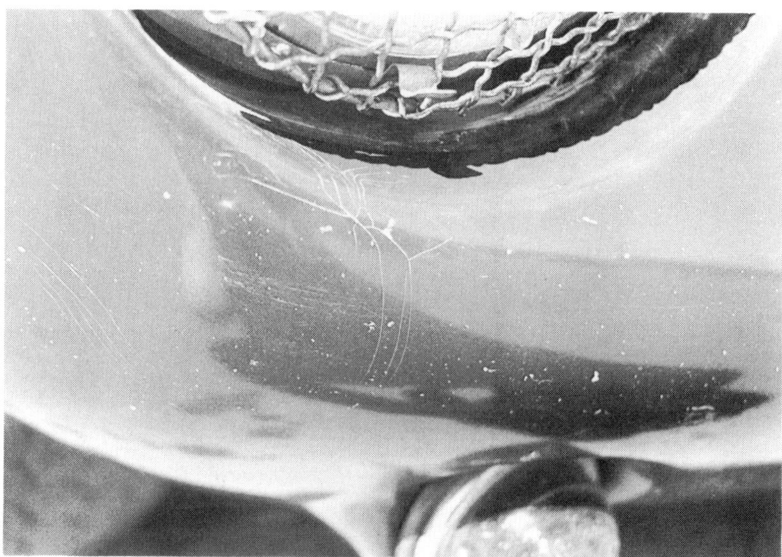

Typical stress crack damage under the headlight of an Elite. (Author)

dom patterns. Any kind of stress crack, if left alone, will ultimately get worse, and might progress from simply a cosmetic imperfection to a structural one.

Places on the Elite which are commonly prone to stress cracking include the areas around the bumpers, fuel filler and door handles. The bonnet's leading edge often has cracks which result from its being dropped shut, and the panel between the boot and the rear window breaks up when the boot lid is forced beyond its normal arc.

Danger

Stress cracks which are warning signs of a more serious problem occur on the inside (or the outside) of the roof adjacent to the shock absorber towers. Breaks in these locations must be considered structural and result from excessive suspension bottoming due to worn-out shock absorbers.

Cracking around the differential mounts (usually the upper ones go first) are also cause for concern. Unfortunately, removal of the differential is necessary to view the front of the box, while the rear can be seen only after removing the petrol tank. One other critical area is the mounting surface for the brake and clutch pedal assembly. This panel is visible from inside the engine bay and the area to examine is around the bolt heads which hold the pedal subframe in place. A catastrophic failure here (if the bolts pulled through the glass) would allow the brake pedal (and clutch) to collapse to the floor, so routine inspection is mandatory.

It will be recalled that Chapman designed the Elite to be raised off the ground (to change a wheel, for example) only by lifting the car at the steel posts which extend slightly below the surface of the undertray at the leading edge of the doors. The entire front and rear of the car can be safely raised as we will examine in a moment, but some Elites suffered damage from uninitiated mechanics placing jacks in other locations. A critical place is the front subframe 'ski', because a jack placed there only bends the frame and breaks the glass.

In order to lift either the entire front or rear of the Elite, a suitable

The correct way to raise the rear of the Elite. A wooden beam is placed on the fibreglass directly aft of the diff. (Author)

piece of wood (a 2 × 4 in piece about 2 feet long will do) is positioned between the jack and the undertray. The contact surface at the front extends from the motor mount bolts on one side of the engine bay to the bolts on the other side. The lifting surface at the rear is just behind the differential, with the wood placed on the fibreglass between the exhaust system recesses. Interestingly, some Elites, very late in production, had these surfaces marked with painted lines on the undertray. All stress cracks, whether cosmetic or structural in nature, are repaired in the same way, by grinding down to below the fissure and laying in enough cloth to restore the surface. Normally, a substantial area around the cracks is ground in order to ease the blending and finishing operation later on. The simple expedient of using filler is at best a temporary cover-up because the structure is left damaged and the cracks will reappear in a short period of time.

Other kinds of damage

The Elite is a difficult car to prepare for *concours d'élégance*, at least in warmer climates, because fibreglass expands and contracts with temperature change. In bright sunshine, on a hot day, the wing tops, for example, will become wavy. As the car cools down the undulations disappear, at least for a time because eventually the surface 'takes a set' and loses its smooth finish permanently.

Another reason why the wings are particularly prone to surface irregularities is that they are subjected to very high torsional and bending loads, especially at the box sections aft of the wheel wells.

As mentioned in an earlier chapter, many Elite doors are also temperature sensitive and tend to develop more dramatic surface imperfections, in extreme cases a texture not unlike cobblestones. Again, the permanence of the effect takes time, in most examples years, but the only solution is to block sand the doors smooth and repaint them. Even then, the texture is likely to return. Apparently the original manufacturing ratio of resin to hardener was inexact which resulted in different rates of expansion and contraction. In time the doors also tended to 'relax' on their hinges and droop. Fortunately, Chapman incorporated an ample range of adjustments, both in and out and up and down, to correct the problem.

The last relatively common form of damage is seam delamination and this occurs where the major mould sections came together in the manufacturing process. Adhesion was dependent on the random placement of epoxy 'glues', but some of these organic compounds have either deteriorated over time, or the original clamping pressure or coverage was insufficient because a few seams have begun to separate. The most common are the bottom of the door openings and the interior (underside) of the roof. In extreme cases the latter panel can actually be seen to sag. The cure here is to cut the section out and reglass in its place, while the door seams respond well to an injection of a resin and chopped glass mush.

Collision repair

As we will see later in this chapter, both the Bristol and the Maximar moulds for the Elite body/chassis still exist, with some of the Bristol fixtures having been completely restored and returned to use. In addi-

Frank Starkey rolled his historic racer at Riverside but large sections of this car were used to restore his 'double dimpled' body/chassis. (Author)

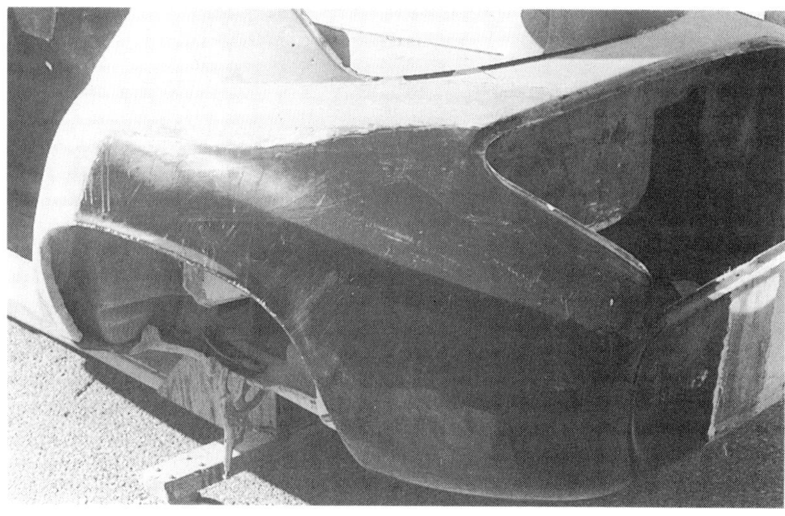

A replacement left rear corner has been grafted on to the main body/chassis. (Frank Starkey)

Frank Starkey's superbly restored 'double dimpled' body/chassis. Notice the dolly which allows the large assembly to be moved about. (Author)

The underside of chassis no 1812 showing the join lines of the new rear body section. (Mike Blackie)

Below *Chassis no 1812 is really three Elites spliced together.* (Mike Blackie)

tion to these moulds, numerous fibreglass repair shops in the UK, Europe and America developed their own moulds to handle collision repairs. The Elite owner is thus in the enviable position of being able to resurrect the most woebegone wreck.

For example, in Southern California (North Hollywood) there is a shop called Bruno's Corvette Repair that has been fixing broken Elites since the days of Jay Chamberlain. In time, the proprietor, Felix Brunelle (who calls himself the original plastic surgeon), built up a collection of moulds and forms to repair the most common kinds of damage. In 1969, chassis number 1812 was brought into Bruno's with the back end of the car broken off and shoved underneath the undertray. Apparently a truck had lost its brakes and used the parked Elite as a bump stop.

Brunelle had earlier acquired an Elite which had substantial front end damage, and the thought occurred to him to splice the two together. The graft was made at the rear window and was so successful that none of the subsequent owners ever guessed they were driving two cars! Only when Mike Blackie of Wilton, California, purchased the car some ten years later and stripped it for historic racing were the seams detected under the carpeting and on the undertray.

Interestingly, by then 1812 had acquired a new nose section as well, so the only part of the car that remained original was the centre section between the wheels. Despite this, the car tracked straight and true and there were no alignment problems. In fact, hands off at a hundred produced no change in direction!

A few words about fire

Although fibreglass does not support combustion, the resins used in the Elite's construction burn with ferocious intensity and, if left alone, the car will incinerate in less time than it takes to say 'Anthony Colin Bruce Chapman'. The most common source of fire in the Elite is backfiring through unfiltered carburettors (especially Webers). The next source is electrical shorts which allow wiring to overheat and melt. Incredibly, the Elite is not fitted with a master circuit breaker and only part of the wiring loom is protected by the car's single fuse! An in-car fire extinguisher should, therefore, be mandatory.

An Elite fitted with 'goose neck' Weber intake manifolds which allow horizontal float levels. This particular car has suffered an engine bay fire. (Adrien Schagen)

Above *Series II rear wishbone mount in the underbody. The bobbins are clearly visible which loosened on some early Bristol bodies.* (Author)

Above right *Frequent replacement of the rear suspension rubber ball is necessary for correct alignment and shock isolation. Here is the Series II arrangement.* (Author)

Right *These pictures illustrate one method to create preload on the rear wheel bearings without assembling the complete hub. Two large washers and a hefty bolt are used to compress the bearings in the hub against the central spacer. If the assembly wobbles, a narrower spacer must be fitted. If the bearings refuse to turn, a wider spacer has to be used.* (Author)

Suspension and drive train

The front and rear suspension on the Series I Elite requires careful and frequent maintenance to keep them in perfect order. Although the Metalastik bushes used at the inboard ends of the wishbones are long-lived and trouble-free, the other end moves on a brass trunnion equipped with two grease nipples which requires lubricant every 5,000 miles or so. The trunnion is attached to the wishbone by means of two cups threaded both on their interior and exterior surfaces. These have to be kept sufficiently tight to eliminate wobbling but loose enough to prevent binding. Unless the threads of these fittings are kept absolutely clean, road grit causes them to seize when they are adjusted.

The anti-roll bar on both series of Elites is clamped to the front sub-frame by two pairs of alloy blocks. The blocks are equipped with grease fittings, but in this case they have to be lubricated very regularly, every 500 miles in hard use, to prevent the anti-roll bar from machining an oval hole and allowing movement and vibration.

The front brakes on both series require no maintenance at all (other than yearly renewal of brake fluid to purge the system of moisture) and are easily inspected for pad wear. Pads, incidentally, usually last 40,000 miles before needing renewal. The rears, whether alloy or late production cast iron, are similarly maintenance free. This is a good thing because a pad change and caliper service (new seals) requires the half shafts to be disconnected from the differential and the discs removed, which is only a step or two away from dropping the diff itself, which some experts recommend anyway.

A word of caution here on rebuilding the hydraulic master cylinders, especially that for the brakes. If the circlip is not fully seated in its recess it can work itself out. This allows the pedal return spring to pull the brake pedal up to the top of the footwell and with it the master cylinder piston, which results in an instant loss of brakes.

The Series I rear suspension is a fiddly set-up which requires routine renewal of the rubber ball at the end of the dog-leg radius arm. After many miles of hard (usually racing) use, the arms bend slightly causing rear wheel steering effects. Correct alignment can be restored by heating the arm (on the bench with a torch) and bending it back the necessary amount. Recall that this arm was attached to the hub carrier by means of two tapered roller bearings which had to be removed in order to be lubricated. In that the seals are of the Nylos type and marginal at best, this lubrication has to be frequent as has the adjustment for pre-load to take up unwanted movement. The hub carrier also contains a pair of roller bearings (albeit huge) which need frequent lubrication as well (again, every 500 miles in hard use) but fortunately a grease fitting exists for this purpose. In the United Kingdom, frequent wheel bearing lubrication is necessary to purge water from the housing because the Nylos seals are ineffective in keeping rainwater out.

The hub carrier bearings are a press fit on to the hub and pre-load is

Below right *This Series II hub carrier has an adjustable spring perch by means of a threaded collar welded to the shock absorber tube. Two threaded rings below the perch lock the assembly at the desired height.* (Author)

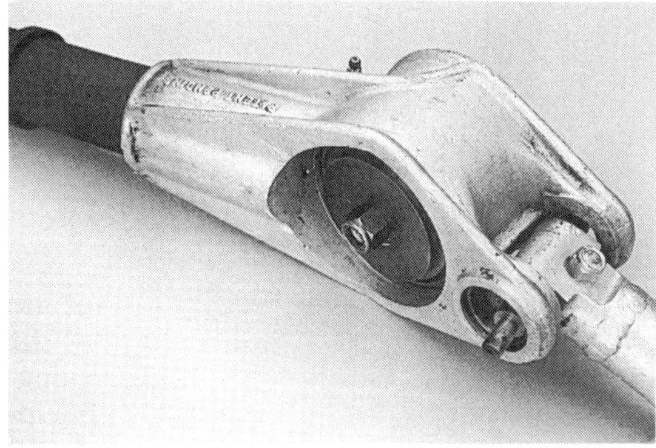

determined by the width of a spacer collar installed between them. When fitting new bearings and races, the press fit can be simulated on the bench by using a long bolt (in place of the hub) and two stout washers to hold the bearings in place. A nut, screwed on the bolt, loads the washers against the inner bearing surface. If the spacer collar is too wide the bearings will wobble; if it is too narrow, the bearings will not turn. Lotus originally supplied spacers in standard + .0015 and + .003 widths to enable bearing adjustment.

The shock absorbers (both front and rear) are rugged items and as long as road salts are hosed off the actuating rods now and again, to prevent rusting and pitting, 50,000 miles on a set is possible. The drive shaft has two U-joints lubricated by grease nipples. The rear joint is accessible at the differential, but the forward joint is exposed by removing an aluminium plate on the right-hand side of the transmission tunnel. The trouble is that the seat has to be removed to get to the cover plate! As a result of this, many Elites suffer from excessively worn U-joints in the front of their drive shafts, although being enclosed by the transmission tunnel does tend to lengthen their life span.

The Elite's half shafts are fixed in length and utilize a universal joint at both ends. Despite the existence of grease fittings and the need for frequent lubrication, these joints wear quickly because they have to endure heavy lateral as well as torsional loads. A major failure of any of the Elite's universal joints can have catastrophic results, so frequent inspection is the rule. The bolts which hold the half shafts and brake discs to the differential stub axles tend to loosen even in normal use, so inspection is critical here also.

The Series II front suspension utilized a newer type of trunnion which attached to the 'A' arm by a through bolt and nylon bushes. It has proved to be long wearing and maintenance free, save for a shot of grease now and again through the single nipple provided. The new rear suspension, besides eliminating rear wheel steering effects, is also easier to service. The hub carrier still needs lots of grease to remain happy and the rubber ball requires frequent inspection, but that is about all! Two types of radius arms were originally manufactured, one with the ball joint on the long tube and the other with the ball on the short tube. The difference provided two angles of attachment which was the only means of adjusting rear wheel toe.

The Koni people made shock absorbers for the Series II Elite which made life easier because they could be adjusted for wear. The rear shocks could also be screwed directly into the old Armstrong housings. To fit a new Armstrong shock absorber, the original unit has to be 'sweated out'. This requires that the hub carrier be heated with a torch while the old shock is driven out. This operation often requires considerable force, although sometimes one is released with a bang. Len Street recalled that there was a large chunk of brick missing in one of the shop walls at Hornsey where an Armstrong exploded from its hub carrier! The Koni's travel is too long, incidentally, for the Series I suspension and bottoming results if they are fitted, which can bend or break the actuating rod.

Happily, the steering gear is trouble free and requires only an injection of grease occasionally. A rubber universal joint was fitted to the steering column on some left-hand drive cars that proved to be robust enough, but a test of patience to replace. The Elite's gearboxes, both the ZF and the MG units, transmit a little noise into the cabin and the

An Elite differential showing a properly vented case and the use of a braided stainless steel brake hose. The brass hexagon plug was originally vented by means of holes drilled in alternate flats. The resulting oil mist quickly covered everything, including the brakes. (Author)

MG's first gear howls whether the box is new or well used, but as long as they are filled with oil neither gives any particular trouble. The differential is equally reliable if the level of oil is kept up (a dip stick, accessible from the spare tyre well, is provided for that purpose) but a little wear makes itself known in the form of a howling noise, especially on the overrun. Fortunately, lash is adjustable to take up for wear.

Unfortunately, however, the top of the differential is fitted with a breather that eventually allows an oil mist to coat everything, including the brakes. An important modification is to replace this breather with a vent and length of hose which directs the oil mist to the ground.

The engine

Happily, the 1216cc Coventry Climax FWE proved to be as robust and reliable an engine as the FWA racing version and was capable of years of service with normal maintenance as long as certain idiosyncrasies were recognized and dealt with. Fortunately, all of the mysteries have been solved and even a major overhaul is within the capability of the amateur.

If the Climax SOHC engine had a weakness it was a particular sensitivity to overheating with blown head gaskets and warped heads the usual result. Alas, the Elite's cooling system was marginal in all but the coldest of climates, so driving in 'stop and go' traffic and motoring on hot summer days was cause to keep a sharp eye on the temperature gauge. The thermostatically controlled electric fan was a rather anaemic device which provided little relief. Even so, many Elites were fitted, at one time or another, with a manual switch (some cars left the works with an auxiliary toggle switch fitted under the dash panel) so that the fan could be turned on in advance of an overheat situation. The trouble was that the fan would not keep the engine from boiling in even tepid weather, so the solution was to park the Elite and let it cool down.

The source of the problem is a radiator with too little coolant capacity. Once under way, even in hellish conditions, the system worked fine, but without a substantial flow of air the radiator simply could not cope. Besides head gasket problems, the Climax never liked warm ambient temperatures and proved it by producing less horsepower than when it was treated to cool air. In fact, the FWE seemed happiest when the temp gauge read between 75 and 85 degrees Fahrenheit.

The solution, of course, is to fit a larger core to the radiator which (on the later style, rounded-corner type) is possible because the top and

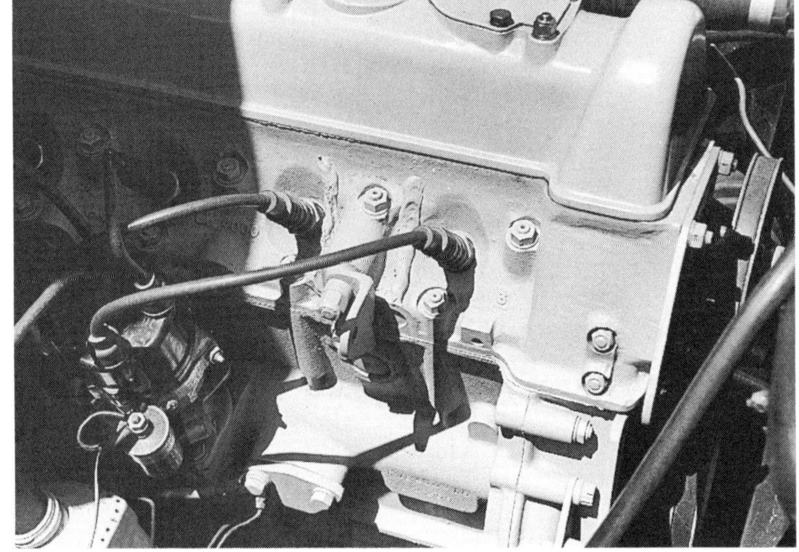

This FWE head has cracked on both sides of the rear generator mount. Since this is a historic racer the driver is able to run a constant loss (battery charge) system. (Author)

The fitting of an alternator in place of the generator is a relatively common modification. Notice the taped message on the cam cover of this historic racer. (Author)

bottom tanks were manufactured slightly oversize. Although this is an expensive cure, it is ultimately more efficient and less troublesome than installing a more powerful fan. The thermostat on the Elite, incidentally, is a curious 'in line' type originally made of plastic but later supplied in brass.

Because the Climax used dissimilar metals in the coolant passages, an electrolytic reaction is an ongoing process that is extremely corrosive to light alloy, although steel and cast iron can eventually be affected as well. In order to prevent the engine from literally eating itself up from the inside out, an inhibiter must be used, such as ethylene glycol in common antifreeze.

The FWE's aluminium castings are also sensitive to torque, and even the greatest care can result in stripped threads in spark plug or oil line holes. An anti-seize compound on the spark plug threads is always a good idea as is the use of a torque wrench. The cam tower studs also have a tendency to pull out of their threaded holes, but helicoils are an effective repair.

As mentioned in the chapter on racing, the Super Series Elites and all others meant for serious competition work were fitted with the steel (some were machined in light alloy) timing gear to replace the fibre item. The penalty for road use with a steel gear is, however, greatly increased noise in an already cacophonous engine. In normal road use, the fibre gear should last 30,000 to 40,000 miles, but since oil saturation is the culprit (besides, of course, normal wear), a coating of polyurethane varnish (as a sealant) prior to installation is a recommended procedure. Once an engine is out of the car, a trip to the balancing shop with the clutch, flywheel, crankshaft, rods, pistons and everything else that goes up, down or around is a mandatory operation. This is because Chapman drove a very hard bargain with Coventry Climax and many of their FWEs suffered from less than perfect machining operations and balancing.

The Elite also suffers from a resonance or droning that usually arrives at about 4,200 revs. Some Elite experts believe the cause to be the exhaust system, while others, including Tony Bates, feel that the high-frequency vibration is related to engine tune and can be adjusted out (with Weber carbs) by careful air/fuel jet selection. When the clutch is apart it is also recommended to replace the spring-type pressure plate with a diaphragm unit. No modifications are necessary and the diaphragm clutch does not suffer from the spring shift and vibration problems of the original.

A special word here about the crankshaft. Whenever the part is removed from the engine it is a good idea to have it cleaned, but the oil galley plugs have to be removed to do so. If these plugs are left in place, wax residue tends to loosen and float around until it blocks the oil passages which leads at best to seized bearings or, worse, a broken crank.

The only other problem area identified in a significant number of Elites is a tendency to burn exhaust valves, but this is usually traced to excessively lean mixtures on cars equipped with a single SU. Much of the FWE's heavy oil consumption (and the Elite's sooty tail after a long run) is due to oil from the cam gear running down the guides and being burned in the combustion chamber. The installation of ordinary valve seals can cut oil consumption by as much as half, besides keeping the rear bodywork clean and tidy.

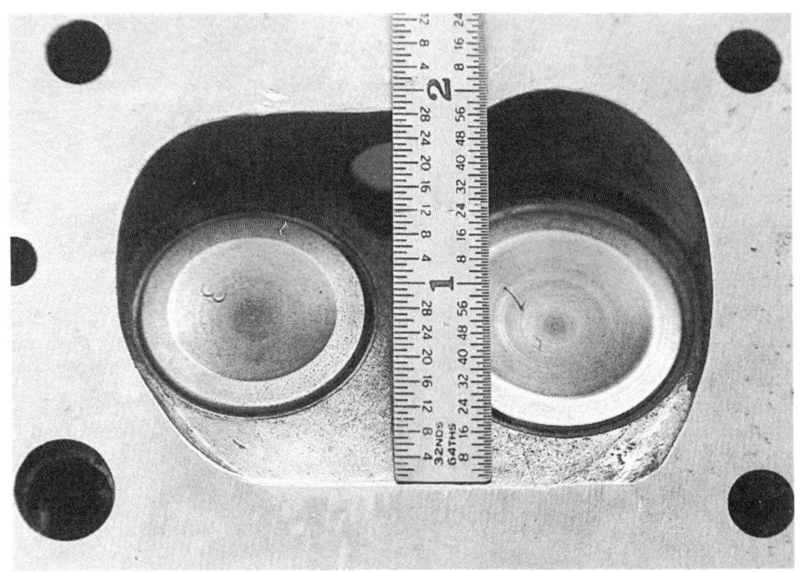

One way to determine how much material has been skimmed off an FWE head is to measure the distance across the combustion chamber; 2 inches is standard, 1⅞ is 40 thousandths less and 1¾ has 80 thou removed. This head has been shaved about 40 thousandths. (Author)

The FWE is otherwise not a leaker, and attention paid to gaskets and to keeping nuts snug on the sump, cam and engine covers yields a dry engine bay and a clean garage floor. The rear main seal is similar to a piston ring and as a result weeps slightly, but the mess is negligible. Fortunately, today's Climax rebuilder is able to obtain everything needed to restore or maintain the engine through the specialists listed in Appendix I. As it happens, some Elite owners look for parts in rather unexpected places—boat shops.

The Bearcat

In the late 1960s, the Fisher-Pierce Company in Rockland, Massachusetts, contracted with Coventry Climax for a supply of single overhead cam engines for a new line of four-cycle marine outboard motors called the Bearcat. In this guise, the featherweight engine was placed on its nose and was contained within a watertight housing. Two versions were available, the Bearcat 55 which displaced 750cc and the Bearcat 85 at 1500cc. The latter, of course, was based on the FWB and today the blocks are highly sought after by Elite owners wishing to modify their cars for a little extra performance.

The pushrod Fords

After the demise of Jay Chamberlain's distributorship, the Elite fell on extremely hard times in America. The technical expertise disappeared and the limited parts stores were quickly depleted. Rather than try to service an engine they knew little or nothing about, or suffer long delays waiting for parts from England, a few well-meaning mechanics decided it would be better to install a common engine in the Elite rather than hassle with the Climax. Inevitably, a few owners lamented over the lack of torque from the Climax engine and the Elite's unsuitability for the 'stoplight Grand Prix' which was considered *de rigueur* in places like Southern California.

Frank Monise of Pasadena, California, was a mechanic who raced Lotus cars and understood the Elite but was also sympathetic to the plight of the owner. His solution in several of the most desperate cases was to perform engine conversions, at first the 1-litre English Ford 105E pushrod and later the enlarged 1340cc (109E) version. The engines were heavier than the Climax but they were quiet and strong and could be serviced at almost any Ford dealer in the country. Whatever the arguments for or against these conversions, there is no question that they saved more than one Elite from the scrapyard.

Miles Wilkins and Fibreglass Services

It all started for Miles Wilkins in 1972 when he bought his first Elite. Already something of a fibreglass expert, having been a manager for Len Street, Wilkins started a boat repair business called Fibreglass Services. During his first 'off season' he rebuilt his Elite, then a friend's and then another, and before long he was doing more cars than boats. His shops were an odd assortment of corrugated metal buildings nestling within the Charlton Saw Mills and located near the old Goodwood circuit, but their forlorn and dilapidated appearance belied the treasures found within.

As Wilkins delved ever deeper into the Elite, his fascination grew along with his understanding of how complex an automobile it was. He passed that knowledge on to his customers in the form of extraordinary enthusiasm in putting right other rebuilders' mistakes and in restoring cars that some might have believed to be hopeless, and all this at a time when the works had essentially forgotten the car and even Lotus dealers and service garages no longer wanted to know. Because parts were next to impossible to obtain through normal channels, even skilled mechanics were reluctant to tackle the Elite. As a result of this, Elites in the UK, not to mention America, fell into uncaring and insensitive hands where service was ignored and repairs were botched.

The Ford pushrod was a common conversion in Southern California, this one having been done by Frank Monise in Pasadena. (A.W. Huberts)

There is no question that were it not for the energy, enthusiasm and industry of Miles Wilkins and two others like him, a good number of Elites would have disappeared from the face of the earth. In Wilkins's case he not only restored, painted and trimmed needy body/chassis, but also overhauled the mechanicals. Slowly, he developed parts stores by searching out old Elite inventories. He even convinced some of the original suppliers to tool up and produce limited runs of new parts. Failing that, he developed new sources to manufacture items like bumpers, windscreen rubber, 'A' arms and the like. In 1977 the works paid Miles the highest compliment by appointing him sole concessionaire to reproduce Elite parts to their original drawings. Advertisements in the enthusiasts' press, including *Motor Sport*, resulted in a thriving business, especially in the sales of parts overseas. As noted in an earlier chapter, Club Elite benefited from his guidance for over a decade.

The specialists: 'A.N.E. Bates'

As mentioned in the previous chapter, Anthony Bates was first smitten by the Lotus Elite while he was a Flying Officer (helicopters) with the RAF. He bought a kit in 1962, another in 1963, and in 1965 he acquired the London Motor Show Car which he transformed into the well-known 'fastback Elite'.

Towards the end of his tour of duty, Tony began to think about ways of making a living as a civilian and decided to pursue fibreglass technology. He studied with a local boatbuilder who had a contract with the Royal Navy and as a result of this made some valuable contacts in the industry, including Strand Glass.

When Tony left the service he continued as a civilian pilot until 1987 when he set up his cottage industry in workshops he built next to his house. Called simply 'A.N.E. Bates—Lotus Elite Specialist', the business

The back of Tony Bates's house reveals the entrance to his Elite restoration services. Here's Tony standing by a customer car. (Photographer unknown)

The centrepiece of Tony Bates's restoration equipment is this chassis alignment jig. (A.N.E. Bates)

catered exclusively to the Lotus Elite although, when pressed, he has been known to work on an Elan or two.

Tony's first goal was to obtain a set of moulds for the Elite and after a great deal of rumour-chasing he finally located the last of the Bristol items. Incomplete and in a generally sorry state, Bates used them as a guide to construct all the pieces necessary to form a complete body/chassis. It took several years to accomplish, but Tony eventually completed not only a full set of brand new body/chassis moulds (including all lids, doors and inner panels), but also jigs and tools for the front subframe and windscreen hoop as well. The centrepiece of his achievement, however, is the full-size alignment jig which allows him to either piece together large repair sections or assemble brand new mouldings as in the original manufacturing process!

The construction of a completely new Elite body/chassis is therefore possible with Tony's equipment, but his strong sense of authenticity has prevented him from doing so. Although he will only work from an original Elite, he also admits that he only needs a small portion, which means even the worst case is not beyond repair. The Bates workshops also include facilities for steam cleaning, bead blasting, machining, welding and milling.

Tony's list of accomplishments includes building two Team Elite 'lookalike racers' and the restoration of DAD 10. The latter was particularly satisfying because of the car's original history and the fact that it has proven to be every bit as fast in modern historic racing. Strand Glass, incidentally, provided Tony with significant technical assistance in DAD 10's rebuild including help in the construction of the body/chassis moulds.

Interestingly, Tony does not advertise, yet he is normally booked two years in advance! In 1988 he heard of some curious car moulds that had been stacked in a garden and were overgrown with weeds. In

Some of the new sections required in the DAD 10 rebuild. (A.N.E. Bates)

DAD 10 after the restoration of its body/chassis. (A.N.E. Bates)

1989 he examined the pieces which turned out to be a set of moulds for the Series I Elite—from Maximar! Alas, they were too worn and too weathered to be used.

The specialists: Hutton Motor Engineering

In 1963 Bill Hutton was in college studying engineering near his home in Clarksville, Tennessee. He had been at his studies for two years when he decided that he needed some practical experience and booked a passage on a freighter bound for Liverpool. At first, this might seem a far-fetched journey to pursue his training, but his love was the automobile and as far as Bill was concerned all of the advances at that time were coming from England.

While seeking employment he saw an advert in *Motor Sport* for the ex-Jim Clark Elite and reckoned it would be ideal for commuting in and around London. The car had the Mecha-Matic gearbox and Hutton recalled that it was great to drive. A hurried cable to his father in the States requesting money was met with the response, 'Buy a bicycle'. For the next few months Bill's transport was just that, a bicycle, but he could not shake the memory of the Elite. When he got a job at Cosworth Engineering Ltd he was able to set aside some cash and convince his father that the Lotus would be a good investment in the US. This time his father sent the money and Bill purchased a red SE, chassis 1369, registered 564 BBL.

In 1966 Hutton returned to Tennessee with his bride Barbara (Keith Duckworth's secretary), the Elite and an idea to import Lotus for fun and profit. In 1969 Hutton Motor Engineering was formed as a rebuilding service for, primarily, Volkswagen engines, but Bill also began importing Elites, ten in fact over the next few years, but inquiries were as much for parts as they were for the cars, so Bill began to develop a small parts inventory. As mentioned in an earlier chapter, he also started the North American version of Club Elite.

In 1977 Hutton learned of Lotus's offer to sell the remaining Elite parts and body/chassis inventory, and although he recalls that he could not afford the 40 or so incomplete Elites, he brought home two tons of parts to establish a bona fide Elite restoration business.

By 1989 Hutton Motor Engineering had branched out to other projects, including development work for Chevrolet. Bill also kept his association with Cosworth Engineering and was involved in the Cosworth Vega (Chevrolet) project. His interest in the Elite is still as strong as ever and besides a worldwide parts business, Bill has the facilities to handle any Elite restoration job including a sophisticated engine dynamometer. Most US Elite owners, incidentally, credit Bill Hutton with saving the car from extinction in America and his address, along with the other Elite specialists, can be found in Appendix I.

Bill Hutton's first Elite posed outside his employer's works, Cosworth Engineering. From left to right, Mike Costin, Bill Brown and Keith Duckworth. This is the same building that housed the construction of the Earls Court prototype (see Chapter 2). (Bill Hutton)

A restoration saga

To many enthusiasts, the spectre of an automobile restoration is akin to an assault on Mount Everest, fraught with trial and tribulation every step of the way with no guarantee of success. The fact that these thoughts have occurred to Elite owners is evidenced by the existence of so many cars that have been taken apart without being put together again. While the restoration of a Lotus Elite is by no means easy, it is certainly possible for an owner to achieve one with professional results, especially with the aid of the Elite specialists and the Elite clubs.

If there is a typical procedure for restoring an Elite, it would probably be pretty close to the method employed by a Californian named Barry Swackhamer. Like many new owners, he flirted with the idea of a complete restoration but hoped to enjoy the car for a while before embarking on so difficult a project. At first glance, chassis 1309 was typical of 'bargain' Elites. 'The left front wing had been damaged but not well repaired, the paint was an unattractive metallic burgundy, the engine compartment was an oil mess and the boot smelled of gasoline, battery acid and decaying jute.' Barry put a few miles on the car but soon learned that the transmission would not hold oil above the minimum mark. 'In one exciting moment I discovered that the master cylinder leaked and there wasn't any fluid in the braking system. The complete restoration would be needed sooner than expected.'

Barry estimated that it took about 50 hours to strip the Elite down to a bare body/chassis. As each component was removed a note was made as to whether to restore or replace, to paint or to plate, and so on. At this stage he also decided to replace all fasteners with aircraft-type AN nuts and bolts. In this way he could choose the right length for each application and be sure that only the shank and not the threads contacted the working surface. Of course, a side benefit was increased strength, and since many aircraft fasteners were cadmium-plated they were cor-

Barry Swackhamer's Elite on its portable body/chassis stand has been primed and is ready for paint. (Barry Swackhamer)

Barry Swackhamer's Elite after the colour coat was applied. The rear body seam is clearly visible in this picture but will be covered by the bumper. (Barry Swackhamer)

rosion resistant as well. Shelves were set aside in the Swackhamer garage for each new or rebuilt component.

The bare body/chassis could easily be moved about by two men, but Barry borrowed a device used by several Elite restorers which suspended the car as on a barbecue spit, so that it could be easily rotated and revolved for inspection and repair. A rented steam cleaning machine removed the last speck of grime but also exposed a damaged (bent) front subframe and radiator mounts which had inexplicably been cut off.

Barry spent weeks hand-sanding the body surfaces down to the gel coat. He believed the resins used in the Elite were vulnerable to damage by chemical paint removers, even those designed for fibreglass, and decided to be ultra-conservative since he wanted to end up with a show-quality paint job. Bob Green (see Chapter 14) did the fibreglass repair and restored the subframe. He also sprayed the body chassis with a catalysed sealer and primer, to produce a strong yet easily sanded gel coat which also, incidentally, provided an effective barrier for previously applied paints, whether enamel or lacquer.

Meantime, Swackhamer worked on the Elite's wiring harness. He discovered that when the fabric cover was peeled away, several wires showed evidence of the plastic insulation having melted. This was because Lotus wired the Elite so that several electrical components shared the same circuit, and when all of them were switched on the wire overheated.

The engine rebuild was straightforward enough with the only modification being the use of a 'forty thou' head gasket to lower the compression ratio. This was done to allow the use of modern low octane fuels, although Barry brought the engine up to Stage II specifications to compensate. Mike Ostrov (Secretary of Club Elite, North America) assisted in testing the engine on a dynamometer. This procedure is highly recommended because it allows the engine to be broken in on the bench while sorting out optimum timing and carb jet-

Boot detail of the Swackhamer Elite. (Barry Swackhamer)

ting, and tending to the inevitable leaks and loose fittings. A 'dyno' also allows some experimentation, and Barry was surprised to see that the use of the original-style air cleaners for the twin SU set-up resulted in a loss of 4 bhp.

The body/chassis was supported on stands and painted lime green (acrylic enamel) in honour of a 1960s West Coast club racer named Al Brizzard, whose Elite was the same colour. After the paint was buffed, the rebuilt and Koni-equipped suspension was installed and new brake piping fitted. Barry was particularly interested in originality and spent some time searching for original (or re-manufactured) decals and markings as well as material in the original colour for the carpeting, upholstery, boot lining and the like. While he was at it, Barry also installed a ZF gearbox and 60-spoke wire wheels.

Barry spent several years of part-time work on his restoration project and believes the most difficult part was the length of time required. Even tasks such as cleaning and storing exceeded the original estimate by a significant margin. But then, the result was essentially a new Elite, and that was well worth the wait.

Chapter 14

Historic racing

The previous chapter alluded to the fact that the current Elite owner is probably in a better position to enjoy his or her car now than ever before. This is because of the existence of clubs and businesses dedicated exclusively to the Elite, run by proprietors who are genuinely interested in the car and its preservation. Thanks to both, the means to keep an Elite healthy and the presence of knowledgeable people to assist in the resurrection of even the neediest example, there is absolutely no reason why the Lotus 14 cannot be enjoyed as much today as when the car was new, and in the same ways, including racing.

Today historic racing (loosely termed vintage racing in the States) is a well-developed sport with clubs and organizations putting together full calendars in Europe, the UK, North America, Australia and Japan. Starting grids are loaded with fascinating cars which recall thrilling periods in the history of road racing. Fortunately, the 'Golden Age' of sports cars (1955–1965) is well represented also, which means that the Elite races in much the same company as it did 30 years ago.

Of course the reasons why the Elite was such an extraordinary racing GT originally hold true today, and the car is not only competitive but is also extremely satisfying to drive. Superlative brakes, handling and chassis rigidity, not to mention good power to weight, are ideally demonstrated on a race-track. The car is so well balanced and stable that it makes average drivers look good, and gifted ones absolutely world class. The Elite has only one vice, which is primarily the result of modern technology, but more on this later.

While a complete Elite racing manual is beyond the scope of this book (although a racing checklist is provided at the end of this section which indicates how detailed such a manual might be), there are some areas of concern which should be dealt with in the interests of safety and minimal levels of car performance. Although some discussion will be given to making the Elite go faster, the real purpose of this section is to encourage an owner to 'blueprint' his car to make sure that it is working the way it is supposed to.

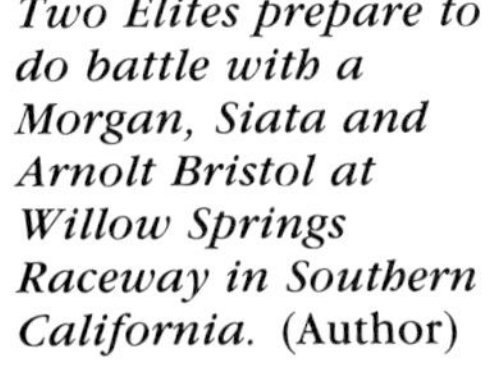

Two Elites prepare to do battle with a Morgan, Siata and Arnolt Bristol at Willow Springs Raceway in Southern California. (Author)

Morris Kindig has campaigned this Elite from the 'sixties to current historic events. It runs in street trim. (Author)

Race preparation: body/chassis

By now, the reader should be familiar with how the body/chassis was constructed and where the weaknesses were discovered. Remember that a repair is obvious by a rough or patched surface, and that the only place the works ever resorted to an 'unfinished' look was in their 'step repair' or Series II wishbone bobbin fix. Careful inspection of these bobbins, whether modified by the works or not, and examination of the diff box is mandatory. If the car came with diff straps they must be used, unless a new, thicker-section diff box is grafted into place. While the differential area is being examined, attention should also be given to the disc brake shields to make sure that they are in place. Some very early Elites were delivered without them, although by now most of these have been retrofitted.

While some stress-cracking on body surfaces is acceptable from a structural point of view, any damage around the shock absorber towers, whether inside the car or on the outside of the cabin, must be repaired. Obviously, any cracking around the front subframe has to be mended as well. The only other critical area to examine is the mounting surface for the brake and clutch pedal assembly. For safety (and a harder pedal), the top surface should be reinforced to prevent the bolts from pulling through the fibreglass. This is usually accomplished by fitting a steel bar to connect the two bolt heads.

A roll bar is a must in the Elite, not only because one is required by most of the historic racing organizers, but due to the fact that, in a rollover, the back of the roof almost always caves in. Fortunately, a variety of designs are possible and all can be made to be removable. Intelligent triangulation and the use of oversize backing plates on both sides of the mounting surfaces will assure a structurally safe installation.

The Elite can be lightened by the removal of the door panels and all of the sound-deadening and carpeting in the cockpit and boot. Full Perspex (plexiglass) screens can be made for the side windows and rear screen, and finally Lotus Formula Junior (or similar GRP buckets) can be substituted for the touring items. A few pounds of unsprung weight can also be saved by fitting Borrani wire wheels which utilize a light alloy rim.

A historic racing Elite with minimum instrumentation. Notice the foot brace on the transmission tunnel left of the clutch pedal. (Author)

The brake and clutch master cylinder cluster have been reinforced with a metal plate. (Author)

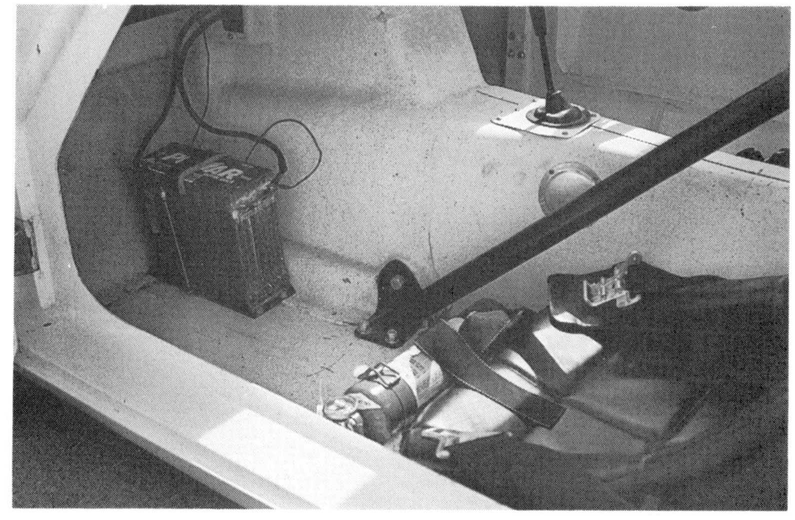

This historic racer utilizes a small racing battery in the left-hand foot well. Notice also that the roll bar picks up the transmission mount. (Author)

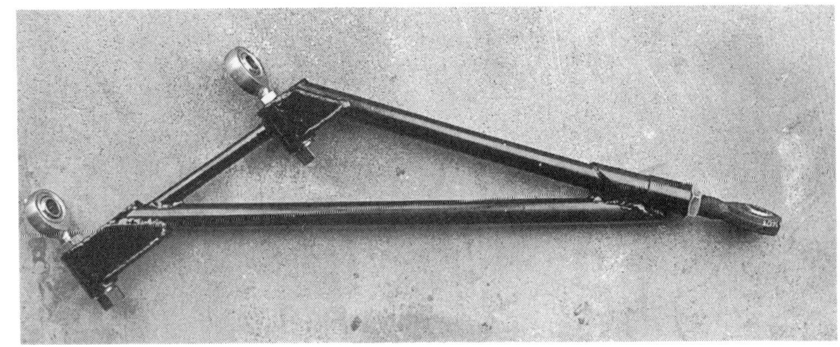

Series II rear wishbone converted to spherical bearings for maximum adjustability. (Author)

Fortunately, John Streets was able to steer his Elite back down on to four wheels without further drama. (Larry Fisher)

Race preparation: suspension and brakes

Accurate tracking is crucial to good handling, but unfortunately it is also somewhat difficult to adjust on the Elite. The first step is to locate and permanently mark the exact body/chassis centreline at the nose and the tail. By means of plumb-lines, a parallelogram can then be determined to set toe. The front is adjusted in the usual way (but remember to keep the steering rack centred) while the rear requires some fiddling unless a rose (heim) jointed and suitably bracketed wishbone is used. The Series I dog-leg arm has to be heated with a torch and bent to adjust toe whereas the Series II requires substitution using the two styles of wishbones supplied by the works. One of these mounted the ball on the long tube of the wishbone while the other style fixed the ball on the short tube. As crude as these methods may be, they are quite necessary because if both rear wheels are out of specification only a degree or two in the same direction, the Elite will steer itself with no help from the driver! If the wheels are 'out' in opposite directions, the car will scrub off speed with every revolution of the wheel.

It should not be necessary to remind that bearings, bushes and U-joints should be in perfect (as new) order with no excessive play. Crack-testing of all suspension components, drive, half shafts and fasteners should also be mandatory and repeated with every teardown. The brake-pipes should be replaced with the braided stainless steel

(Aeroquip) type for fail-safe operation. The use of this kind of line, incidentally, also results in better braking efficiency due to the elimination of expansion. New pads and seals (both caliper and master cylinder) should be fitted with fresh Girling fluid. Larger diameter master cylinders result in a harder, albeit somewhat 'deader', pedal which is preferred by some competitiors. Also, in order to take the remaining 'play' out of the brakes, the master cylinder mounting surface can be re-glassed, or backed with a steel plate.

As to the Elite's only vice on the race-track, it is the car's tendency to get up on two wheels. This is almost always related to too much adhesion caused by the use of modern tyre compounds. The Elite, as discussed earlier, was designed to slide or drift in corners, and when this is prevented by modern race tyres (whose grip cannot be overcome by even a Stage III FWE), the car responds by becoming very light on its inside edge with potentially alarming results. Although strong enough for road use, the standard wheels should be exchanged for double-laced (60-spoke) or triple-laced (72-spoke) wheels for competition.

Race preparation: the engine and drive train

The Stage III Climax is the engine to be chosen for historic racing, not only because of its higher horsepower rating, but also due to its increased reliability at high revs. Fortunately, such an engine can be assembled without having to scour the world for a five-bearing camshaft. A billet cam—machined from a solid steel shaft—will work as well, as long as care is taken in the selection of valve springs. Remember that the five-bearing utilized larger diameter and stiffer items than the standard three-bearing.

A steel timing gear is mandatory as is a diaphragm clutch—both in the interests of reliability—although as we have seen, the latter is related to balance as well. Over the years, just about every speed secret known to man has been applied to the Coventry Climax FWE, including the use of larger bores and 'stroked' crankshafts.

Historic racing FWE fitted with twin SUs and braided stainless steel fuel lines for maximum safety. (Author)

Historic racing FWE fitted with Webers and braided stainless steel fuel lines. Notice also that the coolant hose is of the same fail-safe material. The cam cover on this engine has been highly polished. (Author)

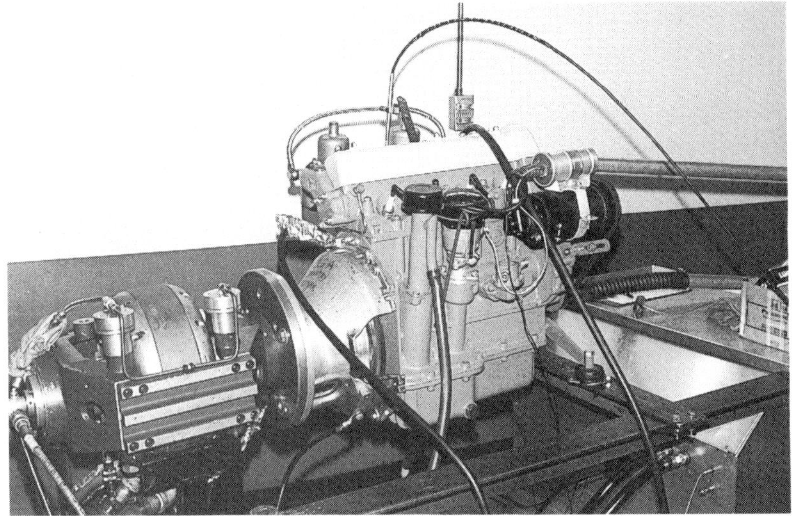

Engine testing on a dynamometer is an easy way of breaking in a freshly rebuilt unit, besides sorting optimum ignition and carburation setting. (Barry Swackhamer)

Inevitably, most engine-builders return to the conclusion that the best way to achieve maximum reliable horsepower is through careful preparation of the cylinder head, with blueprinting (matching ports, equalizing combustion chamber volumes and the like) and gas flowing being the techniques which result in the most dividends. Testing on an engine dynamometer is the ideal way of determining optimum engine timing, carburettor jetting and exhaust system length, but careful experimentation on the road or track can yield similar results. As it happens, the men at Coventry knew all along that the FWE was capable of about 100 reliable brake horsepower at the flywheel. This was an outstanding output from just 1216cc, but consider also that the engine can produce this figure over several seasons of racing with no more maintenance than fresh plugs and regular oil changes. One final word on engine preparation is the recommendation for the Aeroquip type of hose for fuel lines, although some builders like to use the material for the Climax's exterior oil feeds as well. This type of hose is as 'fail-safe' as any component can be.

Lotus Elite racing check list

Date: ____________ **Event:** ____________

Item	Inspected	Comments
Front Suspension		
Wheel bearings		
Upper links and bushes		
Lower 'A' arms and bushes		
Shock absorbers and springs		
Sway bar, bushes and blocks		
Wheels, spokes and knock-offs		
Rear Suspension		
Springs and perches		
Shock metacone		
Hub carrier		
Wheel bearings		
'A' arm (dog-leg)		
Rubber ball and cup		
Brake disc bolts — tighten		
Wheels, spokes and knock-offs		
Half shafts and U-joints		
Steering		
Alignment		
Tie rods		
Rack and mounts		
Ball joints		
Steering arms		
Column mounts and U-joints		
Steering wheel		
Brakes		
Front calipers and mounts		
Pads and flexible lines		
Rear calipers and mounts		
Pads and flexible lines		
Hand brakes		
Rigid lines		
Master cylinder condition		
Master cylinder fluid level		
Pedals and subframe		

Item	Inspected	Comments
Body/Chassis		
Door hinges and latches		
Bonnet hinges and latch		
Boot hinges and latch		
Stress cracks — locations		
Pedal mounts		
Front subframe, skis		
Transmission tunnel		
Differential mounts		
Rear suspension mounts		
Windows and surrounds		
Racing numbers		
Safety		
Seat belts and harness		
Roll bar		
Fire extinguisher		
Seat mounts		
Battery cover		
Mirrors		
Loose items, cockpit		
Drive train		
Clutch master cylinder		
Clutch slave cylinder		
Fluid and line		
Gear lever and knob		
Gearbox mount		
Gearbox oil level		
Differential oil level		
Differential breather		
Engine		
Oil condition and level		
Oil filter		
Coil, points and condenser		
Spark plugs		
Timing		
Valve clearances		
Compression		

Item	Inspected	Comments
Breathers and catch tanks		
Freeze plugs		
Engine mounts		
V belt		
Fuel pump and lines		
Fuel tank straps, hose, cap		
Fuel filter		
Fuel pressure regulator		
Carb jets		
Heat shields		
Carb linkage, return springs		
Exhaust system		
Fluid leaks		
Electrical		
Generator and mounts		
Voltage regulator		
Starter and solenoid		
Battery charge		
Ignition switch		
Instruments		
Brake-lights		
Horn		
Wipers		
Headlamps		
Wiring harness		
Fuel pump		
Cooling		
Air intake		
Radiator mounts, cap, level		
Hoses and clamps		
Expansion tank		
Driver		
Helmet		
Suit, underwear		
Gloves and shoes		
Log book		

The historic racers

Appendix II of this book lists over 40 Elites that were campaigned in historic racing in 1989. While it would be great fun to profile all of the drivers,there simply is not room in this book to do so. Nonetheless, several have been selected who are representative of the current Elite racers. The first is Bob Green, whom the author has known for over 15 years.

Bob Green, California, USA

Bob Green purchased his Elite, chassis 1373, in 1968 and used it regularly on the road for two years during which time he decided to restore the car and participate in the *concours d'élégance*. Progress was slow, due to other commitments, which was probably just as well, because in 1975 he became involved with the Classic Sports Racing Group, a historic racing organization in San Francisco, and decided to race his Elite.

The immediate problem was that his car was not finished, except for a freshly restored engine and gearbox. He did the typical Bob Green thing, which was to borrow a friend's Elite and install his own drive train. Unfortunately, during his first race the steering wheel came off and the car was brought to a stop, off the course, with a cracked 'A' arm and some damaged fibreglass. Green repaired the car and completed four more races in the borrowed Elite without further incident.

In 1977 chassis 1373 was finally completed and painted a bright orange, which led to the nickname 'The Great Pumpkin'. Green ran half-a-dozen races a year until 1981 when he decided to do something completely different and contest the 125 mph class 'H' speed record at the Bonneville Salt Flats. He rebuilt a spare engine to Stage III tune and installed it in 'The Pumpkin'.

Green recalls his first impression of Bonneville: 'The salt is an

Lotus Day at the races. This line-up is led by the ex-Lumsden Elite owned by Matt Carroll. (Adrien Schagen)

Above *Some historic racing Elites are true team efforts. This Elite is pictured at Road Atlanta in 1987; from left to right, Lucien Wilkins (Elite restorer), car owner Watts Hill, Carl Wilson (mechanic) and Bill Hutton of Hutton Motor Engineering (Elite parts supplier).* (Photographer unknown)

Right *While his Elite was undergoing crash repair, Bob Green borrowed a friend's car for the Monterey Historic weekend. He lost control at a corner on some oil and crashed into a tyre wall. Here is the car and Mike Ostrov (current Secretary of Club Elite North America) pointing to the corner where the incident occurred. The owner of the car, George Simmons,is to the left of Mike, and the author (in driving suit) is on the right listening intently.* (Marlene Ortenburger)

awesome experience, 40 square miles of white that crunches like snow when you walk. It's an 11-mile course marked with a 1-foot wide black stripe of used engine oil. The course is graded smooth with a truck towing a weighted 'V' of railroad track. There are actually two lines, one for the over-175-mph cars and the other for all of the rest.

'The Bonneville Salt Flats aren't really flat at all because you can see the curvature of the earth. At the 5 miles mark you would need to be 14 feet tall to see the start line! And the quiet is absolute. I felt very small in the vast whiteness. I'm glad they marked the return road with cones or one could get lost.'

Bob's best run was 117.897 mph, but for an unknown reason his Elite would go no faster despite having revs to spare with his 4.2 differential ratio. No amount of fiddling made any difference (including a run in third gear at 8,000 rpm) so he finished the week of trials second fastest in class without the record he had hoped for.

Bob Green believed a little body damage was all part of the sport. This picture shows 'The Great Pumpkin' after a roll over. (Scott Petersen).

In 1982 Green tried his hand at autocross and emerged the Northern California Champion in 'D' Stock (against Datsun 280ZXs and TR-7s) with five 1sts, four 2nds and one 3rd. Then he loaned his Elite to a friend to use in a vintage racing school. The student spun into a tyre wall which launched the Elite into the air. It landed on the roof and right front wing and did extensive damage to the front subframe.

True to form, Bob removed the engine and gearbox from the wreck and put them into a borrowed Eite so he could make the Monterey Historic weekend. Unfortunately, Bob spun on some oil and crashed, breaking the Elite and his leg in the process!

Undaunted and while still in the cast, he fixed both cars, 'The Great Pumpkin' requiring over 400 hours of work on the body. He recalled: 'In order to repair 1373 I had to remove the bent and twisted front subframe. I also discovered the lousy job that Bristol did on the assembly of the body. The mould release agent was never removed and the parts split along every seam joint.'

In 1983 Green returned to historic racing and has competed in up to half-a-dozen races a year ever since. By 1988 his car had run in 128 races, six of which were two-hour enduros, plus 11 autocross events. He recalled that one of his most memorable races was in 1980 at the Monterey Historic at Laguna Seca when he started 20th on the grid and finished 8th, beating the author of this book at the flag by one foot!

Judy Freeman, Gloucester, UK

'Judy was a keen and successful competitor on horseback and a good, if somewhat forceful, driver on the road, so it seemed right that she should have a go on the track.' So mused Mike Freeman in 1986 about his wife, but the immediate problem was what to race. Mike's Lister Jaguar was on loan to a museum in Belgium and his Brabham BT14 single-seater 'was rather like jumping in at the deep end'.

Both Mike and Judy had long admired the Elite (as a youth, Mike lived close to the garage where DAD 10 was prepared) and when they heard of a restored example for sale nearby they lost no time in making the purchase. What better venue to contest than the Historic Sports

Car Club's 'Classic and Sportscar' Novice Championship? This series was sponsored by *Classic and Sportscar* magazine and was designed for drivers who had no previous racing experience, and sports cars registered from 1960 to 1970. The cars had to be in original production specification and had to be driven to the circuit—no trailers allowed!

Judy attended several drivers' schools while the Elite was race-prepared by fitting an electrical cut-off switch, seat belts and a fire extinguisher. A roll bar was also installed and the fuel filler was moved inside the boot.

The plan was to test the car at Donington before the first round, but two separate sessions were halted because of serious engine oil leaks. Finally, the car was pronounced fit and Judy readied herself for her first race. She recalled, 'At last, the big day arrived. Round one at Thruxton, and I was in the middle of the grid (determined by practice times) ahead of all of the E Types. Keep to the inside at Campbell on the first lap, Mike warned me, the E Types won't stop very well and are liable to go into the back of you if you take the wide racing school line.

'This was the moment the spectators had waited for. A whole grid of novices, their first race and a tricky set of corners—what could be better entertainment? I for one didn't let them down. As we rapidly approached Campbell we seemed to be very well spaced. Enough, I thought, for me to take the line taught by the school. I was wrong, for an E Type hit me hard from behind and spun the Elite right round. I was furious and set off determined to catch them all up, and with the help of Mike's encouraging pit signals, showing a rapid gain on my class mates, I did so, overtaking half the field and winning my class.'

The next race was at Brands Hatch where Mike took the Elite out for a few rounds. He thought it felt a little peculiar in transition from right to left corners and on inspection found the front spring lengths were unequal and that the rear right height was set too high. Still, Judy drove flawlessly and captured another class win and a lead in the Championship!

The six-week break before the next race at Donington was used to fit new front springs and lower the back end. Finally, the weekend ar-

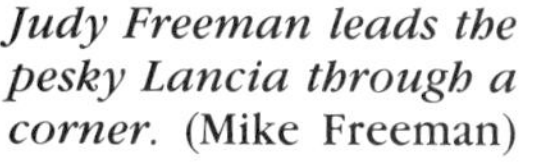

Judy Freeman leads the pesky Lancia through a corner. (Mike Freeman)

Judy Freeman receives the Club Elite trophy from John Chatwin (Chairman) on the left and Mike Raven (Secretary) on the right. (Mike Freeman)

rived and with first practice came the rain. 'Don't worry, Elites go well in the wet.' Which it did, and Judy recalled that the biggest problem was in getting around the spinning cars. Before she could become too confident, however, Mike reported that he smelled a burned clutch and warned her to take it easy. Despite the slippage Judy scored another class win just ahead of a Lancia Fulvia, and everyone agreed that she seemed to be improving dramatically with every race.

The clutch was replaced for the next race at Oulton Park but practice revealed an imbalance that caused the whole car to shake. Judy started well and was dicing with the Lancia for class honours when, suddenly, the Elite went into a violent slide. The cause was a broken Chapman strut, an inch above the alloy casting where it had apparently been previously repaired.

During the next few weeks the clutch was removed and balanced and a new upright installed. A front wishbone mount had broken away from the subframe so this was repaired as well. Unfortunately, during practice the day before the next round at Silverstone, the diff started to part company from the chassis.

The next morning Tony Bates appeared with diff straps and a new differential and after a superlative effort by numerous helpers Judy made the starting grid with 2 minutes to spare. It was raining at flag-fall and Judy made a bad start due to uneven firing. This cleared itself and she started picking off the backmarkers. Mike's pit signals showed that she was gaining on the class-leading Lancia by 3 seconds a lap. Then an Elan spun into the rear wheel of the Elite and bent the wishbone. Judy had to slow considerably to counter the deterioration in handling and she finished well down.

Judy recalled that morale was very low in her pit after the race—good effort spoiled by someone else's mistake. Still, she tied for 2nd place in the Championship and 2nd in her class with two other drivers. There was one race remaining, but Judy's Elite was again bent and broken. However, Mike agreed to pull out all the stops to try to get the car ready despite business and travel conflicts.

A new wishbone was fitted and the fibreglass was pieced together with yellow tape (to match the body colour). The engine still had a misfire but there was only time to install a fresh set of plugs and hope that they would solve the problem.

On the morning of the last round, Mike and Judy walked the circuit to pick out the best racing lines. After practice Judy found herself gridded a second away from the dreaded Lancia. She made a good start and was never overtaken. Her finish put her 1st in Class but 2nd in the HSCC Championship. She was, nonetheless, awarded the 'Classic Car Cup' given by Club Elite and the 'Lotus Trophy' presented by the Historic Sports Car Club for the best performance in a Lotus.

Robin Longdon, Cheshire, UK

Robin Longdon's fascination with Lotus began while he was at University in 1969. He had always been excited about sports cars and owned an MGTC, but when he saw his first Elite he knew he had to have one. His first was acquired in 1971, his second a couple of years later. Both were used extensively on the road and he recalled that they were an absolute pleasure.

In 1977 Longdon met a retired gentleman by the name of John Brown. Brown had been with the Government Foriegn Service in the early 'sixties and had lived for several years in Singapore. The interesting thing was that Brown had purchased an Elite in 1962 and had it shipped to the Far East. Not only that, but he had competed with the car on several occasions, including the Macau Grand Prix in both 1962 and 1963. He had used a Stage III head purchased from Coventry Climax and it was complete with Webers. When Brown told Robin he wanted to sell his car a deal was struck, and Longdon acquired chassis number 1914 in pristine condition with only 21,000 miles on the clock. With Brown's encouragement, Longdon entered it in the Historic Lotus Race at Donington Park in 1978.

As often happens, Longdon was smitten, although he recalled that racing was much harder than he expected. There was no question of not wanting to continue racing, but the ex-Brown Elite was simply

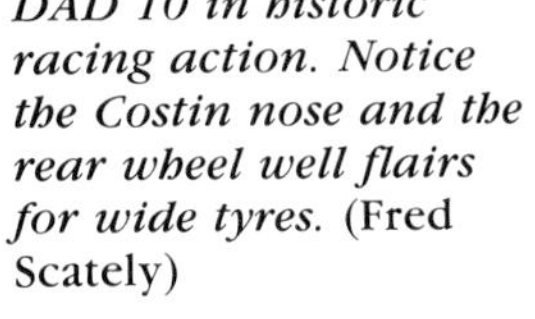

DAD 10 in historic racing action. Notice the Costin nose and the rear wheel well flairs for wide tyres. (Fred Scately)

too nice a car to risk. As luck would have it, Robin happened on two unexpected finds. One was a completely stripped Elite body/chassis almost on his doorstep, and the other a brand new set of Elite running gear—an entire suspension set with an engine and ZF gearbox! Apparently a special builder had purchased the items with an idea for a sports racer, but the project and his resources had faded away.

Longdon bought the bits and proceeded to assemble his own racing Elite. In 1978 he entered his first race at Oulton Park but the car just did not work. Nothing, he recalled, seemed to be right, including his technique, and 'Everyone ran away and hid from me'. Not the least discouraged, Longdon began to sort out himself and the car. He corrected some problems, including oil-soaked rear brake pads, and he fitted stiffer springs, eventually concluding that even the Series I—hard ride—was too soft. He also began to motor considerably faster, beginning at the next outing at Snetterton.

Then came Thruxton where the car took off at the circuit's notorious bump and became airborne. Longdon recalled that it was very windy and reckoned that air got underneath the car and flipped it over. Longdon was in hospital and the Elite was extensively damaged, but in time—about six months to be exact—everything was put back in order.

Oddly enough, both the car and the driver were substantially quicker after the Thruxton crash, and Robin campaigned the car from 1979 to 1982, at which time it was considered the fastest Elite in the United Kingdom. At the end of the season he sold the car to Peter Ecury in Holland and bought an Elva Mark 7.

Meantime, his friend Malcolm Ricketts had found DAD 10 and they set out, as a partnership, to purchase it and, with Tony Bates's help, to restore the car. The first outing for the superbly rebuilt DAD 10 was at Silverstone in 1984 and it proved to be faster than Robin's original racer. By the end of the season he had taken the car to a 2nd overall in class standings. DAD 10 was raced only once in 1984 when Longdon took it to a 1st in the 1300 Class at the Belgium FISA International Cup.

In 1984 Robin campaigned yet another Elite, this time a Team Elite replica. DAD 10 was invited to the FISA round in Zolder as an exhibit, but Longdon decided to race the car rather than simply display it and took 1st overall in the wet!

His thoughts on handling, whether DAD 10 or his other historic racing Elites, are that the cars get around better on 15-inch wheels and 'L' Section rubber than on 13s with Formula Ford tyres. Experimentation with both combinations showed essentially no difference in lap times. Interestingly, Longdon believed that modern technology in the form of engine, exhaust, suspension and tyre development seems to benefit cars like the Elan much more than the Elite. His best results seem to have come when the cars were prepared to a 1960s regime.

Longdon, incidentally, worked for the Champion Spark Plug Company and he stated that the hot set-up for the street was their N87G plug, while for track use he recommended the N84G. He did admit to using rose joints in the rear wishbones and spring rates developed by trial and error, but other than that the specifications were virtually the same as the original Team Elite cars and, as we have already seen, their record speaks for itself.

Brian Caldersmith, Turramurra, Australia

Brian Caldersmith (see Chapter 2 for the story of brother Tony) nurtured a fascination for the Elite for many years but, due to the obligations of family and business, he reckoned he would probably never get around to owning one. Practical fellow, until, that is, he spied an advert for a burned-out Elite being offered for the paltry sum of $900.00! Until that time Brian had never sat in an Elite, let alone driven one, so he did the only sensible thing and bought the car.

The fire had been in the engine compartment, and although the engine bay and the bonnet were extensively damaged, the car was otherwise quite sound. On close inspection, it proved to be even better than that because the engine was an FWB fitted with a Stage III head and Webers. The car also had a ZF gearbox.

Brian began restoring his Elite. He stripped it to the gel coat and repaired the fibreglass. Despite periods of what he described as 'intense activity', there were also 'quite dormant spells' which were fairly lengthy because Brian worked on the Elite for the next ten years!

Finally, in 1984, in large measure due to the help and encouragement given by his brother, the car was finished and given its log book. What better way to wring the car out than by entering the Historic Race Meeting at Amaroo Park in Sydney? This was not as farfetched as it sounded because the organizing body for Australian motor sport (CAMS) specified that cars like the Elite had to be stock and unmodified. Their philosophy is, 'So it was, so it shall be'. As a result of this, Brian could not use the Webers. He could not run adjustable or uniball suspension and the wheels had to be 15 inches with at least 70 per cent aspect ratio for the tyres.

Coincidental with Brian's Elite rebuild was his neighbour's project, which was the restoration of an Albion double-decker bus! In fact, the two restorations were completed at about the same time and the bus's owner, David Griffiths, proposed he fill the double-decker with about

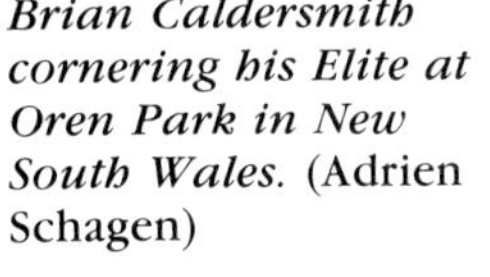

Brian Caldersmith cornering his Elite at Oren Park in New South Wales. (Adrien Schagen)

40 of their neighbours and accompany Brian with his Elite to Amaroo—a kind of Turramurra rooting section with their own grandstand!

A local television station heard of the proceedings and accompanied the entourage to the race-track. Brian's first race (of two that day) was a handicap which he won on the last corner of the last lap! Mind, this was the first race ever for Brian and his Elite. He recalled that 'The win was a fairytale ending just like a Hollywood movie. The car worked like a dream, never missing a beat. When I crossed the finish line my friends went berserk!'

Brian, incidentally, took 2nd place in the class race later in the day, but the die was cast as to where his future lay with the car. Since 1984 he has been a regular competitor in the historic racing scene in Oz and has travelled the length of the country to run at different circuits. Even so, his first encounter with rain was intimidating.

'The course was wet and there were oil flags out all over the circuit as a result of somebody's efforts in the previous race. I remember being very apprehensive, although boys will be boys, and I rationalized it by saying that I would just drive around gently at the back of the field and try to gain some experience of wet weather racing.

'That reasoning lasted until I snatched second gear off the grid. The Elite in the wet was magnificent. The circuit was diabolically slippery and there were people disappearing off the circuit everywhere. The Elite never put a foot wrong, it felt so well balanced and controllable that on the occasions when the rear end twitched out of line in a corner I enjoyed leaving it there all the way around until I felt like straightening it all up.'

Doubtless, Colin Chapman would be proud to see so many of his Elites carrying on so grandly after all of these years.

Epilogue

For years after the Elite ceased production there appeared articles, now and again, in the enthusiasts' press reminding us how great a car it was. Most sounded suspiciously like the old 'driving impressions' with a little history thrown in to modernize the story. They were, nonetheless, all pretty accurate and did their best to convey the special aura about the car. Then *Car and Driver* magazine, in America, published a story by L.J.K. Setright that sought only to define the special appeal of the Elite without describing its nuts and bolts. In his usual eloquence, Setright took us straight to the heart of the matter, and we owe special appreciation to *Car and Driver* for allowing us to reprint the article in its entirety.

L.J.K. SETRIGHT

When "Lotus" meant "tiny" (and Nader meant little).

• In 32 years' driving of cars covering a span of 78 years, I have fallen in love with just three of them. There were others that I admired, some that I lusted after; but only these three produced that special tug at the heartstrings. If I saw one on the road, a deep sigh would well up unsummoned to betray the emotion that any decent psychiatrist could have fed on for years, and passengers would look alarmed or puzzled, wondering whether I had just realized that I had forgotten the way, had forgotten Jerusalem, or had forgotten my wallet. Just three cars—and one motorcycle, about which I may tell you another day—and I still feel about them as I always did. They were the Bristol 405, the Lotus Elite, and the original 1.4-liter Fiat 124S coupe.

To be honest, I am not sure about the Fiat. It was a marvelous car, even though I hated the driving position; driving it on fast roads, or in the snow, or best of all singing through the curves of the Silverstone Circuit with a sweet stability and a speed that it seemed no other production car could match, was cloud-riding of the most heavenly kind. I adored that car; but I am not sure that I truly loved it. The trouble was that the Fiat 2.4 Dino coupe came along and seduced me, and after that I could never be sure which of the two I wanted, while feeling that I should not and did not want both. When you cannot choose between two, I suspect that you do not really love either. Maybe I am wrong; but just to be on the safe side, let us say that i truly loved but two, the Bristol and the Lotus.

What did they have in common? Apart from matter-of-fact things like BSF threads, Lucas electrics, good aerodynamics, and superlative steering, there were two things that mattered. One was that each fitted perfectly, so that driver and passenger alike felt integrated with the car, wrapped up in it and made part of it, so that nothing about the superstructure or the underpinnings felt remote in distance or inappropriate in scale. There was all the room that I wanted, and there was no room that I did not want. Allowing for the one being a two-seater and the other a genuine four-seater, there was in each of them enough car and in neither an excess of car. It is a very special feeling that I have found in an early E-type Jaguar and missed in an early Lamborghini, found in a Ferrari 275GTB and missed in its successor the Daytona. It is a feeling that intimates efficiency by implying economy—economy of substance and of effort, such as prompted Gibbon to praise the emperor Vespasian, for attaining great ends by modest means.

There was one other thing that mattered, one other feature that was shared by my beloved twain. Both the 405 and the Elite had bodies that were built on the edge of Filton Airfield by the Bristol Aeroplane Company, which never made anything less well than anybody knew how. For, you see, the Elite I refer to is not the current cuneiform Lotus that you all know so well, six feet wide and 2400 pounds heavy, but the heartbreakingly lovely little wind-shaped Lotus 14 Elite, less than 60 inches narrow and 1400 pounds light. First seen in 1957, Colin Chapman's idea of uncompromised perfection was not properly realized until, having despaired of getting the body properly made by a boat-building firm that was supposed to be good at fiberglass, he had the Series 2 Elite hull built (from 1960) by the Bristol Aeroplane Plastics Division, then the best workers in resin-bonded fiber to be found anywhere. I believe that they rather enjoyed the job, admiring it for its correct and imaginative use of the material and recognizing how superb was its shape, even if the aerodynamic refinement of the design had been the work of an expert from their rival de Havilland. Frank Costin gave the Elite its reflex-camber chord line, its Kamm tail, and its 0.29 drag coefficient. So light, so little, and so slippery, the Elite needed only 24 bhp to do 60 mph.

The day of the rapier has passed, and the broadsword has come upon us. Look for a little high-performance two-seater with a rigid roof and rapid reactions, and you will find with a shock that the Fiat X1/9 weighs 2030 pounds (2120 in the U.S.A.). The champion of lightweight construction is Volkswagen, but the nearest it comes is with the Scirocco, which in theory (though not in practice) has four seats: the GLI weighs 1800 pounds and is as fast with 110 bhp as the Elite was with 75. Yet it was not especially the lightness of the Lotus, or even its organic, breeze-bating body shape, which gave the Elite its particular charm: they were functions of something more fundamental, its sheer smallness.

It was not alone in its time. In the days when cars were designed to go from A to B—or more probably from A to Z via corners B to Y inclusive—instead of being designed to crash into concrete blocks or shrug off battering rams, there were lots of really little cars, and some of them went like stink. Abarth, Elva, Nardi-Danese, Giannini, and many more, designed with a spring balance and developed with pruning shears, proved that by moving no more than was necessary it could be moved, without much effort, very quickly and precisely. They seldom had engines much bigger than the Elite's 1216cc and were often as small as 750cc (the point from which Chapman really started), they likewise had slim tires on skinny wheels, and they all responded to the slightest touch. Fitting as closely as bathwater, flitting as delicately as butterflies, they flew over the roads of England, France, and Italy, running fast and frugally in TT and Mille Miglia, Bol d'Or and Le Mans, in weekend jaunts and on workaday journeys, just as the microcars from Austin, GN, Amilcar, d'Yrsan, and countless others had in decades before.

You are not allowed to have a car like that now. Maybe you would not appreciate it anyway: apart from the Crosley, I do not think that the Americans have ever made such tiddlers.' Neither have the Germans ever gone in for them, which may partly explain the enthusiasm of Americans for German cars? But the Latins have always done it well, and very occasionally the English have done it brilliantly. There are pride and progress in the fact that the nation which gave us the Nasmyth also bred the Elite; and there are shame and sorrow in the metaphor that we must now revert to the steam hammer to crack a nut. •

Appendix I

Source list

Elite clubs

Club Elite
Nick Raven, Secretary
Little Questing
15 Peatling Road
Countesthorpe
Leicestershire LE8 3RD
England

Club Elite, North America
Michael Ostrov, Secretary
6238 Ralston Avenue
Richmond
California 94805
USA

Elite literature

Richard Spelberg Jr
Kaiser Friedrick Ring 33
4000 Dusseldorf 11
West Germany

Richard Spelberg Jr operates a Lotus literature mail order business and his catalogue (printed in German) lists essentially everything ever printed about the marque including sales literature, books, magazines, blueprints and the like. His inventory features a large section on the Elite.

Elite models and miniatures

Lot:43, The Model Club for Lotus Enthusiasts
Roger Allard, Secretary
11, Old Farm Road
Downley
High Wycombe
Buckinghamshire HP13 5LP
England

As the name suggests, Roger Allard operates a model club exclusively for Lotus enthusiasts. His organization features a regular newsletter which includes colour photos of Lotus models and details the history and availability of various Lotus kits, ready-builts and toys.

Coventry Climax specialist

Climax Engine Services
Tony Mantle
82 Northwick Park Estate
Blockley
Gloucestershire GL56 9RF
England

Elite specialists

Lotus Elite Overhaul and Rebuild Specialist
A.N.E. Bates
Beech House
East Winterslow
Salisbury
Wiltshire SP5 1BG
England

Fibreglass Services
Miles Wilkins
Charlton Saw Mills
Charlton
Singleton
Nr Chichester
Sussex
England

Hutton Motor Engineering
Bill Hutton
PO Box 3333
Clarksville
Tennessee 37043-3333
USA

Elite and Wheel Service
Bob Green
13 Cranham Court
Pacifica
California 94044
USA

Appendix II

The Lotus Elite chassis list

The following pages contain a list of every Elite chassis known to have been produced during, and shortly after, the official production run. At the left-hand side is the chassis number assigned to that particular car. Then follows the original customer and the invoice date. Next to that is the name of the owner in 1989 and his/her country of residence, along with notes of significant interest. The works chassis list (See *The Original Lotus Elite, Racing Car for the Road*, Newport Press, 1977) was a handwritten document, which in some cases was impossible to decipher, both as to the spelling of certain names and the existence of double sets of invoice numbers, customers and invoice dates. They have been sorted as logically as possible in this presentation but no claim is made here for perfect accuracy.

The registry of 1990 owners is the work of Mike Ostrov, the indefatigable Secretary of Club Elite, North America, and is the culmination of two years' work and over 900 individual pieces of correspondence! Our profound appreciation for his allowing the information to be published here.

Examination of the list shows that chassis numbers ran, essentially unbroken, from 1001 to 2000, which was also the extent of the original chassis list. There are some peculiarities, such as a few numbers repeated with the suffix 'B' and a few others which list an invoice date but no customer or a chassis number with no information at all. If all of these chassis were built, the total would be 1,029 (recall that Bristol duplicated the numbers of Maximar's final 29 body/chassis) plus the cars that were built post-production (to 2047) which means a grand total of 1,076 cars. Alas, the exact number remains unknown although it is somewhat less than 1,076 because some chassis numbers were not used at all while others were assigned to a bare body/chassis which was used to restore an accident or racing write-off. What is known from the following is that in 1990 there were 560 Lotus Elites in no fewer than 18 countries. Essentially half the production still existed with 38 of the cars being campaigned in historic racing. Telling testimony to the fitness of Colin Chapman's fibreglass monocoque GT.

NB: CBU signifies 'chassis/body unit'.

Chassis	Original customer and date of invoice	1990 owner and country	Notes
1000(?)	Earls Court		Broken up in 1958 at Hornsey
1001	D. Buxton, 17/9/59		EL 5; Ian Walker raced car for one season
1002		Heinz Schreiber/ Germany	
1003	Peter Lumsden, 11/3/59	Matt Carroll/Australia	WUU 2; Le Mans winner, rebodied 1016
1004	J.P. Williams, 18/2/59	Tony Mantle/UK	JPW 24; club racer
1005	J. Whitmore, 5/2/59		Club racer
1006	G. Warner, 14/3/59	Hiroshi Nakajima/Japan	LOV 1
1007			

Chassis	Original customer and date of invoice	1990 owner and country	Notes
1008	K. Hall, 10/3/59		6 SME
1009	D.C. Barber, 31/12/58		CB 23; club racer
1010	I. Scott Watson, 31/12/58	David Sharlcross/UK	ESH 190; raced by Jim Clark
1011	D. Marguiles, 12/6/59		XLD 141
1012	E. Arnison Newgass, 28/8/59	Deviewers, Belgium	
1013		UK	1959 Sebring racer
1014	Lt Merle Roberson		
1015		Kevin Kilpatrick/USA	1959 Sebring racer
1016	D. Buxton, 10/9/59	Matt Carroll/Australia	Rebodied 1003
1017	R.D. Burrows, 10/4/59	Rowland Long/UK	Ford pushrod vintage racer
1018	J. Walker, 10/4/59		
1019			
1020	E. Lewis, 8/4/59		
1021	D. Buxton, 21/4/59	Peter Stohrmann/ Germany	
1022	D. Buxton, 10/9/59	Jim Castle/UK	Written off, now 1255
1023	J.M. Parkin, 12/5/59		
1024	R. Vincent, 4/5/59		
1025	J.E. Best, 26/6/59		
1026		Humio Kojima/Japan	
1027	J. Wagstaff, 17/6/59		FP 98; Team Elite Le Mans racer
1028		Pirson/Belgium	
1029	C. Gray, 23/6/59		
1030		R. Gravill/UK	
1031	J.L. Wallis, 10/7/59		
1032			
1033		John Skjefstad/Norway	Vintage racer
1034		Olav Glasius/Holland	
1035		Deviewers/Belgium	
1036			
1037	R. Stoop, 10/6/59		
1038	I. Scott Watson, 25/6/59	Peter Herbert/New Zealand	2nd car raced by Jim Clark
1039	Chequered Flag, 2/10/59	Joakim Sjunnesson/ Sweden	
1040			
1041	Lotus Sales, 20/10/59		
1042	Lotus Sales, 29/7/59		
1043	Lotus Sales, 21/9/59		
1044	David Buxton, 19/10/59		
1045	Lotus Development, 17/8/59		
1046	Lotus Sales, 25/8/59	Mike Porter/UK	
1047	J. Chamberlain, 20/7/59		
1048	21/10/59		
1049	D. Jolly, 20/8/59		
1050	Lotus Sales, 17/9/59		
1051	Lotus Sales, 20/7/59		
1052	J. Chamberlain, 20/7/59	Richard Yagami/USA	
1053	J. Chamberlain, 20/7/59	Noble McKay/USA	Original owner
1054	J. Chamberlain, 20/7/59	Rick Snapp/USA	Ex-SCCA racer
1055	J. Chamberlain, 25/9/59	Mark Pedemonte/USA	
1056	J. Chamberlain, 17/11/59		
1057	Lotus Sales, 9/9/59		
1058	21/10/59		
1059	J.R. Bonnell, 7/9/59		
1060	23/11/59		
1061	J. Chamberlain, 25/9/59	Marvin McLaughlin/USA	Ford pushrod
1062	C. Voegele, 30/2/59		
1063	David Buxton, 18/9/59		
1064	J. Chamberlain, 25/9/59	Paul Krusi/USA	
1065	J. Chamberlain, 16/10/59	Jack Fitzpatrick/USA	
1066	J. Chamberlain, 16/10/59	Ron Dietz/USA	

Chassis	Original customer and date of invoice	1990 owner and country	Notes
1067	J. Chamberlain, 27/10/59		
1068	J. Chamberlain, 2/10/59		
1069	J. Chamberlain, 27/10/59		
1070	23/12/59		
1071	3/11/59		
1072	J. Chamberlain, 27/10/59		
1073	D. Jolly, 31/12/59	David Peters/Australia	
1074	6/11/59		
1075	J. Chamberlain, 27/10/59	UK	
1076	R. Stoop, 30/11/59		Body/chassis only
1077	J. Chamberlain, 27/10/59	Richard Cagan/USA	
1078	Lotus Development, 29/12/59		
1079	J. Chamberlain, 30/3/60		
1080	J. Chamberlain, 16/10/59	Mike Ostrov/USA	FWB
1081	J. Chamberlain, 6/10/59		
1082	21/10/59	W.B. Geertsma/ Australia	Written off, now 1449
1083	J. Chamberlain, 27/10/59	Japan	
1084	6/11/59		
1085	20/11/59	Bernard Ducker/UK	FWB
1086	J. Chamberlain, 25/11/59	L. Blake/Cheryl Walker/USA	Ford pushrod
1087	J. Chamberlain, 12/11/59		
1088	J. Allington, 22/6/61	John Pugh/UK	Given to Allington by Chapman
1089	11/11/59		
1090	William Rucker Ort, 20/11/59		
1091	J. Chamberlain, 19/11/59		
1092	J. Chamberlain, 19/11/59		
1093	J. Chamberlain, 17/11/59		
1094	J. Chamberlain, 17/11/59	UK	
1095	J. Chamberlain, 19/11/59	Jim Shannon/USA	Written off
1096	J. Chamberlain, 25/11/59	Joe Marchione/USA	
1097	J. Chamberlain, 4/12/59		
1098	J. Chamberlain, 30/11/59	Henk Resnik/Holland	
1099	Lotus Sales, 20/11/59		
1100	J. Chamberlain, 20/11/59	Tony Clark/USA	
1101	J. Chamberlain, 4/12/59	M. Campbell/UK	
1102	J. Chamberlain, 4/12/59	Karim Abdulla/ Switzerland	
1103	15/1/60		
1104	J. Chamberlain, 4/12/59		
1105	Lotus Development, 11/3/60		
1106	11/12/59	Bill Friend/UK	8 MPG
1107	J. Chamberlain, 4/12/59	USA	
1108	J. Chamberlain, 8/12/59	Ed Clinkscale/USA	
1109	J. Chamberlain, 11/12/59	Terry Elmore/USA	
1110	J. Chamberlain, 8/12/59	UK	
1111	J. Chamberlain, 8/3/60		
1112	J. Chamberlain, 15/12/59	Robert Garbarino/USA	
1113	J. Chamberlain, 23/12/59	Peter Hurlbut/USA	
1114	J. Chamberlain, 15/12/59	Henry Gruver/USA	
1115	J. Chamberlain, 26/1/60		
1116	J. Chamberlain, 15/12/59		
1117	J. Chamberlain, 17/12/59	UK	
1118	J. Chamberlain, 17/12/59	Barney Lenheim/USA	
1119	J. Chamberlain, 8/8/60		
1120	21/12/59	Yoshimichi Miyazawa/Japan	
1121	F. Staumont, 23/12/59		
1122	J. Chamberlain, 23/12/59		
1123	J. Chamberlain, 23/12/59	Terry Elmore/USA	
1124	J. Chamberlain, 23/12/59	John Favro/USA	Original owner

Chassis	Original customer and date of invoice	1990 owner and country	Notes
1125	8/2/60	A. Bradshaw/UK	
1126	J. Chamberlain, 23/12/59		
1127	J. Chamberlain, 23/12/59	Arnold Huberts/ Holland	
1128	F. Staumont, 23/12/59		
1129	J. Chamberlain, 23/12/59	M. Eyre/UK	
1130	J. Chamberlain, 23/12/59		
1131	F. Staumont, 23/12/59	Jason Wright/Italy	Vintage racer
1132	21/1/60		
1133	J. Chamberlain, 23/12/59		
1134	10/3/60		
1135	S.H. Willoughby-Greenhill, 7/3/60	Lennart Almstrom/ Sweden	
1136	J. Chamberlain, 30/3/60	Gary Koller/USA	
1137	J. Chamberlain, 4/3/60		
1138	J. Chamberlain, 26/1/60	Watts Hill Jr/USA	Vintage racer
1139	22/1/60		
1140	J. Chamberlain, 4/3/60	Fritz Bettjer/USA	
1141	D. Jolly, 29/6/60	Bill Mair/Australia	1961 Australian sports car champion
1142	J. Chamberlain, 9/9/60	David Mathison/USA	Ford engine
1143	J. Chamberlain, 4/3/60		
1144	J. Chamberlain, 16/3/60	Charles Ritchie/USA	
1145	J. Chamberlain, 16/3/60	Bob Arp/USA	
1146	J. Chamberlain, 29/1/60	David Stillwell/USA	
1147	J. Chamberlain, 29/1/60	John La Monte/USA	
1148	J. Chamberlain, 26/1/60	Steve Klunk/USA	
1149	J. Chamberlain, 29/1/60	Dave Barnett/USA	

Warranty for Chassis 1157

№ 1157

LOTUS Cars Ltd

DELAMARE ROAD, CHESHUNT, HERTFORDSHIRE   *Telephone : Waltham Cross 26181*

Warranty

The goods supplied by LOTUS CARS LTD. (hereinafter called " the Manufacturer ") are supplied with the following express warranty which excludes all warranties conditions and liabilities implied by common law statute or otherwise.

1. In this warranty " goods " means goods supplied by the Manufacturer but does not include any proprietary articles not manufactured by the Manufacturer which shall be under no liability whatsoever in respect of such articles.
2. For a period of 6 months from the date of delivery of goods to the retail buyer the Manufacturer will repair or replace free of charge any part which needs repairing or replacing due to defective materials or workmanship provided that the defective part or parts are returned carriage paid to the Manufacturer's Works.
3. This warranty is limited to the delivery free at the Manufacturer's Works of the part or parts whether new or repaired in exchange for those acknowledged to be defective. The Manufacturer shall not be liable for any expense incurred in the removal of parts or in the fitting of repaired or replacement parts nor shall the Manufacturer be liable for any injury to persons or property or for any consequential or resulting liability damage or loss howsoever arising.
4. No claim for exchange or repair will be considered unless :—
   (a) the part or parts claimed to be defective are sent carriage paid to the Manufacturer's Works promptly on discovery of the defect ; and
   (b) such part or parts are properly packed for transit and clearly marked for identification with the name and address of the claimant and in case of parts removed from a vehicle with the chassis and manufacturing numbers of such vehicle ; and
   (c) on or before dispatch of such part or parts there is posted to the Manufacturer a full and complete description of the claim and the reasons therefore together with particulars of the date of purchase of the goods alleged to be defective and the name and address of the person firm or company from whom the purchase was made.
5. The Manufacturer shall not be obliged to repair or replace any part which in the opinion of the Manufacturer has been injured by wear or tear or neglect or misuse or has been altered outside the Manufacturers Works.
6. No claim for exchange or repair may be made in respect of a vehicle which has been used for motor racing or competitions of any kind or of which the identification numbers have been removed or altered or of which parts originally fitted by the Manufacturer have been replaced by parts of another origin.
7. The decision of the Manufacturer in all cases of claims and on all questions as to defects and to the exchange of a part or parts shall be final and conclusive. After the expiration of 6 days from the dispatch of notification of the Manufacturer's decision the part or parts submitted for examination may be scrapped or returned carriage forward by the Manufacturer.
8. This warrantee is automatically invalidated if the car is used at any stage of its life in competitive motor racing.

Owner's Name GEORGE R. KREISEL. (BLOCK LETTERS)   *Dealer's Name* LOTUS CARS LIMITED (BLOCK LETTERS)

Address HOHENECKEN/PFALZ, FRIEDENSTRASSE 7, GERMANY.   *Address* D.LAMARE ROAD, CHESHUNT, HERTS.

Chassis No. 1157   *Engine No.* FWE 7646   *Date Supplied* 1ST MARCH, 1960.

Chassis	Original customer and date of invoice	1990 owner and country	Notes
1150	J. Chamberlain, 26/1/60	Jud Cushing/USA	
1151	J. Chamberlain, 26/1/60	Chuck Gardner/USA	Purchased by father
1152	J. Chamberlain, 26/1/60	USA	Ford engine
1153	J. Chamberlain, 9/2/60		
1154	J. Chamberlain, 9/2/60		
1155	J. Chamberlain, 9/2/60		
1156	J. Chamberlain, 10/2/60	Bruce Zemke/USA	
1157	George Kreisel, 25/2/60	G. Tchorznicki/USA	Written off
1158	J. Chamberlain, 9/2/60	John Posselius/USA	Original owner
1159	12/2/60		
1160	J. Chamberlain, 9/2/60	Hans Sifrig/USA	
1161	J. Chamberlain, 10/2/60		
1162	J. Chamberlain, 9/2/60	John Gill/USA	
1163	J. Chamberlain, 10/2/60	Bob Simpson/USA	
1164	J. Chamberlain, 9/2/60	James Gose/USA	
1165	J. Chamberlain, 16/1/60	Robert Fergus/USA	
1166	9/3/60		
1167	28/3/60		
1168	J. Chamberlain, 16/2/60	Jeff Frazier/USA	
1169	J. Chamberlain, 8/3/60	David Parke/USA	
1170	Louis Treadway, 16/3/60		
1171	J. Chamberlain, 8/3/60	D. Bridges/UK	
1172	4/3/60	Roy Yates/UK	
1173	J. Chamberlain, 16/3/60	Allan Brugge/USA	
1174	12/2/60		
1175	J. Chamberlain, 22/3/60		
1176	J. Chamberlain, 8/3/60	Guy Larkins/USA	
1177	J. Chamberlain, 16/3/60	Robert Haug/USA	
1178	J. Chamberlain, 30/3/60	Terry Elmore/USA	
1179	J. Chamberlain, 22/3/60	USA	FWA
1180	J. Chamberlain, 22/3/60	UK	
1181	J. Chamberlain, 22/3/60	Tom White/USA	
1182	6/4/60	UK	Ford engine
1183	J. Chamberlain, 14/4/60		
1184	C. Voegele, 21/4/60		
1185	J. Chamberlain, 30/3/60	Jackie Shea/USA	
1186	J. Chamberlain, 30/3/60	Don Plettenberg/USA	
1187	28/3/60	Peter Kiedrowski/ Germany	
1188	J. Chamberlain, 30/3/60	Mike Ostrov/USA	
1189	J. Chamberlain, 30/3/60	Alan McWain/USA	
1190	J. Chamberlain, 30/3/60		
1191	J. Chamberlain, 30/3/60	UK	
1192	J. Chamberlain, 30/3/60	Bill Greenough/USA	
1193	J. Chamberlain, 30/3/60	Jeff Paquin/USA	
1194	J. Chamberlain, 30/3/60	Wayne Mitchell/USA	Written off
1195	J. Chamberlain, 30/3/60	Mitsuo Kojima/Japan	
1196	J. Chamberlain, 30/3/60	Ray Ozmun/USA	
1197	J. Chamberlain, 8/4/60		
1198	J. Chamberlain, 8/4/60		
1199	8/4/60		
1200	CIT 8/4/60	Mario Ehrensberger/ Switzerland	
1201	J. Chamberlain, 14/4/60	Dick Fryberger/USA	Vintage racer
1202	J. Chamberlain, 8/4/60	Germany	
1203	J. Chamberlain, 8/4/60	Stan Weiss/USA	
1204	Elite Cars, 27/5/60		
1205	J. Chamberlain, 8/4/60	Rich McCormick/USA	
1206	J. Chamberlain, 14/4/60	UK	
1207	J. Chamberlain, 29/4/60		
1208	Woodyatt of Malvern, 4/5/60	Robert Matthews/UK	
1209	21/4/60		
1210	13/4/60	Jamie Morton/Canada	Vintage racer
1211	J. Chamberlain, 14/4/60		

Chassis	Original customer and date of invoice	1990 owner and country	Notes
1212	J. Chamberlain, 8/5/60		
1213	J. Chamberlain, 29/4/60		
1214	J. Chamberlain, 10/5/60	Truett Lawson/USA	Vintage racer
1215	Frosts Cars Ltd, 9/5/60		
1216	Calvin H. Hunt, 17/8/60		
1217	Chequered Flag (Midland) Ltd, 9/5/60		
1218	Chequered Flag (Midland) Ltd, 9/5/60		
1219	11/5/60		
1220	David Buxton Ltd, 9/5/60	D.G. Hales/UK	
1221	Chequered Flag (Comp Cars) Ltd, 9/5/60	Japan	
1222	Dickson Motors (Perth) Ltd, 9/5/60	Bob Akin/USA	
1223	Autosport Equip, 4/8/60	Dennis Wilde/Canada	Vintage racer
1224	J. Chamberlain, 8/8/60	Howdan Ganley/UK	
1225	H. DaSilva Ramos (Malle), 19/5/60	Claude Serre/France	
1226	J. Chamberlain, 20/5/60	John Entwistle/USA	
1227	J. Chamberlain, 12/8/60		
1228	Dickson Motors		
1229	J. Chamberlain, 12/5/60	USA	Written off
1230	J. Chamberlain, 12/5/60	Henry Kight/USA	
1231	Elite Cars, 12/5/60		
1232	J. Chamberlain, 27/5/60		
1233	J. Chamberlain, 27/5/60		
1234	Connaught Cars, 14/5/60	John Lindsey/Canada	
1235	J. Chamberlain, 23/5/60		
1236	J. Chamberlain, 26/5/60	Michael Moore/USA	
1237	J. Chamberlain, 26/5/60	Walter Hironimus/USA	
1238	Provincial Ins Co, 31/8/61	Urban Fassler/ Switzerland	
1239	Elite Cars, 8/6/60	Yoshiho Matsuda/Japan	
1240	J. Chamberlain, 7/6/60	Joe Winterhalter/USA	
1241	Chequered Flag (Comp Cars) Ltd, 24/6/60		
1242	Woodyatt of Malvern, 20/8/60		
1243	J. Chamberlain, 17/4/60	Dan Shanahan/USA	
1244	Chequered Flag (Midland) Ltd, 3/6/60		
1245	J. Chamberlain, 7/6/60	Jerry Morrici/USA	
1246	Jaques Savaye, 16/6/60		
1247	J. Chamberlain, 8/7/60	Frank Miller/USA	Original owner
1248	J. Chamberlain, 29/6/60	Jerry Wachtel/USA	
1249	David Buxton, 17/6/60		
1250	Chequered Flag Ltd, 23/5/60		
1251			SII
1251	J. Chamberlain, 4/7/60	Wallace Hamilton/USA	SI
1252	Dr H. Busch, 27/5/60		SII
1252	J. Chamberlain, 4/7/60	David Grossman/ Germany	SI
1253	J. Chamberlain, 16/8/60	Morris Kindig/USA	SII
1253	J. Chamberlain, 22/6/60	UK	SI
1254	Jim Russell Racing Drivers School, 11/3/60		SII
1254	J. Chamberlain, 4/7/60	Ed Clark/USA	SI written off, now 2041
1255	J. Chamberlain, 30/10/60	UK	SII
1255		Jim Castle/UK	SI–2 litre Le Mans car
1256	J. Chamberlain, 30/10/60	Dick McGovern/USA	SII
1256	Woodyatt, 7/7/60	Roger Barker/Canada	SI
1257	J. Chamberlain, 16/6/60	John Streets/USA	SII
1257	J. Chamberlain, 4/7/60	UK	SI

Chassis	Original customer and date of invoice	1990 owner and country	Notes
1258	J. Chamberlain, 16/6/60		SII
1258	J. Chamberlain, 4/7/60	Dick Lenhart/USA	SI
1259	Elite Cars, 9/8/60	John Scheeman/USA	SII
1259	Dickson Motors, 11/7/60	Raymond Robinson/Canada	SI
1260	J. Chamberlain, 30/6/60	Urban Fassler/ Switzerland	SII
1260	David Buxton, 12/7/60	Gerhard Neitemier/Germany	SI
1261	Elite Cars, 9/5/60	J.B. Skinner/UK	SII; original owner
1261	Chequered Flag, 24/6/60	J.F. Parker/UK	SI
1262	Dickson Motors, 11/7/60	A. McLennan/UK	SII
1262	David Buxton, 30/6/60		SI
1263	Chequered Flag, 9/6/60		SII
1263	Derek Jolly, 13/7/60	Max McCrackan/ Australia	SI
1264	F. Staumont, 28/6/60		SII
1264	J. Chamberlain, 8/7/60		SI
1265	J. Chamberlain, 30/6/60	Jim Shannon/USA	SII
1265	J. Chamberlain, 8/7/60	Terry Elmore/USA	SI
1266	J. Chamberlain, 22/6/60		SII
1266	Elite Cars, 8/6/60	Stan Peterson/USA	SII; original owner
1267	J. Chamberlain, 16/6/60	George Clark/USA	SII
1267	Chequered Flag, 6/7/60		SI
1268	J. Chamberlain, 30/6/60	Read Sigler/USA	SII
1268	J. Chamberlain, 8/7/60		SI
1269	David Buxton, 4/7/60		SII
1269	J. Chamberlain, 8/7/60	USA	SI; written off
1270	J. Chamberlain, 8/8/60		SII
1270	J. Chamberlain, 18/7/60	Karl Bower/USA	SI
1271	J. Chamberlain, 8/7/60	Gary Broeder/USA	SII
1271	J. Chamberlain, 18/7/60		SI
1272	WSU Leech, 17/5/62		SII
1272	Elite Cars, 14/7/60		SI
1273	F. Staumont, 8/7/60	R. Servais/Belgium	SII
1273	J. Chamberlain, 18/7/60		SI
1274	Chequered Flag, 4/7/60	Minor Wilcox/USA	SII
1274	J. Chamberlain, 8/8/60	Bob Green/USA	SI; vintage racer
1275	J. Chamberlain, 22/7/60		SII
1275	J. Chamberlain, 8/7/60	Clem Dwyer/Australia	SI
1276	J. Chamberlain, 8/7/60	Corrado Cupellini/Italy	SII
1276	David Buxton, 18/7/60	Bill Hutton/USA	SI; written off
1277	J. Chamberlain, 8/7/60		SII
1277	David Buxton, 19/7/60		SI
1278	J. Chamberlain, 18/7/60	Bert Curtis/USA	SII
1278	J. Chamberlain, 8/8/60		SI
1279	J. Chamberlain, 18/7/60		SII
1279	J. Chamberlain, 8/8/60	George Wimberly/USA	SI
1280	J. Chamberlain, 8/7/60	Bill Shanklan/Australia	SII
1280	J. Chamberlain, 18/9/60		SI
1281	J. Chamberlain, 16/8/60	Brian Wertheimer/USA	
1282	J. Chamberlain, 8/7/60	Dave Wait/USA	
1283	J. Chamberlain, 18/7/60		
1284	J. Chamberlain, 8/7/60	Jim Duncan/USA	
1285	J. Chamberlain, 8/7/60	Roger Nethercot/ Canada	
1286	J. Chamberlain, 8/8/60		
1287	J. Chamberlain, 8/7/60	Leon Maloski/USA	
1288	J. Chamberlain, 8/8/60	Ed Primosic/USA	
1289	J. Chamberlain, 8/7/60	Mike Ostrov/USA	
1290	J. Chamberlain, 8/8/60		
1291	J. Chamberlain, 8/8/60		
1292	J. Chamberlain, 12/8/60	John Macleod/USA	
1293	Ets L. Beaudoin, 18/7/60		

Chassis	Original customer and date of invoice	1990 owner and country	Notes
1294	J. Chamberlain, 8/8/60	Dwight Cooley Jr/USA	
1295	Ets L. Beaudoin, 18/7/60	M. Beltoise/France	
1296	J. Chamberlain, 8/8/60	Harold Allen/USA	
1297	J. Chamberlain, 8/8/60	UK	
1298	J. Chamberlain, 19/10/60		
1299	J. Chamberlain, 26/8/60		
1300	J. Chamberlain, 8/8/60		
1301	J. Chamberlain, 8/7/60	Richard Shearer/USA	
1302	J. Chamberlain, 8/8/60		
1303	J. Chamberlain, 26/8/60		
1304	J. Nystrom, 28/10/60	Torgany Rojare/ Sweden	
1305	J. Chamberlain, 23/9/60	Shin Yoshikawa/USA	
1306	J. Chamberlain, 26/8/60	Roger Busha/USA	
1307	J. Chamberlain, 19/10/60	Paul Wilson/USA	
1308	J. Chamberlain, 26/8/60	Will Nighswonger/USA	
1309	J. Chamberlain, 23/9/60	Barry Swackhamer/ USA	
1310	J. Chamberlain, 26/8/60		
1311	Peter Lindner, 3/10/60	Mark Rex/USA	
1312	J. Chamberlain, 9/9/60	Wayne Mitchell/USA	
1313	J. Chamberlain, 26/8/60	Dean Price/USA	Written off
1314	J. Chamberlain, 26/8/60		
1315	Peter Lindner, 25/8/60	Bill Hutton/USA	Written off
1316	Peter Lindner, 25/8/60		
1317	David Buxton, 16/12/60	M. Kosellek/France	
1318	J. Chamberlain, 26/8/60	Hale Hunter/USA	Original owner
1319	J. Chamberlain, 26/9/60	R. Bruce McDannald/USA	
1320	J. Chamberlain, 26/8/60		
1321	J. Chamberlain, 8/8/60		
1322	J. Chamberlain, 8/8/60	Morris Kindig/USA	
1323	J. Chamberlain, 8/8/60	Lee Weinstein/USA	
1324	Autosport Equip, 30/8/60	John Lindsey/Canada	
1325	J. Chamberlain, 14/10/60	UK	
1326	David Buxton, 11/7/60		
1327	David Buxton, 29/8/60		
1328	Autosport Equip, 13/7/60		
1329	J. Chamberlain, 8/8/60	Grant Woods/USA	Ford engine

Chassis 1346

Chassis	Original customer and date of invoice	1990 owner and country	Notes
1330	J. Chamberlain, 8/8/60	Wayne Schultz/USA	
1331	J. Chamberlain, 7/10/60	Carl Mumm/USA	
1332	Ets L. Beaudoin, 19/9/60		
1333	Hauri Motor Service, 31/8/60	Japan	
1334	J. Chamberlain, 20/9/60	USA	
1335	J. Chamberlain, 8/9/60	Tim Grindle/USA	
1336	J. Chamberlain, 8/8/60	Ed Gaines/USA	
1337	Ecurie Shirlee, 10/1/63	Bob Sanders/USA	
1338	J. Chamberlain, 8/7/60	Lee Pinto/USA	
1339	I. Neilson, 4/12/61		
1340	J. Chamberlain, 18/7/60		
1341	J. Chamberlain, 9/9/60	Art Siverling/USA	
1342	J. Chamberlain, 26/9/60	Carter Alexander/USA	
1343	J. Chamberlain, 8/7/60	UK	
1344	J. Chamberlain, 9/9/60	Gil Jones/USA	Original owner
1345	J. Chamberlain, 7/10/60	Foster Cooperstein/ USA	
1346	Elite Cars, 13/6/60		
1347	P.J. Ash, 29/3/62		
1348	Ecurie Shirlee, 10/1/63	Tom Schurbert Jr/USA	
1349	F.G. Riggall, 6/4/62		
1350	P. Illion, 9/4/62		
1351	Beaudoin, 29/3/61		
1352	R.W. Messinger, 6/4/62		
1353	Hamilton Leech, 20/7/62	Tom Dickson/USA	
1354	J. Chamberlain, 31/10/60	USA	Flat engine
1355	M. Xilas, 18/4/62		
1356	J. Chamberlain, 7/10/60	Gayle Hicks/USA	
1357	S.W. Morrison, 15/6/62	Gordon Grant/UK	
1358	F.C. Sale, 23/1/62	Bill Orr/USA	
1359	Ecurie Shirlee, 10/1/63		
1360	D.C. Jamson, 17/4/61	J. Faulding/UK	
1361	J. Chamberlain, 12/10/60	Calvin Hefner/USA	
1362	Ecurie Shirlee, 23/10/62		
1363	14/11/62		
1364	Hauri Mtr Serv, 19/6/61	Bruno Schaffner/ Switzerland	Vintage racer
1365	F.A. Hastings, 14/2/62		
1366	Ecurie Shirlee, 17/8/62	David Whiteside/USA	Vintage racer

Chassis 1373

Chassis	Original customer and date of invoice	1990 owner and country	Notes
1367	Beaudoin, 24/4/61	Alain Nogier/France	
1368	Ecurie Shirlee, 23/10/63	Leon Maloski/USA	
1369	Modgeson, 3/5/62		
1370	Ecurie Shirlee, 23/10/62	Gene Kath/USA	
1371	J. Chamberlain, 3/11/60	Austria	
1372	J. Chamberlain, 2/10/60	Japan	
1373	Ecurie Shirlee, 10/1/63	Bob Green/USA	Vintage racer
1374	P.J.Q. Adams, 30/3/62		
1375	E.B. Kay, 10/4/62		
1376	W. Griffiths, 6/3/62		
1377	J. Chamberlain, 20/10/60	David Monett/USA	
1378	R.H. Todd, 18/12/61	George Nuse/USA	Vintage racer
1379	H.E. Avon Esq, 11/4/62	Fred Corporaal/ Holland	Vintage racer
1380	J.B. Blair, 13/8/62	Luca Pedotti/ Switzerland	
1381	Beaudoin, 2/6/61		
1382	P. Sulley, 12/1/62		
1383	J. Chamberlain, 26/9/60	Doug Bentz/USA	
1384	J. Chamberlain, 23/11/60	Paul Ishiyama/Japan	
1385	J. Chamberlain, 12/10/60	Richard Dow/USA	
1386	J. Chamberlain, 14/11/60	George Simmons/USA	Vintage racer
1387	J. Chamberlain, 7/10/60	Clay Vycralek/USA	
1388	J. Chamberlain, 19/10/60	John Bauer/USA	
1389	J. Chamberlain, 7/10/60	USA	
1390	J. Chamberlain, 7/10/60		
1391	Chequered Flag, 27/12/61	John Langford/USA	
1392	J. Chamberlain, 7/10/60	Carol Ann Gent/UK	
1393	Fastamotors, 6/11/62		
1394	J. Chamberlain, 3/11/60	Don Binggeli/USA	
1395	J. Chamberlain, 7/10/60	L. Edwin Viers Jr/USA	
1396	J. Chamberlain, 26/4/60	James Brown/USA	
1397	J. Chamberlain, 12/12/60		
1398	J. Chamberlain, 12/12/60		
1399	J. Chamberlain, 8/9/60	Carl Whitney/USA	
1400	J. Chamberlain, 9/9/60	Jim Rowely/USA	
1401		H. Dutoy Van Hees/Holland	Vintage racer
1402	J. Chamberlain, 8/7/60	Larry Walton/USA	Vintage racer
1403	J. Chamberlain, 8/7/60	Cecil Yates/USA	
1404	Sports Motors, 16/11/60		
1405	David Buxton, 3/10/60	Norman Phillips/ Australia	
1406	J. Chamberlain, 8/9/60	Bill Wayne/USA	
1407	J. Chamberlain, 19/10/60		
1408	H. Jones, 25/1/62	Raymond Bryan/UK	
1409	Alton, 4/4/62		
1410	Ets Jet P. Wouters, 17/12/62		
1411	David Buxton, 8/12/60	Bryn Humphreys/UK	
1412	Chequered Flag, 14/9/60		
1413	Derek Jolly, 30/12/60	Adrian Schagen/ Australia	Original owner
1414	Frost's Ltd, 31/10/60	UK	
1415	Elite Cars, 6/10/60	Mr Raimondi/Italy	
1416	Ecurie Shirlee, 10/1/63	Gail Jacuzzi/USA	
1417	J. Chamberlain, 12/10/60	John Francis/USA	
1418	Autosport Equip, 24/5/61		
1419	J. Chamberlain, 12/10/60		
1420	J. Chamberlain, 26/8/60	George Hamling/USA	
1421	Chequered Flag, 25/10/60		
1422	Ets Beaudoin, 19/9/60	Claude Serre/France	
1423	J. Chamberlain, 12/12/60	Laurn Langhofer/USA	
1424	J. Chamberlain, 31/10/60		
1425	J. Chamberlain, 7/10/60	Japan	

Chassis 1439

Chassis	Original customer and date of invoice	1990 owner and country	Notes
1426	F. Staumont, 16/9/60		
1427	David Buxton, 23/9/60		
1428	Derek Jolly, 14/11/60	Keith Cook/Australia	
1429	Elite Cars, 26/8/60		
1430	Chequered Flag, 16/9/60	William Hope/Scotland	
1431	David Buxton, 10/3/61	C. Hill/UK	
1432	H. Kiviet, 6/10/60		
1433	David Buxton, 21/4/60	Robin Brind/UK	Written off, now 1474
1434	12/11/60	Tommy Paulsson/ Sweden	Super 100
1435	Chequered Flag, 28/10/60	Donald Ross/USA	
1436	J. Chamberlain, 7/9/60	UK	
1437	J. Chamberlain, 31/10/60	David Lambert/USA	
1438	J. Chamberlain, 20/10/60		
1439	J. Chamberlain, 20/10/60	Tom Dunn/USA	
1440	Beaudoin, 12/1/61	Michel Aubarbier/ France	
1441	29/3/61	Tadashi Morita/Japan	
1442	Cheltenham Garage Ltd, 10/1/62		
1443	Chequered Flag, 30/9/60	John Heenan/USA	
1444	J. Chamberlain, 31/10/60	Bret Everett/USA	
1445	Ets L. Beaudoin, 9/11/60		
1446	Chequered Flag (Comp Car), 24/11/60	Hiroshi Yamazaki/ Japan	
1447	J. Chamberlain, 7/10/60		
1448	1/12/60		
1449	Elite Cars, 6/10/60	W.L. Geertsma/ Australia	Was 1082
1450		Ralph Stechow/USA	
1451	Ecurie Shirlee, 23/10/62	Mickey Burns/USA	
1452	J. Chamberlain, 7/10/60		
1453	J. Chamberlain, 12/12/60	Jay Glass/USA	
1454	J. Chamberlain, 12/10/60		
1455	J. Chamberlain, 7/10/60		
1456	David Buxton, 28/4/61	Truett Lawson/USA	Super 95; written off, now 1945
1457	M. Tevsleton, 16/1/61		
1458	Chequered Flag (Comp Car), 25/11/60		
1459		Giorgio Valentini/ Italy	

Chassis	Original customer and date of invoice	1990 owner and country	Notes
1460	David Buxton, 11/4/61	Peter Ecuray/Holland	Ex-David Hobbs car
1461	J. Chamberlain, 19/10/60	Dennis Ortenburger/USA	
1462	26/1/61		
1463	K. McDonald, 29/1/62		
1464	J. Chamberlain, 7/10/60	Gene Young/USA	
1465	George Sheldes, 10/1/63		
1466	Autosport Equip, 21/8/61	George Boorne/Canada	
1467	George Sheldes, 10/1/63		
1468	Ecurie Shirlee, 23/10/62	Harlan Schwartz/USA	
1469	F. Pagani, 2/11/62	R. Corpacci/Italy	
1470	Elite Cars, 26/1/61	Lee Tillotson/USA	
1471	Gilby Eng, 2/1/61		
1472	David Buxton, 6/3/61	Ken Coad/UK	Vintage racer
1473	J.H. Poole, 27/10/60	Naoki Baba/Japan	Vintage racer
1474	David Buxton, 8/12/60	Robin Brind/UK	Was 1433
1475	Chequered Flag (Midlands), 8/2/61	B. Freeman/UK	
1476	Harris Motor Service, 12/10/60	Japan	
1477	20/1/61		
1478	H.P. Clarke, 16/12/61		
1479	Elite Cars, 21/1/61	Ralph Locke/USA	Vintage racer
1480	J. Chamberlain, 19/10/60	Rob Garbarino/USA	
1481	N. Graham, 11/1/62	Tommy Brorsson/ Sweden	
1482	Elite Cars, 27/1/61	R. Thomas Sargent/USA	
1483	Ecurie Shirlee, 10/1/63	Larry Darwin/USA	
1484	J. Chamberlain, 7/10/60	Paul Ishiyama/Japan	
1485	J. Chamberlain, 20/10/60	A.D.Lodge/UK	
1486	Elite Cars, 27/1/61	Switzerland	
1487	M. Cooper Evans, 12/11/61	Michael Gluck/USA	
1488	F. Staumont, 24/8/61	Alex Bressan/ Switzerland	
1489	Ets L. Beaudoin, 12/1/61		
1490	B.W. Parker II, 11/10/62	Brad Parker/USA	Original owner
1491	P. Wood, 8/5/62		
1492	Connaught Cars Ltd, 1/11/60	J. Wagstaff/UK	
1493	Hauri Mtr Serv, 20/1/61	Pierre de Siebenthal/ Switzerland	

Chassis 1479

Chassis	Original customer and date of invoice	1990 owner and country	Notes
1494	Frosts (Cars) Ltd, 7/11/60		
1495	Laystall Ltd, 8/11/60	Jerrold Halverson/USA	750 Le Mans Elite
1496	J. Chamberlain, 14/11/60	Stuart Ralt/UK	
1497	Ecurie Shirlee, 10/1/63	Eric Jewett/USA	
1498	H.A. Foescekson, 21/1/63		
1499	Elite Cars, 27/1/61	Tom Menzies/USA	
1500	I. McLean, 19/12/61		
1501	F.R. Blease, 13/2/62	William Brownlcc/USA	
1502	14/2/63		
1503	Chequered Flag, 20/6/61	Jim Herlinger/USA	Vintage racer
1504	Ecurie Shirlee, 10/1/63	Frank Starkey/USA	Written off
1505	17/1/62		
1506	21/8/62	George Boorne/Canada	
1507	Ets J. Wauters, 17/12/62	Hans Skestool/Holland	
1508	Ecurie Shirlee, 23/10/62	Larry Pugsley/USA	
1509	16/8/63		
1510	Chequered Flag, 30/10/60	Mike Ostrov/USA	
1511	Ecurie Shirlee, 23/10/62		
1512	Western Distributors Inc, 9/10/61		
1513	J. Chamberlain, 12/11/60	UK	
1514	M. Barber, 6/3/62		
1515	Ecurie Shirlee, 6/3/63	Roy Woodcock/USA	
1516	Autosports Equip, 21/8/61	Roger Fountain/UK	
1517	J. Posselues, 31/12/62		
1518	J. Chamberlain, 12/11/60		
1519	Dutchess Auto, 22/4/63	Jack Fitzpatrick/USA	
1520			
1521	J. Chamberlain, 14/11/60	R. Trevor Gersh/USA	
1522	G.E. Turner, 28/6/62		
1523	J. Chamberlain, 18/11/60	Mike Ostrov/USA	FWB, converted to RHD. 5-speed gearbox
1524	M. Walters, 17/1/62	P. Boel/Holland	
1525	Ecurie Shirlee, 6/3/63	Warren Roche/USA	Ford engine
1526	Elite Cars, 26/1/61		
1527	L.B. Flood, 29/12/60	Michael Abramson/USA	
1528	R.N. Vernon, 24/1/62	USA	Written off
1529	H.A. Yoshe, 18/1/62		
1530	J.J. Kilcourse/G.F. Dixon, 26/6/62	G. Thurston/UK	

Chassis 1533

Chassis 1557

Chassis	Original customer and date of invoice	1990 owner and country	Notes
1531	Hauri, 14/3/63	Japan	
1532	D. Harrison, 1/5/62	Arden Sandsnes/USA	
1533	Chequered Flag, 7/3/61	A.N.E. Bates/Robin Longdon/UK	DAD 10
1534	W. Moss, 10/1/62		
1535	Elite Cars, 27/1/61	Terry Elmore/USA	
1536	Ecurie Shirlee, 6/3/63		
1537	29/12/61		
1538	H.P. Clarke, 1/3/62		
1539	Elite Cars, 26/1/61		
1540	D. Lewis, 5/12/61		
1541	J.R. Mount, 30/1/62		
1542	D. Horton, 31/5/62		
1543	Navy Auto Sales, 19/12/62	Geoffrey Griffiths/USA	
1544	Beaudoin, 24/4/61		
1545	F. Pagani, 22/3/63		
1546	F. Pagani, 22/3/63		
1547	Peter Lindner, 14/2/61	Jean Locher/Switzerland	
1548	A.E. Outridge, 21/3/62		
1549	E. Clayton, 3/2/62	Adam Champneys/UK	
1550	Chequered Flag (Comp Cars), 22/12/60		
1551			
1552	16/5/62		
1553	J. Balca, 16/3/62		
1554	J.A. Horton, 28/5/62	Gerrard Raney/USA	
1555	Elite Cars, 9/2/61	Thord Lofgren/Sweden	
1556	Dutchess Auto Co, 22/2/62	Fred Stevenson/USA	Original owner and vintage racer
1557	Elite Cars, 26/1/61	Jay Chamberlain/USA	
1558	J. Cummings, 5/12/61		
1559	R.J. Fuller, 19/12/63		
1560	T.M. Grandon, 14/2/62		
1561	T.H. Cole, 29/1/62	Germany	
1562	F. Staumont, 29/12/60	USA	
1563	A. Foster, 2/5/62	Peter Hall/Australia	Super 95; written off, now 1782
1564	F. Stanley, 30/11/61		

Chassis	Original customer and date of invoice	1990 owner and country	Notes
1565	C.J. Clifton, 11/4/62	M. Dutoy Van Hees/Holland	Vintage racer
1566	J.G. Stewart, 15/4/62	A.N.E. Bates/UK	
1567	Hauri Motor Serv, 6/3/61	Vdo Schurger/Germany	
1568	C.B. Edwards, 30/4/62		
1569	Martin Hoey Esq, 3/4/62	David Springett/USA	
1570	Col Barber, 16/2/62	George Werner/ Germany	Super 95, vintage racer
1571	Mahone, 3/5/62		
1572			
1573	F. Brooks, 17/5/62	Peter John Blincow/UK	Vintage racer
1574		John Hugenholtz/ Holland	Costin nose
1575	G. Hulene, 9/3/62		
1576	Ecurie Shirlee, 17/8/62	John Howe/USA	Written off
1577	B. Barnes, 13/4/62	J.T. Hogg/Switzerland	
1578	E.F. Gleadons, 2/1/62	Jo Robinson/UK	
1579	A.M. Pusser, 3/8/62	David Barraclough/UK	
1580	S.J. Velch, 1/6/62	M.G. Kift/UK	Super 95
1581	R.H. Martin, 10/4/62	Alan Purdy/UK	Written off, now 2033
1582	R.B. Chapman, 25/1/62		
1583	J.A. McLaughon, 4/5/62		
1584	N. Mead, 23/3/62	David Redmond/USA	
1585	J.N. Wylist, 15/8/61		
1586	T.H. Neal, 7/2/62	Mike Ostrov/USA	
1587	Sports Motors, 16/8/62	T. Candlish/UK	
1588	Ets Beaudoin, 16/11/61	Paul Alquier/France	
1589	R.C. Clarke, 7/6/62	A.N.E. Bates/UK	Super 95
1590	K. Lywood, 15/2/62	Alf Blight/Australia	
1591	Chequered Flag, 30/1/61	Brian Caldersmith/ Australia	Vintage racer
1592	Elite Cars, 17/3/61	Gerard W. Carling/UK	Original owner
1593	George Nystrom, 16/8/61	Oves Motor AB/Sweden	
1594	Chequered Flag, 15/2/61		
1595	David Buxton, 27/1/61		
1596	22/2/61		
1597	David Buxton, 29/6/61	E. Seymour/UK	
1598	Sports Motors, 13/2/61	A. Lomas/UK	
1599	David Buxton, 6/3/61	Jay Weidenfeld/USA	Vintage racer
1600	Chequered Flag, 28/4/61	D. Pawson/UK	
1601	Peter Lindner, 28/3/61	Jerrold Halverson/USA	
1602	W. Steiner, 30/3/62	Jim Castle/UK	
1603	J. Blackley, 1/5/62	Ed Jose/USA	
1604			
1605	T.E. Badbury, 26/6/62		
1606	SS Aviation Ltd, 20/1/61	Austria	
1607	G. Nystrom, 10/3/61	Mats Jonsson/Sweden	
1608	Chequered Flag, 6/2/61	John Chatwin/UK	
1609	Frosts (Cars) Ltd, 20/1/61		
1610			
1611	L. Ralph, 25/4/62	Ray Hunter/UK	
1612	J.R. Rouse, 2/5/62	Gunther Dammler/ Germany	
1613	J.A. Marshall, 24/7/62	Gerrit-Jan Caviet/ Holland	
1614	I. McLeod, 24/7/62		
1615	F. Cowlishaw, 23/5/62	Michael Loader/UK	
1616	T. Ward, 22/6/62		
1617	C. Taylor, 9/3/62		
1618	N.N. Nicholls, 24/4/62		
1619	J.R. Nosnarton, 23/11/61		
1620	Chequered Flag, 13/6/61	Charles Levy/USA	
1621	M.S. Cann, 22/6/62	Peter Bergmann/ Germany	Vintage racer

Chassis	Original customer and date of invoice	1990 owner and country	Notes
1622	E.W. Worth, 20/3/62		
1623	Chivens, 26/5/62		
1624	R.G. Smith, 8/3/62	B. Friend/UK	
1625	E. Humphrees, 4/5/62	A.W. Huberts/ Netherlands	
1626	Chequered Flag, 21/3/61		
1627			
1628	Parkin Eng, 28/2/61		
1629	R.B. Broron (Racing) Ltd, 7/2/61	G.F. Tompkins/UK	
1630	Dickson Mtrs Ltd, 27/2/61	Harold Lance/USA	
1631	A. Foster, 2/3/62		
1632	H.F. Collelt, 8/5/62		
1633	B. Tarussell, 23/2/62	D.S. Sammis/USA	
1633B	T. Mermogen, 1/5/62		
1634	W. Taylor, 24/5/62	G. Bryan Hewitt/USA	
1635	Autosport Equip, 6/6/61	Larry Dent/USA	Vintage racer
1636	V.W. Hatton, 8/3/62	Bill Hutton/USA	
1637	J.S. Mchay, 28/3/62		
1638	Fletcher, 2/5/62	Tony Kynaston/UK	
1639	R.S. Smart, 25/4/62		
1640	D.A. Wilus, 16/5/62		
1641	R.L. Culvernover, 30/3/62		
1642	G. Leverton, 7/2/62		
1643	R. Reynolds, 20/2/62	David Buchesky/USA	
1644	D.V. Llewelyn, 4/6/62	Brian Pye/UK	
1645	T.C. Wrey, 14/2/62	UK	
1646	H. Nystrom, 21/3/62	Lars Jonasson/Sweden	Super 100
1647	P.C. Dickson, 19/12/61		
1648	S.C. Thennasen, 18/8/62		
1649	M. Mosley, 23/11/61		
1650	H.P. Jeschambs, 5/4/62		
1651	Chris Ashmore, 27/3/62	Anthony Barry Morse/UK	
1652			
1653	N.V. Burdin, 15/5/62	R.S.F. Wildman/UK	
1654	G.C. Cave, 7/6/62		
1655	B. William Powlott, 8/12/61		
1656	T.W. Boyd, 22/5/62		
1657	J. Smith, 23/3/62		
1658	J.R.F. Berry, 27/7/62		

Chassis 1664

Chassis	Original customer and date of invoice	1990 owner and country	Notes
1659	J. Clark, 31/1/62	A.N.E. Bates/UK	Ex-Jim Clark car
1660	V. Stott, 8/1/62		
1661	N.A. Rodery, 22/3/62		
1662	V.C. Snell, 2/8/62		
1663	R.L. Neill, 15/8/62		
1664	G. Machin, 31/5/62	George Rance/UK	Super 95
1665	A.E. Knight, 20/12/61	Peter Durig/ Switzerland	
1666	G. Clarke, 3/9/62		
1667	J.W. Swan, 8/12/61		
1668	J.F. Guiver, 1/12/61	R. Mummery/USA	Vintage racer
1669	W. Cook, 1/12/61		
1670	J.C. Baxter, 8/3/62		
1671	T. Howarth, 14/10/61		
1672	R.F. Gooch, 2/5/62	Alain Quitton-Rozeubamm/France	Super 95
1673	C. Millet, 12/2/63		
1674		A. Zimmermann/ Switzerland	
1675	F.H. Mann, 3/1/62	H.R.Dare/UK	
1676	R. Radford, 5/1/62		
1677	F. West, 14/12/62	Ean Pugh/UK	Super 95
1678	30/3/62	John Wagstaff/UK	Ex-Team Elite car
1679	W.A. Bell, 18/3/62	W.A. Bell/UK	Original owner
1680	M.A. Zoccola, 18/3/62	Richard Clarke/South Africa	
1681	D. Payne, 4/1/62		
1682	P. Tipple, 6/3/62		
1683	J.M. Wilson, 2/3/62	Wayne Reed/USA	Written off, now 2036
1684	Petook, 9/5/62		
1685	Eastern Auto Co, 28/7/62	Rosso Restorations/ Canada	
1686	T. Williams, 12/12/61	Max Verstappen/ Belgium	Vintage racer
1687	R. Edmunds, 28/11/61	Martin Williams/ Australia	
1688	I.W. West, 11/12/61		
1689	M. Koing, 31/1/62	Peter Aylett/UK	Super 95
1690	J. Robert Shaw, 11/10/62	Noboru Kodaira/Japan	Super 95
1691	I.B. Gillies, 16/5/62		
1692	Saunders Davis, 8/1/62	Craig Bielat/USA	Vintage racer
1693			
1694	T. Burarankovit, 29/3/62		
1695	R. Pushicker, 29/6/61	John Carey/USA	
1696	M.J. West, 15/12/61	Gerrit-Jan Caviet/Holland	Vintage racer
1697	J.P.H. Grosman, 4/1/62		
1698	N. Granville-Smith, 17/4/62		
1699	Beaudoin, 25/4/61		
1700	F.J. Middleton, 17/1/63	Terry Gahl/USA	Super 95
1701	Beaudoin, 28/4/61		
1702	D.H. Strachen, 6/4/62	Masao Sakaguchi/Japan	
1703	Elite Cars, 4/5/61	R. Wilson/UK	
1704	F.F. Clarke, 1/3/62	John Dawson-Damer/Australia	
1705	K.J. Gilbert, 28/6/62		
1706	F.B. Garvey, 16/3/62	E.H. Moses/UK	
1707	Eastern Auto Co, 20/3/62		
1708	Ets F. Staumont, 26/2/62		
1709	D. Jolly, 16/3/62	Barry Bates/Australia	
1710	P.J. Jackson, 21/3/62	Manfred Bode/ Germany	
1711	Ets J. & P. Wauters, 2/10/62		
1712	Weathermatic Corp, 2/2/62		

Chassis	Original customer and date of invoice	1990 owner and country	Notes
1713	Ecurie Shirlee, 18/9/62		
1714	S. McCormick, 11/1/62	W. Wegner/Wales, UK	
1715	S. Maasland, 1/6/62	Wolfgang Wegener/ Germany	
1716	D. Jolly, 16/3/62	Phil Franzone/Australia	
1717	E. Robinson, 4/5/62		
1718	Viscount Gough, 7/5/62	UK	
1719	A.F. Shepherd, 22/3/62		
1720	P.S. Evans, 25/4/62		
1721	J. De La Haye, 9/4/62	Dave Alexander/UK	
1722	Chequered Flag, 20/5/61	Spencer Bates/Australia	Vintage racer
1723	David Buxton, 9/5/61		
1724	David Buxton, 23/6/61		
1725	Elite Cars, 3/5/61		
1726	Autosport Equip, 22/4/63		
1727	Chequered Flag, 18/5/61		
1728	Eastern Auto, 22/6/62	Bruce Mansell/Australia	Ford engine
1729	Peter Lindner, 15/9/61	George Newbauer/USA	
1730	C. Blythe, 19/6/62	David Tattersal/UK	
1731	F. Pagani, 25/7/63		
1732	M.P. Smith, 20/1/62	Peter Ecury/Holland	Vintage racer
1733	M.A. Sizeland, 30/4/62	Roger Brown/UK	
1734	Chequered Flag, 27/6/61	Henry Moore/USA	
1735	J.A. Lister, 15/11/61		
1736	T. Taylor, 10/1/62		
1737			
1738	Chequered Flag (Comp Cars), 27/6/61		
1739	Team Elite (David Buxton), 11/5/61		
1740	C.G. Escott, 15/4/62		
1741	Wolsey, 2/2/62		
1742	H. Janson, 26/3/62		
1743	Y. Nystrom, 22/12/61	Hans Nordstrom/ Finland	
1744	CBU only	Howen Ganley/UK	
1745	R. Vann, 5/11/62	David Snell/UK	
1746	Chequered Flag, 8/6/61	Ricardo Paris/USA	Vintage racer
1747	Russell Yerlett, 12/5/61	Geoff Strachan/ Australia	Super 95
1748	Y. Nystrom, 24/7/61	Thorvald Christensen/ Sweden	
1749	W.A. Bell, 5/5/61	A.N.E. Bates/UK	
1750	D.L. Pergh, 28/2/62	Mike Ostrov/USA	Super 100
1751	Y. Nystrom, 24/7/61		
1752	Chequered Flag, 23/5/61	Roger Walker/UK	
1753	CBU only (Dickson), 21/4/61		
1754	Major A. Wyndham, 2/10/62	Ken Duckworth/ Canada	
1755	CBU only (Alton), 27/7/61		
1756	Ecurie Shirlee, 17/8/62	Dennis Ashley/USA	
1757	G.O. Hutchinson, 1/6/62	Peter Smith/UK	
1758	W.G.U. Hall, 19/4/62	Brian Waite/UK	
1759	3/1/62	E.J. Seymour/UK	
1760	CBU only		
1761	M. Aylvin, 23/11/61		
1762	K. Fenwick, 12/12/61	Howard Tipping/UK	Super 95
1763	Auto Boavista, 13/9/61	L. Leroy/Belgium	
1764	R.C. Perkins, 7/2/62		
1765	E.J. Posey, 19/4/62		
1766	Ecurie Shirlee, 1/8/62	Orville Morrow/USA	
1767	R.K. Meacham, 17/5/62		
1768	R. Brece, 3/11/61	John Wagstaff/UK	Team Elite replica
1769	Bown, 9/11/61	David Lockspeiser/UK	

Chassis	Original customer and date of invoice	1990 owner and country	Notes
1770	Ecurie Shirlee, 23/10/62	Morris Kindig/USA	
1771		Owen Fairbank/USA	
1772	Autosport, 30/8/62	Jim Long/USA	
1773			
1774	J.B. Raven, 22/4/63		
1775	A.W. Schillinger, 14/8/62	Jim Goodman/USA	
1776	R.C. Neal, 11/4/62	Robert Dance/UK	
1777	K.B. Wright, 7/12/61	Bob Green/USA	
1778	G.A. Amato, 16/3/62		
1779	F.H. Richmond, 24/7/62	George Rosenfeld/USA	
1780	29/12/61		
1781	R. Bullfield, 8/12/61	Hiroomi Ogasawara/ Japan	
1782	S. Hedgeson, 13/6/62	Peter Hall/Australia	Was 1563
1783	W.A.B. Jones, 5/10/61	J. Middleton/UK	
1784	M. Davies, 9/11/61	Claude Serre/France	Super 95
1785	Wharton, 3/10/61	B.A. Stock/UK	
1786	Auto Boavista, 13/9/61	Anibal Soares/Portugal	
1787	C.M. Cotton, 27/4/62	Ian Sheppard/UK	
1788	K.D. Lauerton, 12/1/62		
1789	S. Moss, 28/2/62	Richard Richardson/ USA	
1790	R. Robertson, 13/11/61		
1791	C.T.A. Rae, 22/2/62	G. Hunt/UK	
1792	CBU only		
1793	Ecurie Shirlee, 23/10/62		
1794	Ecurie Shirlee, 19/9/62		
1795	Ecurie Shirlee, 18/9/62	Larry Raphael/USA	
1796	Ecuric Shirlee, 17/8/62		
1797	Ecurie Shirlee, 18/9/62	Craig Swayne/USA	
1798	H.W. Porter, 8/5/62	Alan Wilkinson/UK	
1799	S.A. Russell, 18/1/62	Mike Ostrov/USA	
1800	Mrs. H. Templeton, 11/1/62		
1801	T.A. Crawford, 1/2/62	Paul Butler/UK	
1802	Elite Cars, 27/6/61		
1803	H. Eva, 15/11/61		
1804	Hawker, 22/9/61		
1805	G.A. Thomas, 27/2/62		
1806	T. Rogers, 7/2/62		
1807	David Buxton, 23/8/61		
1808	K. Wong, 3/10/61	Alain Crelier/France	

Chassis 1812

Chassis 1841

Chassis	Original customer and date of invoice	1990 owner and country	Notes
1809	Alton, 25/8/61		
1810	S. Maasland, 2/3/62		
1811	P.M. Berry, 28/5/62	Kazunori Takeuchi/ Japan	
1812	L.H. Boring, 4/1/62	William Goldkind/USA	Vintage racer
1813	P.J. Stevenson, 27/2/62		
1814	H.D. Gough, 27/4/62		
1815	W. Bold, 18/2/62	B.T. Williams/UK	
1816	Ets J. & P. Wauters, 22/8/62	Mr Chevel/Belgium	
1817	Autosport Equip, 29/6/62	Bill Griffiths/Canada	
1818	A.B. Biernet, 27/10/61		
1819	29/12/61	Noel Salter/Australia	
1820			
1821	M. Bradford, 27/10/61	David Reilly/USA	
1822	Autosport, 21/8/61	Oliver Clubine/Canada	
1823	Ets L. Beaudoin, 27/6/61		
1824	W.H.S. Pickavance, 17/5/62		
1825	S. Maasland, 2/2/62	Olav Glasius/Holland	
1826	R.C. McLennan, 24/7/62	Michael Baker/UK	
1827	W. Barber, 13/6/62		
1828	C.O. Pilbiam, 14/6/62	William Gubelman/USA	Super 95
1829	W.H. Hill, 12/6/62	Margo Bruyner/USA	
1830	J.G. Edwards, 21/11/61	David Inglis/Australia	
1831	J.R. Blathwayt, 20/11/61	Foster Cooperstein/ USA	
1832			
1833	Ets J. & P. Wauters, 9/8/62	Mr De Viwers/Belgium	
1834	J. Standen, 24/10/61	Sanwa Trading Co/ Japan	
1835	R.A.G. Escot, 16/11/61	B.G. Antill/UK	
1836	13/10/61	John Chatwin/UK	
1837	Fuigo Trading Co, 23/8/61	Sanwa Trading Co/ Japan	
1838	3/10/61	Max Ward/Australia	Super 95
1839	J.S. Ramsbottom, 10/10/61		
1840	D. Jolly, 27/6/61		
1841	Chequered Flag, 29/9/61	Mike Ostrov/USA	
1842	K.D. Gornin, 10/11/61	Judy Freeman/UK	Vintage racer
1843	P.W. McLachlan, 18/10/61		
1844	K. Wildy, 11/10/61		
1845	Grinnes, 27/10/61	W.J. Turner/UK	

Chassis	Original customer and date of invoice	1990 owner and country	Notes
1846	A.M.E. Zats, 11/10/61	C.R. Riley/UK	
1847	T. Anderson, 20/10/61		
1848	CBU only		
1849	J.H. Lapp, 18/10/61	Mike Flanagan/USA	
1850	P.D. Williams, 3/1/62	Masario Nishizawa/ Japan	
1851	Hingley, 9/11/61		
1852	D.C. Alderson, 27/10/61	UK	
1853	Fuigo Trading Co, 23/8/61	Koichi Sugita/Japan	
1854	M. Cooper, 20/10/61	Raymond Gomez/UK	
1855	P. Hutchinson, 13/11/61		
1856	Team Elite, 22/9/61		
1857	5/10/61	Michael Gravill/UK	
1858	13/10/61		
1859	J. Booth, 18/1/62		
1860	CBU only		
1861	Fuigo Trading Co, 23/8/61	Mr Mamizu/Japan	
1862	P. Gourgi, 19/10/61		
1863	22/8/61		
1864	T.F. Padwick, 17/9/61	John Mullen/USA	
1865	D.K. Dungan, 23/8/62	Tim McCoy/USA	Nephew of original owner
1866	J. Cook, 1/6/62		
1867	C.J. Gane, 2/5/62		
1868	P. Seighart, 9/5/62		
1869	Ets Beaudoin, 16/11/61		
1870	Ecurie Shirlee, 1/8/62	Warren Roche/USA	
1871	Ets F. Staumont, 18/7/62	Peter Gantenbein/ Switzerland	
1872	Beaudoin, 19/9/61		
1873	C. French, 20/2/62	Matt Sneddon/USA	
1874	Beaudoin, 30/11/61		
1875	F. Staumont, 20/4/61	Mr Gonzales/Belgium	
1876	D. Lewis, 27/2/62		
1877	C.E. Lake, 16/3/62	Steve Boides/USA	
1878	Dr H. Macpherson, 9/3/62	Japan	
1879	P. Chester, 27/2/62	Peter Chester/UK	Original owner
1880	J.H. Winterbottom, 19/12/61		
1881	A. Berristism, 5/1/62	David Blacklidge/UK	
1882			
1883	J. Ellis, 21/12/61	W. Reichert/Germany	
1884	29/12/61	Bill Kline/USA	
1885	C.W. Hunt, 30/3/62	Masakazu Totsuka/ Japan	
1886	J. Wolton, 5/2/62		
1887	Darwell-Smith, 21/12/61		
1888	CBU only	Mr Pirson/Belgium	
1889	J. Baxter, 2/12/61	Gunther Dammler/ Germany	
1890	E.A. Garside, 12/12/61		
1891	R. Aldridge, 21/11/61		
1892	Mrs Inoie, 2/3/62	M.L. Taylor/UK	
1893	J. Farguhar, 23/8/62	G. Tomkins/UK	
1894	J.P. Hawley, 16/2/62	Richard Lough/Ireland	
1895	Dr D.R. Hill, 5/2/62		
1896			
1897	Beaudoin/Nystrom, 7/6/62	Xavier Valmary/France	
1898	R. Willenghsy, 2/3/62	A. Champneys/UK	
1899	Autosport/Wolfgang Seidel, 12/6/62	Germany	Alfa engine
1900	T.A. Clapham, 27/2/62	Frank Bullock/New Zealand	
1901	T. Dicksons, 6/6/62		
1902	T.R. Fetherstonhaugh, 5/6/62	Barry Clarke/Australia	Super 95
1903	W.B. Stauell, 18/6/62	D.R. Fell/Scotland, UK	

Chassis 1924

Chassis	Original customer and date of invoice	1990 owner and country	Notes
1904	J.C. Chales, 15/6/62	Peter Aylett/UK	
1905	H.R. Groest, 22/6/62	Allan Cruickshank/ Australia	Super 95
1906	H. Radcliffe, 29/6/62		
1907	Saltir, 29/6/62	Ted Lambert/UK	
1908	L.P. Sampson, 7/6/62	Peter Richardson/UK	
1909	R.C. Birnard, 19/6/62		
1910	J.A. Docher, 27/6/62		
1911	S.C. Bentley, 30/7/62		
1912	P. Francis, 10/8/62	Keith Anderson/UK	
1913	L. Galton, 31/8/62	Donald Wilson/UK	
1914	Eastern Auto Co, 28/7/62	Robin Longdon/UK	
1915	B.G. Ranson, 17/7/62		
1916	Goodwin, 23/8/62	Dino Rossetto/France	
1917	Col C.J. Hughes, 17/8/62	Donald Bartlett/USA	Super 95
1918	J.D. Knight, 22/11/62		
1919	Hill, 25/6/62	Frank Starkey/USA	Vintage racer
1920	P.E. Millet, 14/12/62		
1921	Ecurie Shirlee, 10/1/63	Frans Nelson/USA	
1922	Ecurie Shirlee, 30/7/62	USA	
1923	R.E. Bowman, 19/7/62	J.G. Dear/UK	
1924	D.C. Duncan, 24/7/62	Derek Duncan/UK	Original owner
1925	R. Comultren, 23/7/62		
1926	Ecurie Shirlee, 18/9/62	USA	
1927	H.B. Mosher, 18/7/62	Bradley Green/USA	
1928	Ecurie Shirlee, 19/9/62	Alex Bollinger/USA	Super 100; vintage racer, ex-Bob Challman
1929	H.M. Illingworth, 24/1/63		
1930	K. Painter, 28/8/62		
1931	F.P. Hague, 20/8/62	R.C. Cadogan/UK	
1932	D.E. Jolly, 12/9/62	David Bishop/Australia	Super 95, original owner
1933	J. Causer, 23/8/62		
1934	Ecurie Shirlee, 30/7/62	Maury Montag/USA	
1935	D. Miller, 27/7/62	Edward Shaw/UK	
1936		F.T. Riches/UK	
1937	W. Forbes, 8/8/62	A. Lockington/UK	
1938	J. Saxby, 30/8/62		
1939			
1940	C.J. Upjohn, 29/11/62	Nick Raven/UK	
1941	D.E. Jolly, 7/9/62	John B. Roxburgh/ Australia	Super 95

Chassis 1945

Chassis	Original customer and date of invoice	1990 owner and country	Notes
1942	A.W. Books, 6/9/62	Richard T. Maylam/UK	Super 95
1943	C.D. Smith, 18/8/62	John Urwin/UK	
1944	B. Gooch, 8/8/62	Geoff Gillett/Australia	Super 95
1945	W.S. Tingle, 25/7/62	Truett Lawson/USA	Super 95; was 1456
1946		Hiroshi Yamazaki/ Japan	
1947			
1948	B.J. Davis, 29/8/62	M. Ricketts/UK	
1949			
1950	T.H. Turnbull, 6/9/62	Richard Hol/Holland	
1951	14/3/63	Japan	
1951A	Dutchess Auto, 22/4/63	Pat Dennis/USA	
1952	Ecurie Shirlee, 6/3/63	Dean Price/USA	
1953	M.J. Wood, 27/12/62	Mike Ostrov/Hank Mauel Jr/USA	Vintage racer
1954			
1955	G.R. Smith, 16/8/62		
1956			
1957	13/6/63	Tom Mittle/USA	
1958	Dutchess Auto, 5/7/63	Robert LaRoque/USA	
1959	A.J. Micklow, 10/2/62		
1960	J. Hart, 7/12/62	Gene Gully/USA	
1961	J.B. Chattgaley, 2/11/63	Dave Alexander/UK	
1962	Ecurie Shirlee, 6/3/63		
1963	M. Baxtor, 3/9/62		
1964	J. and P. Wauters, 1/5/63		
1965	Fuigo Trading, 14/3/63	Genzo Hisagaki/Japan	
1966	W. Rigg, 19/12/62	Peter Ewart/UK	
1967	L.J. Dawson, 14/2/62	J. Urwin/UK	
1968	Ecurie Shirlee, 6/3/63	Alex Bollinger/USA	Original owner
1969	I.G. Charter, 15/8/63		
1970	M. Kapelowich, 15/11/62	Frank Lugg/UK	Super 95
1971	M. Black, 7/11/62		
1972	M. Capoo, 15/11/62	Jack Bartels/USA	Super 95
1973	F. Rudkin, 11/3/63	C.G. Ross/UK	
1974	Fuigo Trading, 8/11/62	Japan	
1975	J. Halley, 14/11/62	Paul Ellis/UK	
1976	Lotus Automobiles, Andorra, 20/6/63	Michael Jovay/Belgium	
1976B	J.E. Holdes, 25/6/63	Oliver William Ridge/UK	
1977	Ecurie Shirlee, 23/10/62	Walter Jordan/USA	Original owner
1978	N.A. Humell, 18/5/63	A.N.E. Bates/UK	
1979			

Chassis	Original customer and date of invoice	1990 owner and country	Notes
1980	Dutchess Auto, 5/7/63	Joseph Gordon/USA	
1981			
1982		USA	
1983	F.A. Mountford, 5/6/63	P. Ishiyama/Japan	
1984	P.R. Reesan, 24/5/63		
1985	R.J. Asset, 5/10/62		
1986			
1987			
1988	G. Bostock, 23/3/63	David Evans/UK	Written off, now 2018
1989			
1990			
1991		Rainer Brammer/ Germany	Super 105
1992	Fuigo Trading, 14/3/63	Japan	
1993	P. Cesswell, 14/5/62	Robert Matthews/UK	Super 95
1994	E. Winstanley, 20/9/63	Dennis Ganley/New Zealand	
1994B	D.H. Williams, 12/1/64		
1995	W.M. Brodie, 21/11/63		
1996	C. Davies, 20/3/63	Terry Jones/UK	
1997	L. Crawley, 13/2/63		
2001		Brian Stutz/Switzerland	David Lazenby's twin-cam
2003		Holland	
2010		Peter Kiedrowski/ Germany	Super 95
2014		Roger Fountain/Canada	Vintage racer
2015		Bryn Williams/UK	
2016		Miles Wilkins/UK	
2017		Chris Kent/USA	
2018		David Evans/UK	Was 1988
2021		Nick Raven/UK	
2025		Japan	
2028		Hubert Huppauff/ Germany	Vintage racer
2032		Koji Takeguchi/Japan	
2033		Alan Purdy/UK	Was 1581
2036		Wayne Reed/USA	Was 1683
2041		Ed Clark/USA	Was 1254
2046		Christian Jovan/ Belgium	
2047		A.W. Moran/UK	

Chassis 2001

Index